Student Activities Manual

H O R I Z O N S

FIRST CANADIAN EDITION

Joan H. Manley
University of Texas — El Paso

Stuart Smith
Austin Community College

John T. McMinn
Austin Community College

Marc A. Prévost
Austin Community College

Patricia Lee Men Chin
Dalhousie University

NELSON
EDUCATION

NELSON EDUCATION

Student Activities Manual, Horizons, First Canadian Edition

by Joan H. Manley, Stuart Smith, John T. McMinn,
Marc A. Prévost, Patricia Lee Men Chin

Vice President, Editorial Higher Education: Anne Williams	**Developmental Editor:** Theresa Fitzgerald	**Design Director:** Ken Phipps
Publisher: Anne-Marie Taylor	**Content Production Managers:** Susan Lee Imoinda Romain	**Managing Designer:** Franca Amore
Executive Marketing Manager: Amanda Henry	**Copy Editors:** Isabelle Rolland Tannys Williams	**Cover Design:** Courtney Hellam
Technical Reviewer: Kathleen Bush	**Proofreader:** Maude Lessard	**Compositor:** MPS Limited

ISBN-13: 978-0-17-655925-0
ISBN-10: 0-17-655925-6

Credits

Cover: (fair ride) Annette Shaff/Shutterstock, (girl blowing bubbles) © Photolyric/iStockphoto, (lighthouses) Ronald Sumners/Shutterstock, (girl in mirror) © Photolyric/iStockphoto, (bike on street) © pierredesvarre/iStockphoto, (sparklers) © Photolyric/iStockphoto, (road) Chase Clausen/Shutterstock

Table des matières

Preface

This *Student Activities Manual (SAM)* supports the *Horizons* textbook, and provides you with an opportunity to develop the skills needed for effective communication in French. With the exception of the *Chapitre de révision*, there is a chapter in the *Student Activities Manual* with four *Compétences* corresponding to each chapter of the textbook. For each *Compétence* of the *Student Activities Manual*, there are four pages of writing activities followed by two pages of listening activities. These activities give you the opportunity to practise the grammatical structures, vocabulary, and learning skills presented in the textbook. The two pages of listening activities at the end of each *Compétence* also give you the chance to improve your pronunciation and understanding of spoken French. You should always review all of the new words, phrases, grammar rules, and learning strategies presented in each *Compétence* in the *Horizons* textbook before beginning the corresponding section in the *Student Activities Manual*. Also remember that there are two sets of recordings that accompany *Horizons*: the Text Audio and the SAM Audio. The Text Audio contains activities marked with an audio symbol in the textbook. Be sure that you have the SAM Audio when working in the *Student Activities Manual*. Note that an asterisk (*) has been set beside certain written exercises. This is to note the exercises for which the answers will vary.

Writing the *Journal*

At the end of every other *Compétence* in the writing activities, you will write a journal entry. Each entry is a guided composition in which you combine all that you have learned in a global, communicative writing activity. As you begin each *Compétence* in class, look ahead in your workbook to see what you will be expected to communicate in written French after studying the vocabulary and the grammatical structures. This will help you stay focused on the real purpose of learning vocabulary and grammatical structures, which is communication. In class, note down expressions or sentences that you might need for your journal, and as you sit down to write your journal entry, reread the dialogues and readings in the chapter up to that point. This will give you examples of what to say. Try to be creative, but stick to what you know. Do not try to use vocabulary and structures that you have not yet studied in class, unless you feel confident that you understand them. If you do not have enough space to say all that you wish on the page in the workbook, you may write your journal entry on a separate sheet of paper.

Tips for Success with the SAM Audio

It takes time, patience, and practice to understand French spoken at a normal conversational speed. Do not be surprised if at first you find it difficult to understand sections on the SAM Audio recordings. Relax and listen to passages more than once. You will understand a little more each time. Remember that you will not always understand everything and that, for particular activities, you are only expected to understand enough to answer specific questions. Read through listening exercises prior to listening to the recordings so that you know what you are listening for. If you find that you do not have enough time to process and respond to a question before the next one is asked, take advantage of the pause or stop button on your audio player to give yourself more time. Most importantly, stay patient and remember that you can always replay any section and listen again.

Practice, patience, and persistence pay!

On commence! Chapitre

COMPÉTENCE 1

Greeting people

By the time you finish this **Compétence,** you should be able to introduce yourself, meet others, ask how they are, and say goodbye.

Partie écrite

A. Salutations formelles! Complete the following conversations logically by filling in the missing words. Base each conversation on the picture to the right.

— Bonjour, monsieur.

— Bonjour, _____ **(1).**

— Comment _____ **(2)**?

— Je m'appelle Henri Tremblay. Et _____ **(3)**?

— Je _____ **(4)** Hélène Côté.

— Bonsoir, monsieur.

— _____ **(5),** mademoiselle.

— Comment _____ **(6)**?

— Je vais très _____ **(7),** merci. Et vous?

— Assez _____ **(8).**

B. Très bien, merci! How would each man answer the question «**Comment allez-vous?**»

1. _____ 2. _____ 3. _____

C. Ça va ? Complete the following informal (familiar) conversations logically by filling in the missing words. Base each conversation on the picture to the right.

— Bonjour, je m'appelle Philippe. Et _____ **(1)** ?

    Tu _____ **(2)** comment ?

— Je m'appelle Danielle.

— Salut, Jean-Pierre.

— _____ **(3)**, Micheline. _____ **(4)** va ?

— _____ **(5)** va. Et _____ **(6)** ? Comment ça va ?

— _____ mal.

D. Qu'est-ce qu'on dit… ? How might you say goodbye to …

1. your friends until tomorrow?

    _____

2. someone you will see later in the day?

    _____

3. a friend you will visit soon?

    _____

4. someone if you don't know when you'll see him/her again?

    _____

E. Bonjour ! Decide if each of these expressions is appropriate for a formal relationship, for an informal relationship, or for either type of relationship. Put a check mark in the appropriate column. The first one has been done for you.

	Formal	Informal	Either
1. Bonjour, monsieur.	✓	_____	_____
2. Comment vous appelez-vous ?	_____	_____	_____
3. Tu t'appelles comment ?	_____	_____	_____
4. Salut !	_____	_____	_____
5. Comment allez-vous ?	_____	_____	_____
6. Comment ça va ?	_____	_____	_____
7. Je vais très bien. Et vous ?	_____	_____	_____
8. Au revoir !	_____	_____	_____
9. À demain !	_____	_____	_____

F. Situations. What would you say in French in each of the following situations? Remember to use formal or informal (familiar) French as appropriate.

1. to greet your professor and ask his/her name

   _____

2. to ask how your professor is

   _____

3. to greet a classmate and ask his/her name

   _____

4. to ask how your classmate is doing

   _____

*G. Réponses. Imagine that an older married French woman says these things to you and give a logical response for each one. Use *formal* French.

1. Bonjour, monsieur/madame/mademoiselle.

   _____

2. Bonsoir, monsieur/madame/mademoiselle.

   _____

3. Comment vous appelez-vous?

   _____

4. Comment allez-vous?

   _____

5. Au revoir, monsieur/madame/mademoiselle.

   _____

Now imagine that a classmate, Juliette, says these things to you and write a logical response to each one. Use *informal (familiar)* French.

6. Salut!

   _____

7. Tu t'appelles comment?

   _____

8. Comment ça va?

   _____

9. Au revoir! À demain!

   _____

Nom _____ Date _____

Partie auditive

 A. Prononciation : Les consonnes muettes et la liaison. Pause the recording and review the *Prononciation* section on page 6 of the textbook. Then read the following list of words and indicate whether the final consonant of each word is pronounced or silent by underlining those that should be pronounced and crossing out those that should be silent. Turn on the recording and repeat as you hear each word, checking your decision about the final consonant.

EXEMPLES	YOU SEE:	parc	YOU SEE:	pas
	YOU MARK:	par**c**	YOU MARK:	pa~~s~~
	YOU HEAR AND REPEAT:	par**c**	YOU HEAR AND REPEAT:	pa~~s~~

1. Marc   **3.** très   **5.** mal   **7.** actif

2. salut   **4.** assez   **6.** bonjour   **8.** Luc

Now listen and repeat as you hear each of the sentences that follow pronounced. Then listen again and mark where the liaisons occur.

EXEMPLE	YOU SEE:	Comment vous appelez-vous ?
	YOU HEAR AND REPEAT:	**Comment vous appelez-vous ?**
	YOU MARK:	**Comment vous‿appelez-vous ?**

1. Comment allez-vous ?   **4.** Il est trois heures.

2. Je suis en cours.   **5.** Comment dit-on… ?

3. Quelle heure est-il ?   **6.** À tout à l'heure !

 B. Salutations. You will hear three short conversations in which people greet each other. Write the number of each conversation below the picture it matches.

a. _____   **b.** _____   **c.** _____

Now you will hear a series of statements or questions. For each one, decide what would be the most logical response from the choices given. Write the letter of the most logical response next to the number of the statement you hear. One letter will be used more than once.

a. Je vais très bien, merci. Et vous ?

b. Bonjour, mademoiselle. Comment allez-vous ?

c. Je m'appelle Christian Boisvert.

d. Ça va, et toi ?

1. _____   **2.** _____   **3.** _____   **4.** _____   **5.** _____

C. Prononciation : Les voyelles *a, e, i, o, u* et *é*.
Correct pronunciation of the basic vowels is essential to developing speaking and listening skills. Pause the recording and review the ***Prononciation*** section on page 8 of the textbook. Then turn on the recording and listen and repeat the following words.

a [a]	agréable	attitude	art	banane
e [ə]	me	le	regarde	que
é [e]	café	pâté	marié	divorcé
i [i]	quiche	idéaliste	ironie	agile
o [o]	kilo	nos	hôte	abricot
u [y]	université	usage	ultra	tube

Now listen to these words and fill in the missing vowels (**a, e, é, i, o, u**).

1. ____n____m____l
2. p____t____t
3. m____r
4. t____t____
5. n____
6. ____m____

7. qu____
8. t____m____de
9. m____n____
10. j____l____
11. j____p____
12. n____t____

D. Dictée.
You will hear a series of questions or statements. Write each one down. *Do not respond to what you hear, simply write it down* exactly as you hear it. Pause the recording to have sufficient time to respond.

1. _____
2. _____
3. _____
4. _____
5. _____
6. _____

*Now you will hear more questions or remarks. This time, do *not* write what you hear. Instead, *respond* appropriately in French. Pause the recording to have sufficient time to respond.

1. _____
2. _____
3. _____
4. _____

COMPÉTENCE 2

Counting and describing your week

By the end of this **Compétence,** you should be able to count from 0 to 30, ask and tell what day of the week it is, and tell a little about your schedule.

Partie écrite

A. C'est quel nombre? Change these prices from words to numerals.

1. quatre dollars = _____ $
2. cinq dollars = _____ $
3. onze dollars = _____ $
4. trente dollars = _____ $
5. vingt-six dollars = _____ $
6. dix-sept dollars = _____ $

7. vingt-trois dollars = _____ $
8. dix-neuf dollars = _____ $
9. quinze dollars = _____ $
10. dix dollars = _____ $
11. deux dollars = _____ $
12. treize dollars = _____ $

13. seize dollars = _____ $
14. douze dollars = _____ $
15. dix-huit dollars = _____ $
16. quatorze dollars = _____ $
17. vingt-cinq dollars = _____ $
18. vingt-neuf dollars = _____ $

B. C'est combien? You are shopping for a few items you need. Give the price of the following items by spelling out the numbers *in words.*

1. Un sandwich, c'est _____ dollars.

2. Une calculatrice, c'est _____ dollars.

3. Un tee-shirt, c'est _____ dollars.

4. Une plante, c'est _____ dollars.

5. Une affiche, c'est _____ dollars.

6. Un CD, c'est _____ dollars.

Nom _____ Date _____

C. Problèmes de maths. Complete the following math problems by filling in the missing numbers. Spell out the numbers in words.

1. 10 + 5 = 15

   — Combien font _____ et _____ ?

   — _____ et _____ font _____ .

2. 29 − 13 = 16

   — Combien font _____ moins _____ ?

   — _____ moins _____ font _____ .

3. 20 − 17 = 3

   — Combien font _____ moins _____ ?

   — _____ moins _____ font _____ .

4. 30 − 19 = 11

   — Combien font _____ moins _____ ?

   — _____ moins _____ font _____ .

*D. Mon emploi du temps. In French, fill in the days of the week in the left column of the following daily planner. The first one has been done as an example. Then, go back and indicate on the daily planner your typical schedule. Use **Je travaille** to indicate when you work, **Je suis en cours,** for when you are in class, and **Je suis à la maison** for when you are at home.

le jour	le matin	l'après-midi	le soir
le lundi			

*E. Quels jours? Complete the following sentences with the appropriate days. Remember to use **le** in numbers **3 to 7** to say that you do something on a particular day in general. If you do not work, leave numbers **4** and **5** blank.

1. Aujourd'hui, c'est _____.

2. Demain, c'est _____.

3. Je suis en cours de français _____.

4. Je travaille _____.

5. Je ne travaille pas _____.

6. Je ne suis pas en cours _____.

7. Je ne suis pas à la maison le matin _____.

F. Conversation. Complete this conversation between two students, as indicated.

YASMINE: _____ **(1)** aujourd'hui?
                     (What day is it)

HANNAH: C'est _____ **(2)**.
                        (Wednesday)

YASMINE: Tu es en cours _____ **(3)** ce trimestre?
                                      (what days)

HANNAH: _____ **(4)**, je suis en cours de français
                 (In the morning)

_____ **(5)**.
         (every day)

Et _____ **(6)**,
   (from Monday to Thursday)

je suis _____ **(7)** l'après-midi.
             (in another class)

YASMINE: Et _____ **(8)** tes *(your)* cours?
                     (before)

HANNAH: Avant mes *(my)* cours, je suis _____ **(9)**.
                                                   (at home)

YASMINE: Tu travailles _____ **(10)**?
                                      (too)

HANNAH: _____ **(11)** le vendredi soir et
                 (Yes, I work)

_____ **(12)**. Et toi?
         (weekends)

YASMINE: Je travaille le soir _____ **(13)** mes cours.
                                           (after)

_____ **(14)**
         (I'm at home)

le matin et _____ **(15)** l'après-midi.
                  (I'm in class)

*G. Questions. Imagine that a fellow student is asking you these questions and answer them *with complete sentences* in French. In numbers **6 to 8**, start with **oui** to say *yes* or **non** to say *no*.

1. Salut! Comment ça va?

_____

2. Tu t'appelles comment?

_____

3. C'est quel jour aujourd'hui?

_____

4. Tu es en cours quels jours ce trimestre?

_____

5. Tu es en cours de français le matin, l'après-midi ou *(or)* le soir?

_____

6. Tu es en cours de français du lundi au vendredi?

_____

7. Après le cours de français, tu es dans un autre cours?

_____

8. Tu travailles aussi?

_____

At the end of the second and fourth ***Compétences*** of a chapter, you will be asked to write a journal entry. The journal allows you to combine all that you have studied to communicate your own thoughts.

*Journal. Write a paragraph about your typical week. Tell when you are at home, when you are in class, and when you work (or that you don't work).

_____

_____

_____

_____

_____

_____

_____

_____

_____

_____

Partie auditive

 A. Comptez de un à trente ! Repeat each number after the speaker. Notice that the final consonants of some numbers are pronounced, whereas others are silent. Some consonants in the middle of the word are also silent. Repeat this exercise until you feel comfortable counting from 1 to 30 by yourself.

____ 1 un	____ 7 sept	____ 13 treize	____ 19 dix-neuf	____ 25 vingt-cinq
____ 2 deux	____ 8 huit	____ 14 quatorze	____ 20 vingt	____ 26 vingt-six
____ 3 trois	____ 9 neuf	____ 15 quinze	____ 21 vingt et un	____ 27 vingt-sept
____ 4 quatre	____ 10 dix	____ 16 seize	____ 22 vingt-deux	____ 28 vingt-huit
____ 5 cinq	____ 11 onze	____ 17 dix-sept	____ 23 vingt-trois	____ 29 vingt-neuf
____ 6 six	____ 12 douze	____ 18 dix-huit	____ 24 vingt-quatre	____ 30 trente

 B. Quels nombres ? You will hear 12 numbers between 1 and 30 in random order. As you hear each one, place a check mark next to it in the list of numbers in *A. Comptez de un à trente !*

 C. Calculs. You will hear some simple math problems. Pause the recording after each one in order to fill in the numbers and solve the problem. All the problems and answers will be repeated at the end. Listen and verify your responses.

EXEMPLE	YOU HEAR:	Deux et deux font…
	YOU WRITE:	2 + 2 = 4
	AT THE END YOU HEAR:	Deux et deux font quatre.

1. _____ + _____ = _____   3. _____ + _____ = _____   5. _____ + _____ = _____

2. _____ + _____ = _____   4. _____ + _____ = _____   6. _____ + _____ = _____

 D. Prononciation : Les voyelles nasales. Pause the recording and review the *Prononciation* section on page 10 of the textbook. Then turn on the recording and repeat these nasal sounds and the model words and phrases that contain them after the speaker. (Notice that although a final **c** is often pronounced, it is silent at the end of **blanc.**)

$[\tilde{\mathrm{a}}]$:	**an / am**	blanc	avant	dans	chambre
	en / em	trente	enfant	vendredi	temps
$[\tilde{\varepsilon}]$:	**in / im**	cinq	quinze	fin	impossible
	un / um	un	lundi	brun	parfum
	ain / aim	demain	américain	prochain	faim
$[\tilde{\mathrm{o}}]$:	**on / om**	onze	bonsoir	réponse	nom
$[j\tilde{\varepsilon}]$:	**ien**	bien	bientôt	combien	lien
$[w\tilde{\varepsilon}]$:	**oin**	moins	loin	coin	point

un vin / un vin blanc / un bon vin blanc / un bon vin blanc américain

C'est un bon vin blanc américain, Henri.

Now listen to these pairs of words. Fill in the missing letters in both words of the pair with the same choice from the two choices given.

EXEMPLE YOU SEE: en / in   v_____   qu_____ze

YOU HEAR: en / in   vin   quinze

YOU WRITE: en / in   **vin**   qu**in**ze

1. an / on   mais_____   citr_____

2. an / in   vois_____   chem_____

3. en / on   c_____tre   r_____trer

4. en / un   g_____til   souv_____t

5. ien / oin   l_____   c_____

6. un / en   br_____   comm_____

7. an / on   dev_____t   rom_____

E. Les jours de la semaine. Listen and repeat the names of the days of the week. Play this section again until you feel comfortable saying them.

lundi   mardi   mercredi   jeudi   vendredi   samedi   dimanche

F. C'est quel jour ? You will hear the start of a sentence about what day comes *before* or *after* another. Fill in the blank with the day of the week you hear, then complete the sentence logically. After a pause for you to respond, you will hear the correct answer. Pause the recording if you need more time.

EXEMPLE VOUS ENTENDEZ *(YOU HEAR)*:   Avant lundi, c'est…

VOUS ÉCRIVEZ *(YOU WRITE)*:   Avant **lundi,** c'est **dimanche.**

VOUS ENTENDEZ *(YOU HEAR)*:   Avant lundi, c'est dimanche.

1. Avant _____, c'est _____.

2. Avant _____, c'est _____.

3. Avant _____, c'est _____.

4. Après _____, c'est _____.

5. Après _____, c'est _____.

6. Après _____, c'est _____.

G. Mon emploi du temps. You will hear a student describe his schedule. The first time, just listen to what he says. It will then be repeated more slowly with pauses for you to fill in the missing words. Pause the recording and play this section again as needed.

_____ **(1),** *je suis à la maison*

_____ **(2)** *avant mes (my) cours. Le lundi et*

_____ **(3),** *je suis en cours de français*

_____ **(4).** *Après le cours de français, je suis*

_____ **(5).** *Je travaille le soir*

_____ **(6).**

COMPÉTENCE 3

Talking about yourself and your schedule

By the end of this *Compétence,* you should be able to tell a little about yourself and describe your schedule.

Partie écrite

*A. Moi, je... A student is talking about herself. Rewrite her sentences to make them true for you.

1. Je suis étudiante à l'Université Laurentienne.

    Moi, je _____.

2. Je suis canadienne.

    Moi, je _____.

3. Je suis de Sudbury.

    Moi, je _____.

4. J'habite à Sudbury avec ma famille.

    Moi, je/j' _____.

5. Je ne travaille pas.

    Moi, je _____.

6. Je parle français, anglais et un peu espagnol.

    Moi, je _____.

7. Je pense que le français est un peu difficile.

    Moi, je _____.

*B. Qui suis-je ? Imagine three identities of students from your French class. Using the example below, write how each of them would describe themselves. Include their name, their nationality, what city they are from, in what city they live in now, and the college/university in Canada that they are attending.

> **EXEMPLE** **Je m'appelle Paul McBride. Je suis américain. Je suis de Boston et j'habite à Kingston maintenant. Je suis étudiant au Collège militaire royal du Canada.**

1. _____

    _____

    _____

2. _____

    _____

    _____

3. _____

    _____

    _____

C. Conversation. Two people meet at a conference in Montréal. Complete their conversation, as indicated.

MICHELLE NGUYEN: Vous _____ **(1)** canadien, monsieur?
                                    (are)

ANDRÉ GARNIER: Non, _____ **(2)** Paris. Mais _____ **(3)**
                              (I am from)   *(I live)*

ici maintenant _____ **(4)** je travaille ici. J'habite
                          (because)

_____ **(5)**. Et vous, vous êtes _____ **(6)**?
        (with my family)   *(from here)*

MICHELLE NGUYEN: Non, je suis _____ **(7)**.
                                          (American)

ANDRÉ GARNIER: _____ **(8)** vous parlez _____ **(9)** français.
                      (But)   *(very well)*

Vous habitez ici _____ **(10)**?
                          (now)

MICHELLE NGUYEN: Oui, j'habite ici _____ **(11)**.
                                  (with a [female] friend)

Je suis _____ **(12)**.
              (professor at the university)

D. Quelle heure est-il? Tell the time for each clock *in complete sentences*, spelling out all numbers.

EXEMPLE   Il est une heure.

1. _____
2. _____
3. _____

4. _____
5. _____
6. _____
7. _____

E. À la télé. Here are some of the kids' programs on ICI Radio-Canada. What time do the indicated programs start?

EXEMPLE   *Diabolo le petit cochon rigolo* : Ça *(That)* commence **à sept heures moins le quart.**

6 h 45	Diabolo le petit cochon rigolo	8 h 30	Toc toc toc
7 h	Pirates, chercheurs d'art	8 h 55	G Dansé/G Raconté
7 h 15	Babar	9 h 45	Edgar & Ellen
8 h 05	Max & Ruby	12 h 20	Les aventures de Tintin

1. *Pirates, chercheurs d'art* : Ça commence _____.

2. *Babar* : Ça commence _____.

3. *Max & Ruby* : Ça commence _____.

4. *Toc toc toc* : Ça commence _____.

5. *G Dansé/G Raconté* : Ça commence _____.

6. *Edgar & Ellen* : Ça commence _____.

7. *Les aventures de Tintin* : Ça commence _____.

F. Le lundi. Here is a friend's typical schedule on Monday. He is at home before class in the morning. Translate these sentences, and then finish them as he would with the times. *Include the French expressions equivalent to a.m. and p.m. with the times.*

1. I am at home before . . . a.m.

_____

2. I am in class from . . . a.m. to . . . p.m. My class (**Mon cours**) starts at . . . a.m. and ends at . . . p.m.

_____

_____

3. I work from . . . p.m. to . . . p.m.

_____

4. I am at home after . . . p.m.

_____

*G. Une interview. Answer the following questions *with complete sentences* in French.

1. Vous êtes canadien(ne)? Vous êtes de quelle ville *(from what city)*?

_____

_____

_____

_____

2. Vous habitez ici maintenant? Vous habitez seul(e)?

_____

_____

_____

_____

3. Vous travaillez quels jours? De quelle heure à quelle heure? Vous travaillez beaucoup?

_____

_____

_____

_____

4. Vous parlez un peu français? Le français est assez difficile ou très facile?

_____

_____

_____

_____

5. Vous êtes en cours tous les jours? Vous êtes en cours quels jours et de quelle heure à quelle heure?

_____

_____

_____

_____

6. Vous êtes en cours de français quels jours? Le cours de français commence à quelle heure et finit à quelle heure?

_____

_____

_____

_____

Partie auditive

 A. Masculin ou féminin ? When the masculine form of an adjective ends in a consonant other than **c, r, f,** or **l,** the final consonant is usually silent. Since the feminine form of an adjective usually ends in **-e,** this consonant is no longer final and is pronounced. You will hear several pairs of adjectives. Repeat each pair after the speaker.

Masculine	Feminine		Masculine	Feminine
1. _____ américain	_____ américaine	4. _____ anglais	_____ anglaise
2. _____ français	_____ française	5. _____ canadien	_____ canadienne
3. _____ intéressant	_____ intéressante	6. _____ étudiant	_____ étudiante

Now you will hear either the masculine or feminine form from each pair. Listen and place a check mark next to the form you hear.

 B. Un étudiant. Listen as a student talks about himself. Repeat each pair of sentences after he says them.

1. Je ne suis pas professeur. Je suis étudiant.

2. Je ne suis pas français. Je suis canadien.

3. Je ne suis pas d'ici. Je suis de Regina.

4. Je n'habite pas avec ma famille. J'habite seul.

5. Je ne travaille pas. Je suis étudiant.

6. Je ne parle pas espagnol. Je parle anglais et un peu français.

7. Je pense que le français est un peu difficile mais intéressant.

C. Autoportraits. You will hear two people give a short description of themselves. The first time, just listen to each one. Then, as you hear them a second time, write in the missing words from each description. Play this section again as needed.

1. WILLIAM :

_____ (1) William et _____ (2) canadien. Je suis de Red Deer,

_____ (3) mais j'habite à Ottawa _____ (4). J'habite

_____ (5) et j'étudie _____ (6). Je suis aussi étudiant à

l'Institut des langues officielles et du bilinguisme de _____ (7) où j'apprends

_____ (8).

2. MARIE :

Je m'appelle Marie et je suis _____ (1). _____ (2) de Chicoutimi,

_____ (3) mais _____ (4) à Ottawa avec une amie. Je suis

_____ (5) à l'Institut _____ (6) et du _____ (7)

de l'Université d'Ottawa où j'étudie _____ (8).

Nom _____ Date _____

D. Prononciation : L'heure et la liaison. Pause the recording and review the *Prononciation* section on page 16 of the textbook. Remember that the pronunciation of some of the numbers changes in liaison with the word **heures**. Listen and repeat as you hear each time pronounced. Then listen again, marking where you hear liaison occur.

EXEMPLE VOUS LISEZ *(YOU READ)*:   Il est dix heures.
             VOUS ÉCOUTEZ ET RÉPÉTEZ *(YOU LISTEN AND REPEAT)*: **Il est dix heures.**
             VOUS MARQUEZ *(YOU MARK)*:   **Il est dix‿heures.**

1. Il est deux heures dix.

2. Il est trois heures et quart.

3. Il est cinq heures et quart.

4. Il est six heures et demie.

5. Il est huit heures moins le quart.

6. Il est neuf heures moins vingt.

E. Quelle heure est-il? You will be asked what time it is for each of the following clocks. After a pause for you to respond, you will hear the correct answer. Verify your response and your pronunciation.

EXEMPLE VOUS VOYEZ *(YOU SEE)*:

VOUS ENTENDEZ *(YOU HEAR)*:   Quelle heure est-il?
VOUS DITES *(YOU SAY)*:   **Il est une heure.**
VOUS ENTENDEZ *(YOU HEAR)*:   Il est une heure.

1   2   3   4

5   6   7   8

F. L'heure. Listen and write down the time of day. Pause the recording after each question to allow enough time to respond.

EXEMPLE VOUS ENTENDEZ *(YOU HEAR)*:   Il est trois heures et quart du matin.
             VOUS ÉCRIVEZ *(YOU WRITE)*:   **3:15 a.m.**

1. _____   **3.** _____   **5.** _____   **7.** _____   **9.** _____

2. _____   **4.** _____   **6.** _____   **8.** _____   **10.** _____

COMPÉTENCE 4

Communicating in class

By the end of this *Compétence,* you should be able to follow instructions in class and ask your professor for clarification.

Partie écrite

A. Les instructions en classe. What did the professor say to these students? Write the appropriate phrase from the list in the blank corresponding to the matching illustration.

Allez au tableau.
Écoutez la question.
Répondez à la question.
Écrivez la réponse en phrases complètes.

Ouvrez votre livre à la page 23.
Prenez une feuille de papier et un stylo.
Donnez-moi votre examen.
Fermez votre livre.

1

2

3

4

1. _____
2. _____
3. _____
4. _____

5

6

7

8

5. _____
6. _____
7. _____
8. _____

B. Des instructions logiques. Using vocabulary you have learned, list at least three things that logically complete the following commands. (With **Ouvrez...** and **Faites,** list only two things.)

1. Écoutez...

_____

_____

2. Lisez...

_____

_____

3. Ouvrez...

_____

_____

4. Prenez...

_____

_____

5. Écrivez...

_____

_____

6. Faites...

_____

_____

C. Les accents. In French, accents do not indicate stress. They may indicate how a word is pronounced, and sometimes the presence or absence of an accent changes a word's meaning entirely. For example, the word **ou** means *or*, whereas the accented word **où** means *where*. With the exception of the **cédille,** which occurs on the letter **c (ç),** you will find accents only on vowels.

a. An **accent circonflexe (â, ê, î, ô, û)** frequently indicates that an **s** has been dropped from the spelling of a word. Knowing this will help you recognize the meaning of more words. Can you guess what the following words mean in English by inserting an **s** after the vowel with the **accent circonflexe**? Write the English words in the blanks.

1. hôpital : _____

2. hôtesse : _____

3. forêt : _____

4. hâte : _____

5. honnête : _____

6. île : _____

7. ancêtre : _____

8. quête : _____

b. When writing in French, pay close attention to accents. With practice, you will learn to determine where the accents should go on a word. In the meantime, learn accents as part of the spelling of words. To get started, copy the following words, making sure to place the accents where they belong.

1. À bientôt. _____

2. répétez _____

3. le français _____

4. Noël _____

5. Ça s'écrit... _____

D. Comment? Using phrases learned in *Compétence 4,* tell or ask your professor the following.

1. Ask him/her how to say *book* in French.

_____

2. Ask him/her to repeat something.

_____

3. Tell him/her that you don't understand.

_____

4. Ask him/her what the word **prenez** means.

_____

5. Ask him/her how **prenez** is written.

_____

6. Tell him/her that you don't know the answer.

_____

7. Thank him/her.

_____

E. Vous parlez anglais? Someone asks or says the following things to you. Respond to each *with a complete sentence* in French, except in the last one.

1. Vous parlez anglais?

_____

2. Comment dit-on **exercice** en anglais?

_____

3. *Exercise* s'écrit avec un *c* ou avec un *s* en anglais?

_____

4. Je ne comprends pas le mot **prochain**. Qu'est-ce que ça veut dire en anglais?

_____

5. Vous comprenez les mots **ouvrez** et **fermez**?

_____

6. Que veut dire : **Fermez votre livre**?

_____

7. Merci bien.

_____

Nom _____   Date _____

F. Ça s'écrit comment? Explain to a student from France how to spell the English equivalents of the following French words.

EXEMPLES hôpital
En anglais, *hospital,* **ça s'écrit sans accent circonflexe et avec un *s*.**

biologie
En anglais, *biology,* **ça s'écrit avec un *y*.**

1. philosophie

En anglais, *philosophy,* _____.

2. mariage

En anglais, *marriage,* _____.

3. forêt

En anglais, *forest,* _____.

4. intellectuel

En anglais, *intellectual,* _____.

5. adresse

En anglais, *address,* _____.

---

*Journal. Write two paragraphs introducing yourself. Include the following information.

In paragraph 1, tell your name, where you are from originally, where you live now, and with whom you live.

In paragraph 2, tell which days you are in class and from what time to what time. Then say whether you work, where, which days, and from what time to what time.

_____
_____
_____
_____
_____
_____
_____
_____
_____
_____
_____
_____
_____
_____

Partie auditive

 A. Qu'est-ce qu'on fait? You will hear a series of classroom commands. Write the number of each command under the picture that best represents it.

a. _____

b. _____

c. _____

d. _____

e. _____

f. _____

g. _____

h. _____

 B. Prononciation: Les voyelles groupées. Pause the recording and review the *Prononciation* section on page 21 of the textbook. Then turn on the recording and repeat each of the words after the speaker, paying attention to the pronunciation of the vowel combinations. Repeat this exercise as needed.

EXEMPLE   VOUS ENTENDEZ *(YOU HEAR)*:   seize
                VOUS RÉPÉTEZ *(YOU REPEAT)*:   **seize**

au, eau [o]:	au	aussi	beaucoup	tableau
eu [ø]:	deux	peu	jeudi	monsieur
eu [œ]:	heure	neuf	professeur(e)	seul(e)
ou [u]:	vous	douze	jour	pour
ai [ɛ]:	français	je vais	je sais	vrai
ei [ɛ]:	treize	seize	beige	neige
oi [wa]:	moi	toi	trois	au revoir
ui [ɥi]:	huit	minuit	aujourd'hui	suis

Nom _____ Date _____

Now repeat these pairs of words after the speaker.

1. _____ cuisine   _____ cousine   5. _____ poire   _____ peur
2. _____ fou   _____ feu   6. _____ suivant   _____ souvent
3. _____ saison   _____ Soisson   7. _____ toile   _____ tuile
4. _____ chou   _____ chaud   8. _____ lait   _____ loup

Now you will hear one word pronounced from each of the preceding pairs. Place a check mark next to the one you hear.

C. À vous maintenant! You will hear a series of words. Complete each one with the correct missing vowel combination from the two choices given.

EXEMPLE VOUS VOYEZ *(YOU SEE)*:   eu / oi   coul_____r
            VOUS ENTENDEZ *(YOU HEAR)*:   couloir
            VOUS ÉCRIVEZ *(YOU WRITE)*:   coul**oir**

1. au / ai   f_____t   5. au / eu   chev_____x
2. ui / ou   c_____vre   6. ai / ou   v_____s
3. eu / au   chev_____x   7. eu / ou   d_____x
4. eu / oi   cr_____x   8. ui / ou   c_____r

D. L'alphabet. Say each letter of the alphabet after the speaker. Repeat this exercise until you feel comfortable reciting the alphabet by yourself.

a b c d e f g h i j k l m n o p q r s t u v w x y z

Now fill in the blanks with the words you hear spelled out. You have not seen all of these words before.

EXEMPLE VOUS ENTENDEZ *(YOU HEAR)*:   b-e-a-u-c-o-u-p
            VOUS ÉCRIVEZ *(YOU WRITE)*:   **beaucoup**

1. _____   5. _____
2. _____   6. _____
3. _____   7. _____
4. _____   8. _____

E. En cours. You will hear a series of statements and questions. For each one, decide in which of these situations it would be used. Put the number of the statement or question you hear next to the situation to which it corresponds.

_____ **a.** You need something repeated.
_____ **b.** You want to know how a word is spelled.
_____ **c.** You want to know what a word means.
_____ **d.** You need to excuse yourself.
_____ **e.** You want to thank someone.
_____ **f.** You want to know how to say *zero* in French.
_____ **g.** You don't understand what was said.

À l'université   Chapitre **1**

COMPÉTENCE 1

Identifying people and describing appearance

By the time you finish this ***Compétence***, you should be able to identify friends and classmates and tell a little about them.

Partie écrite

A. Félix et Emma. In the left-hand column below, write new sentences about Félix using an antonym for each of the words in boldface. Then, in the right-hand column, describe Emma, who is very similar to Félix, by rewriting both sentences about Félix. Remember to use the feminine form of the adjective.

EXEMPLE   Il n'est pas **gros**.
Il est mince.

EXEMPLE   **Elle n'est pas grosse.**
Elle est mince.

1. Il n'est pas **vieux**.

1. _____

_____

2. Il n'est pas **grand**.

2. _____

_____

3. Il n'est pas **marié**.

3. _____

_____

B. Conversation. Reread the conversation between Félix and Emma on page 35 of the textbook. Then, complete this conversation between two other students with the indicated words.

Olivier et Louise se rencontrent *(meet)* pendant la _____ **(1)** des cours.
                                                                        (first week)

OLIVIER : Salut ! Je suis Olivier Leclerc. _____ **(2)** dans le _____ **(3)** cours de biologie, non ?
                                                        (We are)   *(same)*

LOUISE : Oui, c'est ça. _____ **(4)**, bonjour. Moi, _____ **(5)** Louise Mackay.
                            (So)   *(my name is)*

        Tu es _____ **(6)** ?
                (from here)

OLIVIER : Oui, je suis d'ici. Et toi? Tu es _____ **(7)**?
                                              (from where)

LOUISE :   Je suis _____ **(8)** Edmonton.
                        (from)

C. *C'est ou il/elle est*? In the left-hand column below, complete the sentences about Félix. Remember to use **c'est** if you are identifying him with *a noun* and **il est** if you are describing him with *an adjective*. Next, in the right-hand column, change the sentences so that they describe Emma.

FÉLIX
EXEMPLE   **Il est** québécois.

EMMA
EXEMPLE   **Elle est ontarienne.**

1. _____ un ami.
2. _____ Félix.
3. _____ petit.
4. _____ beau.
5. _____ jeune.

1. _____.
2. _____.
3. _____.
4. _____.
5. _____.

Now use **ce sont** and **ils sont** to complete the sentences about Félix and Jean in the left column below. Then, in the right column, rewrite the same sentences to talk about Emma and Olivia.

FÉLIX ET JEAN
EXEMPLE   **Ils sont** québécois.

EMMA ET OLIVIA
EXEMPLE   **Elles sont canadiennes.**

1. _____ mes amis.
2. _____ Félix et Jean.
3. _____ célibataires.
4. _____ beaux.

1. _____.
2. _____.
3. _____.
4. _____.

D. Comment sont-ils? Complete these descriptions with the appropriate form (masculine, feminine, singular, plural) of the indicated adjective. The first one has been done as an example.

Emma et Olivia sont sœurs ____**jumelles**____. Elles ne sont pas
                                      (twin)

_____ **(1)**; elles sont _____ **(2)**.
         (Québeckers)   *(Ontarians)*

Elles sont assez _____ **(3)**, _____ **(4)** et _____ **(5)**.
                      (short)   *(young)*   *(thin)*

Elles ne sont pas _____ **(6)**. Elles sont _____ **(7)**.
                        (married)   *(single)*

Félix n'est pas très _____ **(8)**; il est assez _____ **(9)**. Il est
                          (tall)   *(short)*

_____ **(10)** et il est très _____ **(11)**. Il est _____ **(12)**
     (thin)   *(handsome)*   *(Québecker)*

et il habite avec son *(his)* frère, Jean. Jean et Félix ne sont pas frères _____ **(13).**

(twin)

Jean est moins *(less)* _____ **(14),** mais il n'est pas _____ **(15).** Il est

(young)   *(old)*

plus *(more)* _____ **(16)** et un peu plus _____ **(17)** que *(than)* Félix.

(tall)   *(heavy)*

Jean et Félix sont tous les deux *(both)* _____ **(18)** et _____ **(19)** !

(young)   *(single)*

E. Pour mieux lire : *Using cognates and familiar words to read for the gist.* Guess the meaning of each boldfaced cognate, writing your answer in the blank.

1. Je comprends **généralement.** _____

2. **Normalement,** le cours de français est facile. _____

3. Les examens sont **probablement** difficiles. _____

4. Je suis **frustré(e).** _____

5. Je suis **fatigué(e).** _____

F. Mots apparentés. Scan this list of courses offered during the spring session and *identify at least 20 cognates.* Then, read the list and answer the questions that follow. Let the cognates guide you as you read.

SESSION DE PRINTEMPS
Du 5 mai au 20 juin

Les étudiants doivent s'inscrire à un minimum de 3 crédits jusqu'à un maximum de 9 crédits.

Anthropologie
- Anthropologie sociale et culturelle (6 crédits)
- Peuples autochtones des Amériques (3 crédits)

Criminologie
- Introduction à la criminologie (3 crédits)

Études anciennes
- La civilisation grecque (3 crédits)
- Latin I (3 crédits)
- Latin II (3 crédits)

Études canadiennes
- Langue et gouvernement au Canada (3 crédits)
- Panorama de la littérature canadienne-française (3 crédits)

Français
- Culture et littérature françaises du Moyen Âge (3 crédits)
- Poésie québécoise (3 crédits)
- Théâtre français (3 crédits)

Langues et littérature modernes
- Cours élémentaire de chinois (6 crédits)
- Cours élémentaire d'allemand (6 crédits)
- Culture de l'Amérique latine (3 crédits)

Science politique
- Partis politiques au Canada (3 crédits)
- Fédéralisme canadien (3 crédits)
- Gouvernement et politique des provinces (3 crédits)

Sociologie
- La société canadienne (3 crédits)
- Minorités et groupes ethniques (3 crédits)

---

1. How many weeks does the spring session last?

2. What is the minimum number of credits a student can take? _____ The maximum? _____

3. What courses could you recommend for…

    a. someone interested in social sciences?

    _____

    b. someone interested in politics?

    _____

    c. someone interested in Canadian culture?

    _____

G. Qui est-ce ? Reread the story *Qui est-ce ?* on pages 38–39 of the textbook. Then complete the paragraph, using the following choices.

Emma / suis / Vous ne comprenez pas / arrive / la situation / elle ne parle pas / pense / sœurs jumelles / sauvée / comprend

Félix _____ **(1)** au Musée des beaux-arts et il voit Olivia. Il dit : « Salut, Emma ! »

parce qu'il _____ **(2)** que c'est son amie Emma. Olivia répond avec difficulté

parce qu' _____ **(3)** très bien français. Elle dit : « _____ **(4)**. Je ne suis

pas Emma. Je _____ **(5)** Olivia. » Félix ne _____ **(6)** pas. Finalement,

_____ **(7)** arrive et Olivia est _____ **(8)**. Félix comprend _____ **(9)**.

Emma et Olivia sont _____ **(10)**.

*H. Un autre étudiant. You run into a student from your French class. Answer his questions *with complete sentences* about yourself.

1. Tu t'appelles comment ?

    _____

2. Tu es d'où ?

    _____

3. Tu es étudiant(e) à l'université, non ?

    _____

4. Tu es en cours de français quels jours *(which days)* ? De quelle heure à quelle heure ?

    _____

5. Nous sommes dans le même cours de français, non ?

    _____

6. Tu es marié(e) ?

    _____

Partie auditive

 A. C'est qui ? You will hear a series of sentences. Decide if each is about a male (**Jean-Marc**), a female (**Sophie**), or a group (**des amis**) and indicate the number of the sentence you hear in the appropriate column. The first one has been done as an example.

EXEMPLE   VOUS ENTENDEZ :   **1.** C'est un jeune homme.
VOUS MARQUEZ :

Jean-Marc	Sophie	des amis
1	_____	_____
_____	_____	_____
_____	_____	_____
_____	_____	_____

 B. Prononciation : *Il est* + adjectif / *Elle est* + adjectif. Pause the recording and review the *Prononciation* section on page 37 of the textbook. Then turn on the recording, listen, and repeat the sentences you hear. Be careful to differentiate between the masculine and feminine forms of the pronouns and some of the adjectives. Remember some adjectives sound the same in the masculine and feminine forms.

Il est canadien. / Elle est canadienne.   Il est jeune. / Elle est jeune.

Ils sont français. / Elles sont françaises.   Ils sont mariés. / Elles sont mariées.

Il est petit. / Elle est petite.   Il est québécois. / Elle est québécoise.

Ils sont grands. / Elles sont grandes.   Ils sont célibataires. / Elles sont célibataires.

 C. On parle de qui ? You will hear a series of sentences. For each one, decide who is being described: **Félix, Emma, Emma et Olivia,** or **tous les trois** *(all three)*. Mark the appropriate column.

EXEMPLE   VOUS ENTENDEZ : Il est québécois.
vous écrivez :

	Félix	Emma	Emma et Olivia	tous les trois
Exemple	✓	_____	_____	_____
1.	_____	_____	_____	_____
2.	_____	_____	_____	_____
3.	_____	_____	_____	_____
4.	_____	_____	_____	_____
5.	_____	_____	_____	_____
6.	_____	_____	_____	_____

Nom _____ Date _____

D. Première rencontre. Listen as two people meet for the first time. Then pause the recording and complete the statements about them by indicating which of the words in italics are appropriate.

1. Ils sont dans le même cours *de français / de sociologie / d'histoire.*

2. Le jeune homme s'appelle *Alex / Daniel / Jean-Luc / Alain.*

3. La jeune femme s'appelle *Marie / Sophie / Alice / Catherine.*

4. Elle est d' / de *Edmonton / Montréal / Calgary / Moncton.*

5. Elle est à Montréal pour *étudier / voir le Québec.*

6. Il habite *seul / avec sa* (his) *famille / à l'université.*

E. Lecture : *Qui est-ce ?* Pause the recording and reread the story ***Qui est-ce ?*** on pages 38–39 of the textbook. Then turn on the recording. You will hear three excerpts based on the encounter between Olivia and Félix. Listen to each one and decide which illustration depicts what is happening. Fill in the number of the excerpt in the blank below the appropriate picture.

a. _____   b. _____   c. _____

F. Dictée. You will hear a friend talking about Jean-Marc and his sister Céline. The first time, just listen to what she says at normal speed. Then fill in the missing words as it is repeated more slowly. Pause the recording as needed to allow enough time to fill in the words.

_____ (1) Jean-Marc, un _____ (2) québécois.

_____ (3) étudiant. Jean-Marc est _____ (4),

_____ (5) et _____ (6). Jean-Marc

et moi, _____ (7) d'histoire.

C'est Céline, _____ (8) de Jean-Marc.

_____ (9) étudiante.

Elle _____ (10). Céline est

_____ (11) et elle est _____ (12)

aussi. Jean-Marc et Céline _____ (13).

Nom _____ Date _____

Describing personality

By the time you finish this *Compétence,* you should be able to describe a person's personality and compare two individuals.

Partie écrite

A. Qui est-ce? Decide who from each pair of drawings is best described by each of the following adjectives. Then translate each adjective into French and write a sentence.

Éric ou André?

Éric

    EXEMPLE   *(very active)* **André est très dynamique.**
                     (unpleasant) **Éric est désagréable.**

  1. *(lazy)* _____

  2. *(fun)* _____

  3. *(a little boring)* _____

  4. *(athletic)* _____

  5. *(rather pessimistic)* _____

André

Monique ou Isabelle?

Monique

    EXEMPLE   *(very young)* **Monique est très jeune.**

  6. *(a little mean)* _____

  7. *(nice)* _____

  8. *(very shy)* _____

  9. *(divorced)* _____

10. *(little)* _____

11. *(fairly big)* _____

Isabelle

Pierre et Marie ou Emma et Olivia?

Pierre et Marie

    EXEMPLE   *(Ontarian)* **Emma et Olivia sont ontariennes.**

12. *(young)* _____

13. *(old)* _____

14. *(married)* _____

15. *(single)* _____

16. *(beautiful)* _____

17. *(French)* _____

Emma et Olivia

B. Astérix et Obélix. First impressions can be misleading, but what impressions do these pictures give you of the famous French comic characters **Astérix** and **Obélix**? Complete the following comparisons.

Astérix

Obélix

EXEMPLES   (optimiste) Astérix **est plus optimiste qu'**Obélix.
(beau) Obélix **est moins beau qu'**Astérix.

1. (gros) Astérix _____ Obélix.

2. (mince) Astérix _____ Obélix.

3. (petit) Astérix _____ Obélix.

4. (grand) Obélix _____ Astérix.

5. (dynamique) Astérix _____ Obélix.

6. (amusant) Obélix _____ Astérix.

C. Conversation. Reread the conversation between Félix and Marie-Louise on page 40 of the textbook. Then, complete this conversation between two other students with the indicated words.

PAUL: Tes amis et toi, vous êtes étudiants, _____ **(1)**?
                                                    (right)

ANNE: Mes amis _____ **(2),** mais moi,
                          (are students)

les études, _____ **(3).**
                (that's not my thing)

_____ **(4)** intellectuelle. Mais je suis
        (I am not at all)

_____ **(5).**
        (rather athletic)

PAUL: Alors, _____ **(6)** le sport?
                  (you like)

ANNE: Oui, _____ **(7)** beaucoup _____ **(8)**
              (I like)   *(soccer)*

et _____ **(9).** Et toi?
      (football)

PAUL: J'aime bien _____ **(10),** mais _____ **(11)** beaucoup
                      (tennis)   *(I don't like)*

le football. En fait (*In fact*), je suis _____ **(12).**
                                          (more intellectual than athletic)

D. Quel pronom ? Emma is talking to a new friend. Complete what she says with the logical subject pronoun: **je, tu, il, elle, nous, vous, ils,** or **elles.**

1. Ma famille et moi, _____ sommes de Sault-Sainte-Marie, en Ontario. Et ta *(your)* famille et toi,

   _____ êtes d'où ? Ma sœur Olivia est ici pour voir le Québec mais _____ ne parle pas très bien

   français. Moi, _____ parle très bien français ! Mes parents ne sont pas ici au Québec. _____ sont

   à l'Île-du-Prince-Édouard.

2. C'est mon ami Félix. _____ est étudiant. Et toi ? _____ es étudiante aussi ? Les amies d'Olivia

   ne sont pas étudiantes. _____ travaillent.

E. Des présentations. Félix is introducing his friends. Complete their conversation with the correct form of **être.**

FÉLIX :   Emma, Olivia, c' _____ **(1)** mon ami Thomas. Il _____ **(2)** aussi étudiant à

            l'Université de Montréal. Nous _____ **(3)** dans le même cours de maths. Thomas, ce

            _____ **(4)** mes amies Emma et Olivia. Elles _____ **(5)** de Sault-Sainte-Marie.

THOMAS :   Bonjour, Emma ! Bonjour, Olivia ! Vous _____ **(6)** ontariennes, alors ?

EMMA :   Oui, nous le _____ **(7)**. Moi, je _____ **(8)** à Montréal pour étudier. Olivia

            n' _____ **(9)** pas étudiante. Et toi ? Tu _____ **(10)** d'où ?

THOMAS :   Je _____ **(11)** d'ici.

F. Questions. A classmate is asking Emma questions. In the first blank, rephrase her classmate's question, using **est-ce que.** Then, using the information given in the preceding activity, *E. Des présentations,* answer each question as Emma would. *Use complete sentences.*

> **EXEMPLE**   Tu es étudiante ?
> — **Est-ce que tu es étudiante ?**
> — **Oui, je suis étudiante.**

1. Olivia est étudiante ?

   — _____

   — _____

2. Et Olivia et toi ? Vous êtes d'ici ?

   — _____

   — _____

3. Tu es ontarienne ?

   — _____

   — _____

4. Félix et Thomas sont ontariens ?

   — _____

   — _____

G. Encore des questions. A new friend is asking Olivia questions. Based on the answers she gives, supply her friend's questions. Use **est-ce que.**

EXEMPLE — **Est-ce que tu es intellectuelle?**
— Non, je ne suis pas très intellectuelle.

1. — _____.

— Oui, je suis sportive.

2. — _____.

— Oui, j'aime le sport.

3. — _____.

— Oui, Emma est assez sportive aussi.

4. — _____.

— Oui, Emma est étudiante.

5. — Et Emma et toi? _____.

— Emma et moi? Non, nous ne sommes pas québécoises.

6. — _____.

— Oui, nous sommes célibataires.

7. — _____.

— Oui, Félix et Jean sont d'ici.

*Journal. Your new roommate from Québec is arriving next week. Below, write an e-mail message to a new roommate. Tell her your name and where you are from. Then describe yourself in three sentences. Finally, ask her questions to find out her name, if she is from Montréal, and if she is married or single.

Nom _____ Date _____

Partie auditive

 A. Jean-Marc et Céline. You will hear several sentences describing Jean-Marc. After each sentence, say that the same is true for Céline, changing the form of the adjective as needed. After a pause for you to respond, you will hear the correct answer.

EXEMPLE   VOUS ENTENDEZ: Jean-Marc? Il est grand. Et Céline?
              VOUS DITES: **Elle est grande aussi.**
              VOUS ENTENDEZ: Elle est grande aussi.

Now you will hear a friend talking about Jean-Marc and Céline. Complete his sentences.

1. Jean-Marc n'est pas _____.

   Il est un peu _____.

2. Céline est _____, mais Jean-Marc

   n'est pas _____.

3. Jean-Marc et Céline sont _____.

   Ils ne sont pas _____.

4. Ils ne sont pas _____.

   Ils sont _____.

5. Céline n'est pas _____.

   Elle est _____. Jean-Marc est _____

   aussi. Il n'est pas _____ non plus *(either)*.

 B. Les adjectifs. Since the final **e** and **s** of adjective agreement are often not pronounced, forms that are spelled differently may be pronounced the same. You will hear one pronunciation of each of the following adjectives. Indicate all the forms of the adjective that have the pronunciation you hear.

EXEMPLE   VOUS VOYEZ: petit _____   petits _____   petite _____   petites _____
              VOUS ENTENDEZ: petite(s)
              VOUS INDIQUEZ: petit _____   petits _____   petite __✓__   petites __✓__

1. ennuyeux _____   ennuyeux _____   ennuyeuse _____   ennuyeuses _____

2. jeune _____   jeunes _____   jeune _____   jeunes _____

3. américain _____   américains _____   américaine _____   américaines _____

4. sportif _____   sportifs _____   sportive _____   sportives _____

5. marié _____   mariés _____   mariée _____   mariées _____

6. célibataire _____   célibataires _____   célibataire _____   célibataires _____

 C. Prononciation: Les pronoms sujets et le verbe *être*. Listen and repeat the subject pronouns and the verb **être,** paying particular attention to the pronunciation.

être	
je suis	nous sommes
tu es	vous êtes
il est	ils sont
elle est	elles sont

Now complete the sentences you see with the correct form of the verb **être** as you hear the narrator read them. Stop the recording as needed.

1. Moi, je _____ Félix Simard.

2. Bruno, c' _____ mon ami.

3. Il _____ de Marseille.

4. Bruno et Martine _____ très sympathiques.

5. Nous _____ dans le même cours d'espagnol.

6. Et toi, tu _____ étudiante aussi ?

7. Olivia et toi, vous _____ ontariennes, non ?

D. Les pronoms sujets. Bruno is speaking to Emma, but his remarks are incomplete. Fill in the number of the sentence you hear next to its logical completion. The first one is done as an example.

_____ **a.** Je suis étudiant à l'Université de Montréal.

___1___ **b.** Ils sont sympathiques.

_____ **c.** Il est étudiant aussi.

_____ **d.** Vous êtes sportives ?

_____ **e.** … elle est plutôt sportive.

_____ **f.** Tu es étudiante ?

_____ **g.** Nous sommes assez sportifs.

*E. Toujours des questions. You will hear a series of questions about your French class asked with rising intonation. Rephrase each one using **est-ce que.** After a pause for you to respond, you will hear the correct answer.

EXEMPLE	VOUS ENTENDEZ :	Vous êtes en cours maintenant ?
	VOUS DITES :	**Est-ce que vous êtes en cours maintenant ?**
	VOUS ENTENDEZ :	Est-ce que vous êtes en cours maintenant ?

Now play this section again. This time, *do not write* the questions, but *answer* them. Pause the recording as needed.

EXEMPLE	VOUS ENTENDEZ :	Vous êtes en cours maintenant ?
	VOUS ENTENDEZ :	Est-ce que vous êtes en cours maintenant ?
	VOUS ÉCRIVEZ :	**Oui, je suis en cours maintenant.**
		Non, je ne suis pas en cours maintenant.

1. _____

2. _____

3. _____

4. _____

5. _____

6. _____

COMPÉTENCE 3

Describing the university area

By the time you finish this *Compétence,* you should be able to describe your campus and tell what's in the surrounding neighbourhood.

Partie écrite

A. Qu'est-ce que c'est? Identify the following places or things. Remember to use **c'est** or **ce sont** when identifying something with a noun.

EXEMPLE   C'est un cinéma.

1

2

3

4

5

6

7

8

9

10

1. _____
2. _____
3. _____
4. _____
5. _____

6. _____
7. _____
8. _____
9. _____
10. _____

B. Conversation. Reread the conversation on page 47 of the textbook. Then, complete this conversation between two friends.

MARCEL: _____ **(1)** à ton université?
               (What's the campus like)

PHILIPPE: Il est trop *(too)* _____ **(2)** et il n'est pas _____ **(3)**. Il y a
                              (big)   *(very pretty)*

_____ **(4)** avec des _____ **(5)**
            (lots of buildings)   *(classrooms)*

et des _____ **(6)** et il n'y a pas _____ **(7)**.
           (offices)   *(enough trees)*

MARCEL: Qu'est-ce qu'il y a _____ **(8)**?
                                      (in the university neighbourhood)

PHILIPPE: _____ **(9)**, il y a une librairie et un cinéma
               (Near the university)

_____ **(10)**. Il y a _____ **(11)**,
            (with foreign films)   *(a lot of fast-food restaurants)*

mais il n'y a pas de _____ **(12)**.
                              (good restaurants)

C. Près de l'université. According to these individuals' preferences, what sort of place might they ask about? Compose logical questions for them to ask.

> **EXEMPLE**   **J'aime beaucoup les hamburgers.**
>   **Est-ce qu'il y a un resto rapide** près de l'université?

1. J'aime beaucoup les films étrangers.

   _____ près de l'université?

2. J'aime beaucoup les cours d'aérobique.

   _____ près de l'université?

3. J'aime beaucoup les livres.

   _____ près de l'université?

4. J'aime beaucoup le cappuccino.

   _____ près de l'université?

D. À l'université. Indicate whether each of these things is found on your campus. Be sure to use the correct form of the indefinite article **(un, une, des)** and remember that after **ne... pas, un, une,** and **des** become **de (d')**.

> **EXEMPLE**   *(rock concerts)* Sur le campus, **il y a des concerts de rock / il n'y a pas de concerts de rock.**

1. *(a nightclub)* Sur le campus, _____.

2. *(lecture halls)* Sur le campus, _____.

3. *(dorms)* Sur le campus, _____.

4. *(houses)* Sur le campus, _____.

E. Votre université. Complete these sentences with the correct indefinite article (**un, une, des**). Remember that these articles change to **de (d')** after **ne... pas** or after quantity expressions such as **beaucoup** or **assez**, and also directly before plural adjectives. Then indicate if each sentence describes your university by checking **vrai** or **faux**.

EXEMPLE   Il y a beaucoup __de__ vieux bâtiments dans le quartier.   ✓ vrai ____ faux

1. Il y a _____ grands bâtiments dans le quartier.   ___ vrai ___ faux

2. Il y a _____ salles de classe modernes sur le campus.   ___ vrai ___ faux

3. Il y a _____ théâtre sur le campus.   ___ vrai ___ faux

4. Il y a _____ grande bibliothèque sur le campus.   ___ vrai ___ faux

5. Il y a _____ résidences sur le campus.   ___ vrai ___ faux

6. Il n'y a pas _____ boîte de nuit sur le campus.   ___ vrai ___ faux

7. Il y a assez _____ stationnements sur le campus.   ___ vrai ___ faux

8. Il y a beaucoup _____ librairies dans le quartier.   ___ vrai ___ faux

F. Descriptions. Write the adjective that best describes each noun in the blank before or after it. Remember that most adjectives are placed after the noun in French, but review the 14 adjectives that are generally placed before the noun and the special forms **bel, nouvel,** and **vieil** on page 50 of the textbook before you begin.

EXEMPLE

C'est une _____ ville _intéressante_.
(ennuyeuse, intéressante)
C'est une ___jolie___ ville _____.
(jolie, laide)

1. C'est une _____ ville _____.
(grande, petite)

C'est une _____ ville _____.
(américaine, canadienne)

2. C'est un _____ quartier _____.
(vieux/vieil, moderne)

C'est un _____ quartier _____.
(agréable, désagréable)

3. C'est un _____ bâtiment _____.
(vieux/vieil, nouveau/nouvel)

C'est un _____ bâtiment _____.
(beau/bel, laid)

4. C'est un _____ homme _____.
(jeune, vieux/vieil)

C'est un _____ homme _____.
(méchant, sympa)

G. Optimiste ! Emma is always positive and enjoys everything. Complete what she would say by writing the French equivalent of the appropriate adjective given in English in the correct position in the sentence. Pay attention to the form of the adjective (masculine, feminine, singular, plural).

EXEMPLE   C'est une _____*jolie*_____ maison _____. *(pretty, ugly)*

1. Félix est un _____ homme _____. *(ugly, handsome)*

2. C'est un _____ ami _____. *(mean, nice)*

3. C'est un _____ homme _____. *(optimistic, pessimistic)*

4. Jean est un _____ homme _____. *(intelligent, stupid)*

5. Ce sont des _____ amis _____. *(interesting, boring)*

6. Olivia est une _____ femme _____. *(young, old)*

7. C'est une _____ femme _____. *(athletic, lazy)*

8. Il y a un _____ restaurant _____ près d'ici. *(bad, good)*

9. Il y a un _____ parc _____ près d'ici. *(pretty, ugly)*

10. Il y a un _____ stationnement _____ à l'université. *(small, large)*

*H. Comment est l'université ? A friend is asking you about your university. Answer his questions *in complete sentences.*

1. Est-ce que tu aimes le campus ? Comment est le campus ?

_____

_____

2. Est-ce qu'il y a plus de *(more)* vieux bâtiments ou plus de nouveaux bâtiments sur le campus ? Est-ce qu'il y a beaucoup d'arbres ? Est-ce qu'il y a assez de stationnements ?

_____

_____

_____

3. Est-ce qu'il y a un restaurant sur le campus ? Si oui *(If so)*, est-ce que c'est un bon restaurant ?

_____

4. Qu'est-ce qu'il y a sur le campus ? (Nommez au moins trois choses. *[Name at least three things.]*)

_____

5. Comment est le quartier universitaire ?

_____

6. Qu'est-ce qu'il y a près de l'université ? (Nommez au moins trois choses.)

_____

Partie auditive

 A. Identification. You will hear the following places identified. Fill in the number of each sentence you hear under the picture it identifies.

> **EXEMPLE**   VOUS ENTENDEZ : C'est un cinéma.
> VOUS ÉCRIVEZ :

a. _____

b. _____

c. <u>Exemple</u>

d. _____

e. _____

f. _____

g. _____

h. _____

Now look at the illustrations again as you hear each place named in the order it appears on the page. Repeat what you hear.

> **EXEMPLE**   VOUS ENTENDEZ : C'est un gym.
> VOUS RÉPÉTEZ :   **C'est un gym.**

Now you will hear a student say whether or not each of these places is located on campus or in the university neighbourhood. List each place that is found there. Do not write anything for the places that are not on campus or in the neighbourhood.

> **EXEMPLE**   VOUS ENTENDEZ :   **1.** Il y a un cinéma dans le quartier universitaire.
> VOUS ÉCRIVEZ :

Il y a <u>un cinéma,</u>_____

_____ .

 B. Prononciation : L'article indéfini. Pause the recording and review the ***Prononciation*** section on page 48 of the textbook. Then turn on the recording and fill in the form of the indefinite article, **un** or **une,** that you hear with each noun.

_____ cours	_____ classe	_____ bibliothèque	_____ bâtiment
_____ gym	_____ boîte de nuit	_____ ami	_____ amie
_____ résidence	_____ laboratoire	_____ quartier	_____ librairie

C. Quelle forme ? You will hear a series of questions about your university. Indicate the form of the indefinite article you hear in each one.

1. un _____   une _____   des _____   4. un _____   une _____   des _____

2. un _____   une _____   des _____   5. un _____   une _____   des _____

3. un _____   une _____   des _____   6. un _____   une _____   des _____

*Now play this section again and *answer* the questions about your university *with complete sentences* in French.

1. _____

2. _____

3. _____

4. _____

5. _____

6. _____

D. L'université. Listen as two students talk about one of their courses. Then pause the recording and complete each sentence logically.

1. Les étudiants sont dans le même cours _____.

2. Ils sont en cours le mardi et _____.

3. Le cours est à _____ heure _____.

4. Le professeur est _____.

5. Annick n'aime pas _____.

E. Dictée. You will hear a student talking about his university. The first time, just listen to what he says at normal speed. Then fill in the missing words as it is repeated more slowly.

1. Sur le campus, il y a _____

   _____.

2. Il y a _____

   et _____ pour les profs.

3. _____ l'université,

   il y a _____

   et _____.

4. Dans le _____, il y a

   _____.

5. _____, il y a _____

COMPÉTENCE 4

Talking about your studies

By the time you finish this **Compétence,** you should be able to talk about the activities and courses at your university and say what you are studying.

Partie écrite

A. Préférences. Fill in the name of each of these courses in the logical category.

le marketing / l'histoire / le théâtre / la chimie / l'anglais / la psychologie / l'espagnol /
la musique / l'informatique / la biologie / les sciences politiques / le français / la physique / l'allemand /
la comptabilité / les mathématiques

LES LANGUES	LES SCIENCES	LES SCIENCES HUMAINES
_____	_____	_____
_____	_____	_____
_____	_____	_____
_____		

LES BEAUX-ARTS	LES COURS DE COMMERCE	LES COURS TECHNIQUES
_____	_____	_____
_____	_____	_____

*Now complete these sentences about your studies.

1. Ce trimestre, j'étudie _____.

2. Je n'étudie pas _____.

3. Je comprends bien _____.

4. Je ne comprends pas très bien _____.

5. J'aime le cours de _____ parce qu'il est _____.

*Now express your feelings about these courses, activities, and places at your university by writing each of them in the appropriate category.

la philosophie / la littérature / les fêtes / les devoirs / les examens / les matchs de basket /
le laboratoire d'informatique / la bibliothèque / les cours à huit heures du matin

J'aime beaucoup...	J'aime assez...	Je n'aime pas...
_____	_____	_____
_____	_____	_____
_____	_____	_____
_____	_____	_____
_____	_____	_____

B. Comparaisons. Thomas loves all math and science classes, but he finds all other courses difficult and boring. How would he compare the following courses for the quality indicated in parentheses? Use the expressions **plus… que** and **moins… que** and remember to use the correct form of the adjective (masculine, feminine, singular, plural).

> **EXEMPLE** physics / German (interesting)
> **La physique est plus intéressante que l'allemand.**

1. chemistry / philosophy (easy)

   _____

2. psychology / math (interesting)

   _____

3. biology / history (difficult)

   _____

4. literature / chemistry (boring)

   _____

C. Conversation. Reread the conversation on page 52 of the textbook. Two friends are talking about their studies. Complete their conversation.

ISABELLE : _____ **(1)** ce trimestre?
                    (What are you studying)

RACHID : _____ **(2)** l'anglais, _____ **(3)**,
                (I'm studying)   *(history)*

_____ **(4)**, _____ **(5)** et
(computer science)   *(chemistry)*

_____ **(6).**
(accounting)

ISABELLE : _____ **(7)**?
                              (How are your classes)

RACHID : _____ **(8)** mon cours d'histoire
                (I prefer)

_____ **(9)** le prof est _____ **(10).**
      (because)   *(very interesting)*

Et toi? _____ **(11)** tes cours?
                    (Do you like)

ISABELLE : _____ **(12)**, j'aime beaucoup mon cours d'histoire.
                  (Like you)

D. Mon université. A friend is asking about life at your school. Complete her questions by filling in the correct form of the definite article: **Le, La, L', or Les.**

1. _____ université est grande?   4. _____ étudiantes sont sympas?

2. _____ cours sont faciles?   5. _____ campus est agréable?

3. _____ professeurs sont sympathiques? 6. _____ bibliothèque est moderne?

Now answer each of her questions, using the appropriate pronoun, **il, elle, ils,** or **elles,** to replace the subject. The first one has been done as an example.

1. Oui, elle est grande. / Non, elle n'est pas grande. / Non, elle est petite.

2. _____

3. _____

4. _____

5. _____

6. _____

*E. Quel article ? Complete a friend's questions with the correct form of the definite article (**le, la, l', les**), the indefinite article (**un, une, des**), or **de (d').** Then answer each question *with a complete sentence.*

1. Comment est _____ cours de français ?

   _____

2. Est-ce que _____ langues sont faciles pour toi ?

   _____

3. Combien _____ étudiants est-ce qu'il y a dans le cours ?

   _____

4. Est-ce qu'il y a _____ étudiants étrangers dans le cours ?

   _____

5. Est-ce qu'il y a _____ cinéma dans le quartier universitaire ?

   _____

6. Est-ce que tu aimes _____ films étrangers ?

   _____

F. Qui est-ce ? Complete these sentences using **c'est, ce sont, il/elle est,** or **ils/elles sont.** The first blank has been done as an example.

1. _____ *Ce sont* _____ mes amis.

   _____ à la maison.

   _____ américains.

   _____ sympas.

2. _____ une femme.

   _____ étudiante.

   _____ en classe.

   _____ timide.

3. _____ Félix et Olivia.

_____ à Montréal.

_____ mes amis.

_____ sympas.

---

*Journal. Write an email to a new French-speaking classmate from your chemistry class.

In the first paragraph, tell her:
• your name, where you are a student, and what you are studying

In the second paragraph, tell her:
• whether or not you like the university and why
• three things there are on campus and one thing there is not

In the third paragraph, ask her:
• if she is a student
• if she is married or single

_____

_____

_____

_____

_____

_____

_____

_____

_____

_____

_____

_____

_____

_____

_____

_____

_____

_____

_____

_____

_____

_____

Partie auditive

 A. Les cours. You will hear the names of various courses. For each one, indicate the field to which it belongs.

EXEMPLE VOUS ENTENDEZ : l'anglais

VOUS SÉLECTIONNEZ : C'est une langue. ___ ✓ C'est une science. ___

 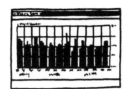 

1. C'est une langue. _____   C'est une science. _____
2. C'est une science humaine. _____   C'est un cours technique. _____
3. C'est une science. _____   C'est une science humaine. _____
4. C'est une langue. _____   C'est une science. _____
5. C'est un cours technique. _____   C'est un cours de commerce. _____
6. C'est un cours de commerce. _____   C'est une langue. _____
7. C'est une science humaine. _____   C'est un cours technique. _____
8. C'est un cours technique. _____   C'est une science humaine. _____

 B. Quels cours ? Listen as two students talk about their classes. Then complete the following statements according to the conversation.

1. Le cours d'informatique de la jeune femme est à _____ heures.
2. Elle pense que le cours d'informatique est un peu _____.
3. Le prof de théâtre du jeune homme est très _____.
4. La sœur du jeune homme étudie la _____.

 C. Prononciation : L'article défini. Pause the recording and review the *Prononciation* section on page 54 of the textbook. Then turn on the recording and practise pronouncing the forms of the definite article by repeating these words after the speaker.

le campus   la bibliothèque   l'université   les cours   les activités

le français   la comptabilité   l'informatique   les langues   les arts

 D. Préférences. You will hear the names of places or activities common to university life. Fill in the form of the definite article (**le, la, l', les**) that you hear for each one. Pause the recording between items to allow enough time to respond.

1. _____   2. _____   3. _____   4. _____   5. _____   6. _____   7. _____

*Now play this recording again and, as you hear each one, decide how much you like it and write it under the appropriate column. Stop the recording to have enough time to respond.

EXEMPLE VOUS ENTENDEZ : les fêtes
VOUS ÉCRIVEZ :

J'aime beaucoup...	J'aime assez...	Je n'aime pas du tout...
les fêtes		

*E. Colocataires. The following people are looking for housemates. Listen to each description. Then pause the recording and indicate the names of two students who, in your opinion, would make good housemates. Finally, explain your choice in English.

Daniel / Ahmad / Philippe / Pierre / Annette / Hyemi

_____

_____

Now play this section again. Then complete the statement you see, explaining which person you would prefer to live with and why.

Je préfère habiter avec _____ parce que (qu') _____

_____.

*F. Vos cours. A friend is asking about your courses this term. Answer her *with complete sentences* in French.

1. _____
2. _____
3. _____
4. _____
5. _____
6. _____
7. _____
8. _____

Après les cours   Chapitre 2

COMPÉTENCE 1

Saying what you like to do

By the time you finish this **Compétence,** you should be able to tell how you spend your free time and invite a friend to do something.

Partie écrite

A. Est-ce que vous aimez…? Félix finds certain activities fun or interesting and others boring. Does he say that he likes to do each pictured activity? Start each sentence with **J'aime…** or **Je n'aime pas…** based on whether he says the activity is fun/interesting or boring.

EXEMPLES **J'aime aller au cinéma.** C'est amusant.
Je n'aime pas faire du jogging. C'est ennuyeux.

1. _____ C'est ennuyeux.
2. _____ C'est amusant.
3. _____ C'est ennuyeux.
4. _____ C'est amusant.
5. _____ C'est intéressant.
6. _____ C'est ennuyeux.
7. _____ C'est intéressant.

B. Quel verbe? Fill in each blank on the left with a logical infinitive. Then indicate whether you generally go out with friends or to the park or stay at home to do the activity.

		A SORTIR AVEC DES AMIS OU AU PARC	B RESTER À LA MAISON
EXEMPLE	dîner au restaurant	X	
1.	_____ au cinéma	_____	_____
2.	_____ un verre avec des amis	_____	_____
3.	_____ un texto	_____	_____
4.	_____ la radio	_____	_____
5.	_____ au tennis	_____	_____
6.	_____ de la guitare	_____	_____
7.	_____ du vélo	_____	_____
8.	_____ au téléphone	_____	_____
9.	_____ sur l'ordinateur	_____	_____
10.	_____ des courriels	_____	_____

C. Conversation. Reread the conversation between Félix and Emma on page 71 of the textbook. Then complete this conversation between two other students with the indicated words.

ADRIEN: Est-ce que tu voudrais _____ **(1)** avec moi
_____ *(to do something)*

cet *(this)* après-midi?

LUCILE: _____ **(2)** cet après-midi, mais je voudrais bien
_____ *(I'm not free)*

_____ **(3)** avec toi ce soir.
_____ *(to go out)*

ADRIEN: Tu aimes la musique classique? Il y a un concert à l'université.

LUCILE: _____ **(4)**. Je préfère aller au concert de rock
_____ *(No, not really)*

au stade en ville à huit heures.

ADRIEN: Bon, _____ **(5)**.
_____ *(okay)*

LUCILE: On va souper _____ **(6)**?
_____ *(before)*

ADRIEN: _____ **(7)**. _____ **(8)** au restaurant Beauchamp.
_____ *(Okay)* _____ *(I would like to go)*

LUCILE: Bon. Alors, _____ **(9)** au restaurant Beauchamp.
_____ *(around six thirty)*

ADRIEN: Oui. À _____ **(10)**.
_____ *(later)*

D. Trop fatiguée. Emma is very tired and wants to put off doing the more demanding activities until later, and do those that take less energy now. Complete her statements with the indicated activities.

> **EXEMPLE** Je préfère **aller danser en boîte** demain soir. Je voudrais **rester à la maison** ce soir. (rester à la maison / aller danser en boîte)

1. Je voudrais bien _____ cette fin de semaine, mais cet (*this*) après-midi je préfère _____. (jouer au tennis / regarder un match à la télé)

2. Je préfère _____ demain matin. Je voudrais _____ aujourd'hui après les cours. (dormir / faire mes devoirs)

3. Je préfère _____ plus tard. Je voudrais _____ maintenant. (faire du jogging / lire)

4. Je préfère _____ demain et _____ ce soir. (rester à la maison / souper au restaurant)

5. Je préfère _____ samedi. Aujourd'hui, je voudrais _____. (inviter des amis à la maison / être seule)

E. Pourquoi ? Emma is explaining why she likes to go to different places. Which words in parentheses go in which blanks? Remember that **pour** means *in order to*, rather than *for*, when it is used before infinitives.

> **EXEMPLE** J'aime **aller au cinéma Odéon** pour **voir un film.** (voir un film, aller au cinéma Odéon)

1. J'aime _____ pour _____ _____. (prendre un verre avec des amis, aller au café Hugo)

2. Je préfère _____ pour _____ _____. (dîner avec des amis, aller au restaurant Roma)

3. Je n'aime pas beaucoup _____ pour _____ _____. (sortir en boîte, danser).

4. J'aime _____ pour _____ _____. (jouer au volleyball, aller au parc).

5. Quelquefois, j'aime _____ pour _____ (rester à la maison, dormir).

*F. Projets. Choose two activities you would like to do during your free time this week. Indicate with whom, on what day, and at what time you want to do each.

Activité	Avec qui (*whom*)?	Quel jour?	À quelle heure?
EXEMPLE aller au cinéma	avec Kim	samedi soir	à 8 h
_____	_____	_____	_____
_____	_____	_____	_____

*G. On sort? Write a conversation in which you invite one of the people listed in *F. Projets* to do the suggested activity.

EXEMPLE   aller au cinéma   avec Kim   samedi soir   à 8 h

— Kim, tu es libre samedi soir? Tu voudrais aller au cinéma avec moi?
— Oui, je veux bien. Vers quelle heure?
— Vers huit heures, d'accord?
— D'accord. À samedi!
— Au revoir!

_____

_____

_____

_____

_____

_____

*H. Et vous? A friend is making plans with you for this weekend. Answer his/her questions *with complete sentences*.

1. Est-ce que tu préfères sortir vendredi soir ou samedi soir?

   _____

2. Tu préfères aller au cinéma ou à un concert?

   _____

3. Vers quelle heure est-ce que tu voudrais sortir?

   _____

4. Tu voudrais dîner au restaurant avant d'aller au cinéma?

   _____

5. Est-ce que tu es libre dimanche après-midi?

   _____

Nom _____ Date _____

Partie auditive

 A. Loisirs. You will hear expressions for several leisure activities. Repeat each phrase after the speaker. Then, write both the number of the item and the verb under the corresponding picture. The first one has been done as an example.

EXEMPLE   VOUS ENTENDEZ: **1.** LIRE UN LIVRE
                 VOUS RÉPÉTEZ: **lire un livre**
                 VOUS ÉCRIVEZ: **1. lire** *under* **k**

a. _____

b. _____

c. _____

d. _____

e. _____

f. _____

g. _____

h. _____

i. _____

j. _____

k. 1. lire _____

l. _____

m. _____

n. _____

o. _____

 B. Prononciation: La consonne *r* et l'infinitif. Pause the recording and review the ***Prononciation*** section on page 72 of the textbook. Then turn on the recording and repeat these infinitives after the speaker. Place a check mark under the verbs where you hear the boldfaced **r** in the infinitive ending pronounced.

manger *(to eat)* inviter surfer rester aller sortir dormir voir faire échanger prendre être
     ___   ___   ___   ___   ___   ___   ___   ___   ___   ___   ___   ___

Now, stop the recording and complete the following questions between two friends with the logical infinitives from the preceding list. Use each infinitive only once. Then turn on the recording and check your work, repeating after the speaker. The first blank has been completed as an example.

1. Tu préfères __sortir__ avec des amis la fin de semaine ou _____ des amis à la maison?

2. Tu préfères _____ au cinéma ou _____ un film en ligne?

3. Tu voudrais _____ un verre ou _____ un sandwich?

4. Tu préfères _____ avec des amis sur Facebook ou _____ sur le Net?

5. Tu aimes _____ le dimanche matin ou tu n'aimes pas _____ au lit *(in bed)*?

6. Tu voudrais _____ quelque chose avec moi ou tu préfères _____ seule?

C. Pour mieux comprendre: *Listening for specific information.* Listen to three conversations in which people are making plans. For each one, select the correct option from the list given to indicate what they decide to do, where, what day, and at what time.

Activité: jouer au soccer / regarder la télé / prendre un verre / souper / aller voir un match de soccer

Où: à la maison / au café / au stade / au parc / au restaurant

Le jour: mercredi soir / jeudi / aujourd'hui / samedi / mardi soir

L'heure: vers sept heures / à quatre heures et demie / à deux heures / à midi / à cinq heures et quart

CONVERSATION A: Activité: _____ Où: _____

Le jour: _____ L'heure: _____

CONVERSATION B: Activité: _____ Où: _____

Le jour: _____ L'heure: _____

CONVERSATION C: Activité: _____ Où: _____

Le jour: _____ L'heure: _____

D. On fait quelque chose? Listen to a conversation in which Félix invites Emma and Olivia to do something tomorrow. Afterward, pause the recording and complete these statements.

1. Félix aime _____, mais Olivia préfère _____

et Emma préfère _____.

2. Félix voudrait _____ avec Olivia demain matin et

_____ avec Olivia et Emma demain après-midi.

*E. Une invitation. A friend is inviting you to do something. Answer in *complete sentences in French*.

1. _____
2. _____
3. _____
4. _____
5. _____
6. _____
7. _____

COMPÉTENCE 2

Saying how you spend your free time

By the time you finish this **Compétence,** you should be able to tell what you and those around you do regularly and how often and how well you do them.

Partie écrite

A. Talents et connaissances. Complete the sentences saying whether or not you often do these things on Saturday.

> **EXEMPLE** Je **joue** souvent au soccer le samedi matin.
> Je **ne joue pas** souvent au soccer le samedi matin.

1    **2**   **3**

1. Je _____ souvent au lit jusqu'à dix heures.

2. Je _____ souvent mes cours le samedi après-midi.

3. Le samedi soir, je _____ souvent au cinéma.

Now say whether you do the following things well.

> **EXEMPLE** Je **joue** bien au hockey.
> Je **ne joue pas** bien au hockey.

4   **5**   **6**

4. Je _____ bien.

5. Je _____ bien au tennis.

6. Je _____ bien.

B. Adverbes. Number the adverbs in the top line from 1 (most often) to 5 (least often), according to how often they indicate that people do something. Then number the adverbs in the bottom line from 1 (best) to 5 (worst), according to how well someone does something.

____ rarement | ____ ne... jamais | ____ quelquefois | ____ presque toujours | ____ souvent

____ assez mal | ____ comme ci comme ça | ____ très mal | ____ très bien | ____ assez bien

C. Conversation. Reread the conversation between Félix and Emma on page 77 of the textbook. Then, complete this conversation between two other students with the indicated words.

ÉRIC: _____ **(1)** le samedi _____ **(2)**?
             (What do you do)   *(usually)*

SOPHIE: Le samedi matin, _____ **(3)** au parc pour faire du jogging ou pour jouer au tennis,
                                    (I go)

l'après midi, _____ **(4)** et le soir j'aime sortir avec des amis.
                          (I stay home)

ÉRIC: Tu voudrais _____ **(5)** avec moi cette fin de semaine?
                                (to play tennis)

SOPHIE: Oui, oui, je veux bien. _____ **(6)** vers dix heures généralement.
                                            (I play)

ÉRIC: Je _____ **(7)** vers neuf heures et demie?
                  (pass by your house)

SOPHIE: D'accord! Tu voudrais _____ **(8)**?
                                            (to eat something afterward)

ÉRIC: Oui, je veux bien. Alors, à samedi!

SOPHIE: Au revoir. À samedi!

D. Une fille dynamique. If *Olivia leaves home early, spends a lot of time with friends, and usually only returns home to sleep*, which adverb in parentheses goes with which sentence? Rewrite the sentences inserting the logical adverb.

EXEMPLE   Elle aime sortir avant neuf heures du matin. / Elle reste au lit après huit heures.
                (ne... jamais, toujours)
                **Elle aime toujours sortir avant neuf heures du matin. Elle ne reste
                jamais au lit après huit heures.**

1. Elle reste à la maison. / Elle préfère sortir avec des amis. (ne... presque jamais, presque toujours)

   _____

   _____

2. Elle préfère voir des films au cinéma. / Elle regarde des films en ligne. (rarement, toujours)

   _____

   _____

3. Elle bricole la fin de semaine. / Elle joue au tennis. (ne... jamais, quelquefois)

   _____

   _____

4. Elle mange à la maison la fin de semaine. / Elle dîne au restaurant avec des amis. (presque toujours, rarement)

   _____

   _____

5. Elle passe la fin de semaine avec des amis. / Elle est seule. (presque toujours / ne... presque jamais)

   _____

   _____

Nom _____ Date _____

E. La famille d'Emma. Emma is talking to a new friend about her family. Complete her statements with the correct conjugated form of the verb in parentheses.

Ma famille _____ **(1)** (habiter) à Sault-Sainte-Marie. Mes parents _____ **(2)**

(être) à la retraite *(retired)*. Ils _____ ne **(3)** (travailler) pas. Mon père *(father)*

_____ **(4)** (rester) souvent à la maison. Il _____ **(5)** (regarder)

la télé et il _____ **(6)** (bricoler). Ma mère *(mother)* préfère sortir

et elle _____ **(7)** (inviter) souvent des amies à la maison. Elles

_____ **(8)** (parler) et elles _____

(9) (jouer) au bridge. Ma mère _____ **(10)** (aimer) la musique. Elle

_____ **(11)** (danser) et elle _____

(12) (chanter) très bien. Ma sœur Olivia _____ **(13)** (travailler) dans

un club de gym. Elle _____ **(14)** (aimer) beaucoup le sport et elle

_____ **(15)** (jouer) très bien au tennis.

Moi, j' _____ **(16)** (habiter) à Montréal maintenant, parce que j' _____ **(17)**

(étudier) à l'Université de Montréal. Olivia _____ **(18)** (être) ici à Montréal

maintenant. Nous _____ **(19)** (aimer) être ensemble *(together)*. Le soir, nous

_____ **(20)** (souper) ensemble et après nous _____ **(21)**

(inviter) des amis à sortir.

F. Chacun ses goûts. Emma is talking about what people prefer to do in their free time. Review the spelling change verbs on page 82 of the textbook. Then, complete each sentence with a conjugated form of **préférer** and the logical infinitive from the list.

       voir   faire   écrire   jouer   lire   prendre   surfer   dîner   aller danser

    EXEMPLE   Moi, je **préfère lire** des magazines.

1. Mes amis _____ au soccer au parc.

2. Moi, je _____ un film au cinéma.

3. Mon meilleur ami _____ sur Internet.

4. Mes amis et moi, nous _____ au restaurant la fin de semaine.

5. Olivia _____ des courriels à des amis le soir.

6. Félix et Jean _____ un verre au café.

7. Quelquefois, mes amis et moi _____ en boîte.

8. Et toi, qu'est-ce que tu _____ avec tes amis ?

*G. Mes amis et moi. Say how often the following people do the indicated things. Remember to conjugate the verb and to place the adverb in the correct position in the sentence. The verbs in **5, 6,** and **7** have spelling changes, as explained on page 82 of the textbook.

toujours / souvent / quelquefois / rarement / ne… jamais

EXEMPLE moi, je / jouer au golf la fin de semaine
Moi, je joue rarement au golf la fin de semaine.

1. mes amis / regarder la télévision la fin de semaine

_____

2. moi, je (j') / envoyer un texto à un(e) ami(e)

_____

3. ma meilleure amie / inviter des amis à la maison la fin de semaine

_____

4. les étudiants de l'université / étudier la fin de semaine

_____

5. en cours de français, les étudiants / répéter après le prof

_____

6. en cours de français, nous / commencer à l'heure *(on time)*

_____

7. nous / manger pendant les cours

_____

*Journal. Write a paragraph describing how you typically spend your time on the weekend. If you want to use the verb **aller**, or verbs that do not end in **-er**, such as **dormir** or **sortir**, see the *Note de grammaire* in the margin on page 78 of the textbook.

EXEMPLE Le vendredi soir, je reste souvent à la maison parce que je suis fatigué(e) *(tired).*
Quelquefois, je préfère sortir avec des amis. Le samedi matin, je reste au lit jusqu'à…

_____

_____

_____

_____

_____

_____

_____

_____

_____

Partie auditive

 A. La fin de semaine. Listen and repeat as a woman says how often she does different things on weekends. Pause the recording and write the adverb saying how often under the corresponding illustration.

EXEMPLE   VOUS ENTENDEZ :   D'habitude, je rentre à la maison à 4 h le vendredi.

VOUS RÉPÉTEZ :   **D'habitude, je rentre à la maison à 4 h le vendredi.**

VOUS ÉCRIVEZ :

a. _____   **b.** _____   **c.** d'habitude   **d.** _____

e. _____   **f.** _____   **g.** _____   **h.** _____

 B. Prononciation : Les verbes en -er. Pause the recording and review the *Prononciation* section on page 79 of the textbook. Then read the following sentences and cross out the boldfaced verb endings that are not pronounced. Finally, turn on the recording and repeat the sentences after the speaker, checking your work.

_____ Emma et Olivia préfèr**ent** le restaurant Le Lion d'Or.

_____ Où est-ce que vous mang**ez** ?

__1__ Tu rest**es** à la maison ce soir ?

_____ Emma aim**e** passer beaucoup de temps avec toi, non ?

__6__ Oui, je pass**e** beaucoup de temps avec elle.

_____ Non, Emma, Olivia et moi soup**ons** au restaurant.

Now stop the recording and reorder the preceding sentences to create a logical conversation between Félix and his brother Jean by numbering them from **1** to **6**. The first one and the last one have been done for you. Then turn on the recording and listen to their conversation to check your work.

C. Prononciation: Les verbes à changements orthographiques. Pause the recording and review the *Prononciation* section on page 82 of the textbook. Then turn on the recording and repeat these verb forms after the speaker.

je préfère   nous préférons   tu répètes   vous répétez

Pause the recording, look at the following words, and decide how the underlined **c** or **g** is pronounced. Where **c** is pronounced like **s,** write an **s** in the blank. Where **g** is pronounced like **j,** write **j.** If the indicated **c** or **g** has a hard sound, leave the blank empty. Finally, turn on the recording and check your work, repeating each word after the speaker.

_____ café   _____ culture   _____ gare   _____ guitare

_____ célèbre   _____ créole   _____ général   _____ gosse

_____ ici   _____ commençons   _____ gré   _____ voyageons

_____ cocorico   _____ gitane

D. La fin de semaine. Pause the recording and review the verbs with spelling changes on page 82 of the textbook. Then turn on the recording and listen as Félix's friends, Thomas and Gisèle, say what they do. The first time, just listen to their conversation at normal speed. Then listen as it is repeated in short phrases at a slower speed, with pauses for you to fill in the missing words.

THOMAS: Qu'est-ce que tu fais _____ (1) la fin de semaine?

GISÈLE: Le samedi après-midi, je _____ (2), mais le samedi soir, j'aime

_____ (3).

Nous _____ (4) souvent ensemble au

restaurant et nous _____ (5) beaucoup.

Et toi, Thomas, tu _____ (6) beaucoup de

temps à la maison ou tu _____ (7) sortir?

THOMAS: Moi, je _____ (8) inviter des amis à la maison. Beaucoup

de mes amis _____ (9) de la musique. Nous_____ (10)

et nous _____ (11). Et toi Gisèle, tu _____ (12),

non? Tu es libre samedi? Tu voudrais jouer de la musique avec nous?

GISÈLE: Oui, je veux bien, mais je _____ (13)!

Je _____ (14) chez toi à quelle heure?

THOMAS: Nous _____ (15) à jouer vers huit heures généralement.

*E. Et toi? Listen as a friend asks you questions about what you do on the weekend. Answer each question *with a complete sentence.*

1. _____

2. _____

3. _____

4. _____

5. _____

COMPÉTENCE 3

Asking about someone's day

By the time you finish this **Compétence,** you should be able to ask how people typically spend their day and tell how you spend yours.

Partie écrite

A. Ma journée. Write each possible answer from the list after the logical question word. The first one has been done as an example.

avec mon petit ami (ma petite amie) / tous les jours / parce que c'est amusant / toute la journée / parce que j'aime ça / chez moi / dans un resto rapide / avec mon mari (ma femme) / pour dîner / à la bibliothèque / le matin / seul(e) / de deux heures à quatre heures

Quand? _____

_____

Où? _____

_____

Avec qui? *avec mon petit ami (ma petite amie),*

_____

Pourquoi? _____

_____

B. Conversation. Reread the conversation between Jean and Emma on page 84 of the textbook. Then, complete this conversation between two other friends with the indicated words.

ABDUL: _____ **(1)** est-ce que tu travailles?
_____(When)_____

YANN: Je travaille _____ **(2)** la fin de semaine.
_____(every day, except)_____

ABDUL: Tu travailles _____ **(3)**?
_____(all day long)_____

YANN: Oui, _____ **(4)** huit heures _____ **(5)** cinq heures, mais _____ **(6)** à la
(from)   _(to)_   _(I return)_

maison à midi pour _____ **(7)**.
_____(to have lunch)_____

ABDUL: Et le soir, qu'est-ce que tu fais _____ **(8)**?
_____(in general)_____

YANN: _____ **(9)** à la maison vers cinq heures et demie.
(I return)

_____ **(10)** un peu avant de souper.
_____(Sometimes, I sleep)_____

ABDUL: Et après?

YANN: Je parle au téléphone _____ **(11)** ou
_____(with my girlfriend)_____

_____ **(12)**.
_____(I surf the Web)_____

C. Une lettre. Emma is writing to her former French teacher in Sault Ste Marie about her new experiences in Montréal. Complete her statements with the correct form of the indicated verb. Pay attention to the verbs with spelling changes.

Chère Madame Filloux,

Je _____ **(1)** (être) très contente ici à Montréal.

J' _____ **(2)** (aimer) beaucoup mes cours et l'université. Les

étudiants _____ **(3)** (être) sympas et les cours _____ **(4)**

(être) intéressants. Je _____ **(5)** (être) à l'université tous

les jours sauf la fin de semaine. Le matin, je _____ **(6)** (préparer)

mes cours à la bibliothèque. Je _____ **(7)** (préférer) étudier

avec une amie. Nous _____ **(8)** (commencer) à travailler vers

neuf heures et l'après-midi, je _____ **(9)** (être) en cours. Je ne

_____ **(10)** (passer) pas tout mon temps _____

(all my time) à l'université, bien sûr *(of course)*. J'_____ **(11)**

(aimer) sortir avec des amis. Nous _____ **(12)** (aimer) aller

au cinéma et nous _____ **(13)** (manger) souvent ensemble.

Quelquefois, nous _____ **(14)** (dîner) ensemble dans un

resto rapide et d'autres fois _____ *(other times)* nous **(15)**

_____ (souper) ensemble au restaurant. J'_____

(16) _____ (aimer) mieux aller au restaurant ! Olivia **(17)**

_____ (être) ici et nous **(18)** _____ (passer)

beaucoup de temps ensemble. Elle **(19)** _____ (être) très

sportive et elle **(20)** _____ (aimer) beaucoup jouer au tennis.

Moi, je n' **(21)** _____ (aimer) pas beaucoup jouer avec elle

parce qu'elle **(22)** _____ (gagner) toujours. Quelquefois, nous

_____ **(23)** (voyager) la fin de semaine pour voir un peu le Québec.

Cordialement,
Emma Clark

Now complete the following questions by translating the question words in parentheses. Then answer each question according to what Emma says in the preceding letter.

1. _____ *(How)* sont les étudiants et les cours ?

_____

2. _____ *(What days)* est-ce qu'Emma est à l'université ?

_____

3. _____ *(With whom)* est-ce qu'Emma aime sortir ?

_____

4. _____ *(What)* est-ce qu'ils aiment faire ensemble ?

_____

5. _____ *(Where)* est-ce qu'Emma aime mieux manger ?

_____

6. _____ *(Why)* est-ce qu'Emma n'aime pas jouer au tennis avec Olivia ?

_____

7. _____ *(When)* est-ce qu'Emma et Olivia voyagent ?

_____

D. Projets. Two friends are talking about plans for the evening. Complete their conversation with the logical question words.

à quelle heure / pourquoi / qui / que (qu') / où / comment

— _____ **(1)** est-ce que tu voudrais faire ce soir ? Tu voudrais faire quelque chose avec moi ?

— Pas ce soir. Je vais chez mon amie Florence.

— _____ **(2)** est-ce que tu vas *(are going)* chez elle ?

— Parce qu'il y a une fête pour son anniversaire *(birthday)*.

— _____ **(3)** est-ce qu'elle habite ?

— Elle habite près de l'université.

— _____ **(4)** est-ce que la fête commence ?

— À sept heures.

— _____ **(5)** est-ce que tu vas chez Florence ?

— Une amie passe chez moi vers six heures et demie.

— _____ **(6)** est-ce ?

— C'est mon autre amie Yasmine.

E. Beaucoup de questions. Emma is answering a friend's questions. Based on the italicized part of each of Emma's answers, provide the question her friend asked.

EXEMPLE — **Quels jours est-ce que tu es à l'université ?**
— Je suis à l'université *tous les jours sauf la fin de semaine.*

1. _____?

Je suis à l'université *de neuf heures à trois heures.*

2. _____?

Je dîne *avec Olivia.*

3. _____?

Nous aimons manger *au café Le Trapèze.*

4. _____?

Nous mangeons *vers une heure et demie* d'habitude.

5. _____?

Je rentre *à trois heures et demie.*

6. _____?

Je prépare les cours *avec une amie.*

7. _____?

Elle préfère étudier *à la bibliothèque.*

8. _____?

Le soir, j'aime faire *quelque chose avec mes amis.*

F. Mon meilleur ami. Using inversion, rewrite the following questions about you and your best male friend.

EXEMPLE Est-ce que ton meilleur ami habite ici ou dans une autre ville?
Ton meilleur ami habite-t-il ici ou dans une autre ville?

1. Est-ce que ton meilleur ami travaille la fin de semaine?

_____

2. Est-ce que vous aimez sortir ensemble la fin de semaine?

_____

3. Quel jour est-ce que vous préférez sortir?

_____

4. Est-ce que ton ami préfère aller danser ou aller au cinéma?

_____

5. Est-ce qu'il danse bien?

_____

6. Est-ce que vous mangez souvent ensemble au restaurant?

_____

7. Est-ce que tu préfères dîner ou souper au restaurant?

_____

*G. Mon ami et moi. Answer the questions about you and your best male friend from *F. Mon meilleur ami* with complete sentences.

EXEMPLE Ton meilleur ami habite-t-il ici ou dans une autre ville?
Il habite ici. / Il habite à Regina.

1. _____

2. _____

3. _____

4. _____

5. _____

6. _____

7. _____

Partie auditive

 A. C'est logique ? For each item, you will hear two questions. Repeat the question that would logically elicit the response shown. Indicate whether it was the first or second option by indicating **1ʳᵉ** or **2ᵉ** and write out the question word used. Finally, check your work as you hear the correct answer.

EXEMPLE VOUS VOYEZ : tous les jours **1ʳᵉ** ____ **2ᵉ** ____ _____

VOUS ENTENDEZ : Quand est-ce que vous êtes à l'université ?

Pourquoi est-ce que vous êtes à l'université ?

VOUS DITES : **Quand est-ce que vous êtes à l'université ?**

VOUS INDIQUEZ : tous les jours **1ʳᵉ** √ **2ᵉ** ____ **quand**

VOUS ENTENDEZ : Quand est-ce que vous êtes à l'université ?

1. au café du quartier **1ʳᵉ** ____ **2ᵉ** ____ _____

2. avec une amie **1ʳᵉ** ____ **2ᵉ** ____ _____

3. un sandwich **1ʳᵉ** ____ **2ᵉ** ____ _____

4. vers quatre heures **1ʳᵉ** ____ **2ᵉ** ____ _____

5. chez moi **1ʳᵉ** ____ **2ᵉ** ____ _____

6. avec mon petit ami (ma petite amie) **1ʳᵉ** ____ **2ᵉ** ____ _____

7. jouer au tennis **1ʳᵉ** ____ **2ᵉ** ____ _____

 B. Prononciation : Les lettres qu. Pause the recording and review the **Prononciation** section on page 86 of the textbook. Then turn on the recording and repeat these questions after the speaker. When you have finished, turn off the recording and match the questions to their logical responses by writing the number of the question in the blank next to the corresponding answer.

1. Est-ce que tu travailles ?   ____ **a.** À l'université.

2. Où est-ce que tu travailles ?   ____ **b.** Avec Ali.

3. Quand est-ce que tu travailles ?   ____ **c.** Parce que j'aime le sport.

4. Avec qui est-ce que tu travailles ?   ____ **d.** Tous les jours sauf la fin de semaine.

5. Qu'est-ce que tu aimes faire la fin de semaine ? ____ **e.** J'aime jouer au soccer.

6. Pourquoi ?   ____ **f.** Oui, je travaille beaucoup.

 C. Prononciation : L'inversion et la liaison. Pause the recording and review the **Prononciation** section on page 88 of the textbook. Decide whether the final consonants *of the verbs* in the following questions should be pronounced. Cross out those that are silent and mark those that are pronounced in liaison with a link mark [‿]. Then turn on the recording and repeat the sentences after the speaker, checking your pronunciation.

EXEMPLE Le café est-il près d'ici ?

1. Voudrais-tu aller au café ?   3. Félix voudrait-il aller prendre un verre ?

2. Olivia et Emma sont-elles au café ?   4. Aiment-ils aller au café ?

Nom _____ Date _____

D. Quelle est la question? You are eavesdropping on your friend Jean-Luc, who is talking on the phone about plans for this weekend. You cannot hear the questions of the person on the other end of the line, but you figure them out from Jean-Luc's answers. Complete the questions asked by the other person by writing the logical question word.

À quelle heure / Quand / Avec qui / Que (Qu') / Où / Pourquoi

EXEMPLE   VOUS ENTENDEZ: Je voudrais aller danser samedi soir.
               VOUS ÉCRIVEZ: **Qu'**est-ce que tu voudrais faire samedi soir?

1. _____ voudrais-tu souper?

2. _____ est-ce que tu voudrais aller danser?

3. _____ voudrais-tu aller danser?

4. _____ voudrais-tu sortir avec elle?

5. _____ est-ce que tu préfères étudier?

E. À l'université. Listen as Emma asks a friend, Bruno, about his day and complete the following statements according to what he says.

1. Bruno est à l'université _____.

2. Il prépare ses cours _____ et

   _____, bien sûr.

3. _____ il étudie à la maison, mais il étudie aussi

   _____ à la bibliothèque.

4. Après les cours, il aime _____ et quelquefois, il

   _____.

*F. Et vous? Answer the following questions about your typical day *with complete sentences*.

1. _____

   _____

2. _____

   _____

3. _____

   _____

4. _____

   _____

5. _____

   _____

COMPÉTENCE 4

Going to the café

By the time you finish this **Compétence,** you should be able to say what you like to eat and drink at a café.

Partie écrite

A. Je voudrais un/une/des... Some people are discussing food and drinks and ordering at a café. Complete their sentences with the name of the pictured item. Remember to use **un, une,** or **des.**

EXEMPLE   Je voudrais **un café.**

1   2   3   4   5

1. Je voudrais _____.

2. Pour moi, _____.

3. Pour mon ami, _____.

4. Félix voudrait _____.

5. Je vais prendre _____.

B. Préférences. Some people are discussing their eating habits or ordering at a café. Complete their sentences with the logical noun in parentheses, including the appropriate article. Remember to use **un, une,** or **des** to say *a* or *some,* but use **le, la, l',** or **les** after verbs indicating likes or preferences (**J'aime le café. Je préfère le thé.**).

EXEMPLE   Je mange souvent **des frites,** mais je n'aime pas **les sandwichs au jambon.** Je suis végétarien. (sandwichs au jambon, frites)

1. Le matin, je préfère _____. Je n'aime pas

_____ parce que je n'aime pas prendre de boissons avec de la caféine.

(café, jus de fruits)

2. J'ai soif. Je voudrais _____. J'ai faim aussi, alors je vais prendre

_____ avec ça. (sandwich au fromage, chocolat chaud)

3. _____ pour mon ami. Moi, je préfère quelque chose de chaud, alors je

vais prendre _____ (bière, thé au citron)

4. Je mange souvent _____ avec un hamburger et je commande

_____ comme boisson d'habitude. (Orangina, frites)

5. Au café, je commande _____ d'habitude. Je voudrais prendre

_____ quelquefois, mais je suis diabétique. (verre de vin, eau minérale)

*C. Et vous? Do you like to go to cafés? Complete the following questions with the logical question words, according to the answers suggested in parentheses. Then answer each question about yourself. One of the words will be used twice.

où / que (qu') / comment / qui / pourquoi / quand / quelle / combien

EXEMPLE **Combien** de temps est-ce que vous passez au café? (beaucoup de temps, peu de temps)
Je passe beaucoup de temps au café.

1. Avec _____ est-ce que vous aimez aller au café? (avec mes amis, avec

mon petit ami, avec ma petite amie, seul[e], …)

_____

2. _____ est-ce que vous préférez aller? (chez Tim Hortons, chez Van

Houtte, chez Starbucks, …)

_____

3. _____ est-ce que vous aimez ce *(that)* café? (parce que le café est très

bon, parce que la clientèle est intéressante, parce qu'il est près de l'université, …)

_____

4. _____ est le service dans ce café? (toujours très bon, quelquefois

mauvais, …)

_____

5. _____ est-ce que vous préférez aller au café? (le matin, l'après-midi, le

soir)

_____

6. À _____ heure est-ce que ce café ferme? (à minuit, à neuf heures du

soir, …)

_____

7. _____ est-ce que vous aimez prendre au café? (un café, un coca, un

thé, …)

_____

8. _____ est-ce que vous aimez faire au café? (lire, parler avec des amis,

écouter de la musique, surfer sur Internet, faire des devoirs, écrire des courriels, …)

_____

D. Conversation. Reread the conversation in which Félix and Emma order at a café on pages 90–91 of the textbook. Then, complete the following conversation in which Emma is at the café with another friend.

EMMA: _____ (1) et _____ (2). Et toi?
                        (I'm very hungry)   *(I'm thirsty too)*

GISÈLE: _____ (3).
                     (Me too)

EMMA: Monsieur, _____ (4).
                             (please)

LE SERVEUR: Bonjour, mesdemoiselles. Vous désirez?

EMMA: _____ (5) un coca et _____ (6).
              (I would like)   *(some fries)*

GISÈLE: _____ (7).
              (For me, a glass of white wine and a ham sandwich)

LE SERVEUR: Très bien.

Après, Emma et Gisèle _____ (8).
                                 (pay)

EMMA: _____ (9), monsieur?
              (That comes to how much)

LE SERVEUR: _____ (10) vingt dollars _____ (11).
              (That comes to)   *(fifty)*

EMMA: _____ (12) trente dollars.
                     (Here are)

LE SERVEUR: Et _____ (13). Merci bien.
                         (here is your change)

E. Les prix. Write the following prices in numerals.

    EXEMPLE   quarante-huit dollars **48 $**

1. soixante-quatre dollars _____ $
2. soixante-quatorze dollars _____ $
3. quatre-vingt-un dollars _____ $
4. cinquante-quatre dollars _____ $
5. cinquante-sept dollars _____ $
6. quarante-deux dollars _____ $
7. quatre-vingt-dix-neuf dollars _____ $
8. soixante-quinze dollars _____ $
9. quatre-vingt-huit dollars _____ $
10. cent dollars _____ $

F. C'est combien ? Emma is writing some cheques. Write out these amounts as they would appear on her cheques.

    EXEMPLE   84 $ **quatre-vingt-quatre** dollars

36 $ _____ dollars   100 $ _____ dollars

92 $ _____ dollars   83 $ _____ dollars

76 $ _____ dollars   95 $ _____ dollars

88 $ _____ dollars   55 $ _____ dollars

47 $ _____ dollars   89 $ _____ dollars

65 $ _____ dollars   41 $ _____ dollars

71 $ _____ dollars   74 $ _____ dollars

---

*Journal. Write a paragraph describing your activities the days you go to school. Include the following information. You may change the order as needed to fit your day.

- what days you are at the university
- what time you are at the university on one of those days
- where, at what time, and with whom you have lunch that day
- what you like to do after class
- how often you go to a café, with whom, what you order, and what you like to do there
- what time you return home
- what you do in the evenings usually

    EXEMPLE   **Je suis à l'université tous les jours sauf la fin de semaine. Le lundi, je suis à l'université toute la journée, de neuf heures à cinq heures…**

_____

_____

_____

_____

_____

_____

_____

_____

_____

_____

_____

_____

_____

_____

Nom _____ Date _____

Partie auditive

 A. Au café. Order each of these items by repeating the order after the speaker.

un expresso
_____

un jus de fruits
_____

un Orangina
_____

un café au lait
_____

un coca
_____

un sandwich
au jambon
_____

un thé au citron
_____

un verre de vin rouge
et un verre de vin blanc
_____

un sandwich
au fromage
_____

une eau minérale
_____

une bière
_____

des frites
_____

 B. Je voudrais… You will hear a conversation in which a family is ordering at a café. As they order, check off the items they ask for in the illustrations in *A. Au café.*

 C. Comptons! Listen to the numbers and repeat after the speaker.

30… 40… 50… 60… 70… 80… 90… 100

D. Prononciation : Les nombres. Pause the recording and review the *Prononciation* section on page 92 of the textbook. Decide whether the final consonants of these numbers should be pronounced. Cross out those that are silent and mark those that are pronounced in liaison with a link mark [‿] as in the first item, which has been done as an example. Then turn on the recording and repeat after the speaker, checking your answers.

1. un / un‿étudiant / un livre
2. deux / deux étudiants / deux livres
3. trois / trois étudiants / trois livres
4. six / six étudiants / six livres
5. huit / huit étudiants / huit livres
6. dix / dix étudiants / dix livres

CHAPITRE 2 *Compétence 4 • Partie auditive*   **71**

E. Prix moyens. You will hear the average price for beverages at cafés in Québec. Write the name of the beverage and the price.

      EXEMPLE   VOUS ENTENDEZ ET VOUS ÉCRIVEZ : Une bouteille *(bottle)* de **bière,** c'est **3,50 $.**

1. Un _____, c'est _____ $.

2. Un _____, c'est _____ $.

3. Un _____, c'est _____ $.

4. Un _____, c'est _____ $.

5. Un _____, c'est _____ $.

F. On va au café ? Listen to a conversation in which two students who just met in class at the **Université de Montréal** are making plans to go to a café together. Fill in the missing numbers *using numerals.*

— Tu voudrais aller prendre quelque chose avec moi au café ?

— Maintenant, je voudrais rentrer rapidement chez moi, mais peut-être dans _____ **(a)** minutes.

— Où est-ce que tu habites ?

— À la résidence universitaire.

— Moi aussi ! Je suis dans la chambre _____ **(b).**

— Moi, je suis dans la chambre _____ **(c).** Quel est ton numéro de téléphone ?

— C'est le 514 _____-_____ **(d).**

— Mon téléphone, c'est le 514- _____-_____. **(e).**

— Alors, je passe chez toi dans _____ **(f)** minutes ?

— D'accord.

G. Au café. Review the dialogue on pages 90–91 of the textbook, in which Félix and Emma order something at the café. Then listen as they order at the café another time and complete the following sentences.

1. _____ voudrait manger, mais _____ n'a pas faim.

2. Félix commande _____ et _____.

    Emma commande _____.

3. Ils paient _____ dollars _____.

Un nouvel appartement

Chapitre **3**

COMPÉTENCE 1

Talking about where you live

By the time you finish this *Compétence,* you should be able to describe where you live in French.

Partie écrite

*A. Chez Thomas. Read about where Thomas lives, then say what is true for you. To say *my apartment, my house,* or *my room,* use **mon appartement**, **ma maison**, or **ma chambre**.

> **EXEMPLE** Thomas est étudiant à l'Université d'Ottawa.
> Moi, je **suis étudiant(e) à l'Université…**

1. Thomas habite dans un appartement avec un colocataire.

   Moi, j' _____.

2. Thomas habite au centre-ville. Sa *(His)* famille habite en banlieue. Son *(His)* meilleur ami habite à la campagne.

   Moi, j' _____.

   Ma famille _____.

   Mon meilleur ami (Ma meilleure amie) _____.

   _____

3. L'appartement de Thomas n'est pas trop loin de l'université. C'est très commode.

   _____

   _____

4. L'appartement de Thomas est grand et il n'est pas trop cher. Le loyer est de 825 $ par mois.

   _____

   _____

   _____

B. Une maison. Tell what rooms there are in this house by filling in each blank to identify the room. Use the indefinite article **un, une,** or **des.**

Dans cette *(this)* maison, il y a six pièces :

1. _____.
2. _____.
3. _____.
4. _____.
5. _____.
6. _____.

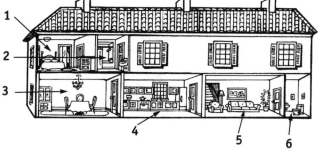

C. L'immeuble de Thomas. Change these cardinal numbers to their ordinal equivalents.

> **EXEMPLE**   deux → **deuxième**

1. un → _____   4. cinq → _____

2. trois → _____   5. neuf → _____

3. quatre → _____   6. dix → _____

Now, identify parts of Thomas's apartment building by filling in items **1–8** below.

> **EXEMPLE**   **l'ascenseur**

1. la _____

2. la _____

3. l' _____

4. le _____ étage

5. le _____ étage

6. le _____ étage

7. le _____

8. le _____

l'appartement de Thomas

Exemple

Now, complete the statements that follow to say what is going on in the building. In the first blank, identify the floor. In the second blank, say what the indicated person is doing. Remember to use **au** to say *on the* or *in the* with a floor.

> **EXEMPLE**   **Au troisième étage,** trois étudiants **préparent les cours.**

1. _____, Thomas et son ami _____

_____ .

2. _____, une jeune femme _____

_____ .

3. _____, la mère et deux de ses enfants _____

_____ . Les deux autres enfants _____

au ballon.

4. _____, un vieux monsieur _____

_____ .

D. Une conversation. Philippe is asking Thomas about his apartment. Complete their conversation.

PHILIPPE : _____ **(1)** est ton appartement ?
(On what floor)

THOMAS : J'habite _____ **(2)**
(on the second floor)

d'un _____ **(3).**
(large apartment building)

PHILIPPE : Tu habites _____ **(4)** l'université ?
(near)

THOMAS : Mon appartement n'est pas _____ **(5)** l'université
(too far from)

et il y a _____ **(6)** tout près.
(a bus stop)

PHILIPPE : Quelles _____ **(7)** est-ce qu'il y a chez toi ?
(rooms)

THOMAS : Il y a trois _____ **(8)**, _____ **(9)**,
(bedrooms) _(a modern kitchen)_

_____ **(10)** et _____ **(11).**
(a living room) _(a small dining room)_

E. En quelle année ? Fill in the following important years from Québec's history in numerals.

EXEMPLE **1534** Jacques Cartier prend _(takes)_ possession du Canada pour la France
en **mille cinq cent trente-quatre.**

_____ **1.** La ville de Québec est fondée _(founded)_ en **mille six cent huit.**

_____ **2.** La France cède ses territoires canadiens aux Anglais en **mille sept cent soixante-trois.**

_____ **3.** Le Parti québécois a été fondé en **mille neuf cent soixante-huit.**

_____ **4.** Près de _(Nearly)_ cinquante pour cent des Québécois ont voté pour un Québec libre en **mille neuf cent quatre-vingt-seize.**

_____ **5.** En **mille neuf cent quatre-vingt-dix-huit,** la Cour suprême du Canada a affirmé que le Québec ne pouvait pas _(could not)_ procéder unilatéralement à la souveraineté.

F. Des chiffres. People are writing cheques for the amounts shown. Complete the amounts.

1. 300 $ = trois _____ dollars

2. 2 204 $ = deux _____ deux cent quatre dollars

3. 1 718 000 $ = _____ sept _____ dix-huit

_____ dollars

4. 492 $ = _____ dollars

5. 3 925 $ = _____ dollars

6. 2 685 050 $ = _____ dollars

*G. Pour mieux lire: *Guessing meaning from context*. Use what you know and the context to guess the meaning of the **boldfaced** words below. The verbs are all in the *present* tense.

Philippe ouvre la lettre de Thomas et **vérifie** l'adresse. Il **lit**: «*Mon appartement **se trouve** au 2065, rue Lisgar. J'habite au deuxième étage.* » «Oui, c'est bien là», pense-t-il. Il **descend de** la voiture, **entre** dans l'immeuble et **monte** l'escalier.

1. vérifie = _____   4. descend de = _____

2. lit = _____   5. entre = _____

3. se trouve = _____   6. monte = _____

*H. Un nouvel appartement. Reread the story *Un nouvel appartement* on pages 112–113 of the textbook. Then answer the following questions with *short answers in English*.

1. What floor does Thomas live on?

    _____

2. What floor did Philippe first go to?

    _____

3. Who is the Claude that Philippe speaks to? Who does Philippe think she is?

    _____

4. What *two* things was Philippe confused about? Why?

    _____

    _____

*I. Et vous? Answer the following questions about your living situation *with complete sentences*.

1. Est-ce que vous habitez dans un appartement, dans une maison ou dans une chambre à la résidence universitaire?

    _____

2. Est-ce que vous aimez l'appartement / la maison / la résidence où vous habitez? Pourquoi?

    _____

3. Est-ce que c'est au centre-ville, en ville, en banlieue ou à la campagne? C'est près de l'université ou loin de l'université?

    _____

4. À quel étage est-ce que vous préférez habiter?

    _____

5. Il y a un ascenseur ou un escalier chez vous?

    _____

6. Quelles pièces est-ce qu'il y a chez vous? (Si vous habitez dans une résidence universitaire, quelles pièces est-ce qu'il y a chez vos parents)? (To say *at my parents' house*, say **chez mes parents**.)

    _____

    _____

    _____

Partie auditive

 A. Qu'est-ce que c'est ? Identify the places and things in this house as in the example. After a pause for you to respond, you will hear the correct answer. Verify your response and your pronunciation.

> **EXEMPLE**   VOUS ENTENDEZ : C'est une chambre ou une salle de bains ?
> VOUS DITES :   **C'est une chambre.**
> VOUS ENTENDEZ : C'est une chambre.

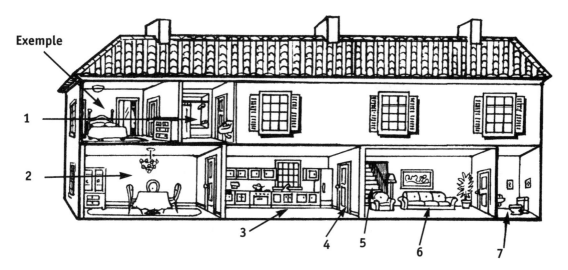

 B. Où habitent-ils ? Pause the recording and review the expressions used to talk about where you live on page 108 and in the dialogue between Philippe and Thomas on page 109 of the textbook. Then turn on the recording and listen as three students, Didier, Sophie, and Caroline, talk about their living arrangements. The first time, just listen to what they say. Then listen again, stop the recording, and complete these statements by indicating the correct expressions in italics.

1. Didier habite *en ville / en banlieue / à la campagne.*

2. Il habite *au rez-de-chaussée / au premier étage / au deuxième étage / au troisième étage.*

3. Il habite *dans une vieille maison / dans un vieil immeuble / à la résidence universitaire.*

4. Son *(His)* appartement est *tout près de l'université / assez loin de l'université.*

5. Sophie habite *dans un appartement / dans une maison / dans une chambre à la résidence.*

6. Sa *(Her)* chambre est *grande et moderne / petite et moderne / petite et vieille.*

7. Le loyer est *plus de / moins de* cinq cents dollars par mois.

8. Caroline habite *seule / avec sa famille / avec une amie.*

9. Elle habite *au centre-ville / en ville / en banlieue / à la campagne.*

10. Sa maison est *petite / vieille / moderne.*

C. Les nombres. Listen and repeat these numbers after the speaker, paying careful attention to your pronunciation.

105 _____	454 _____	700 _____	1 000 _____	1 000 000 _____
220 _____	500 _____	800 _____	2 150 _____	1 304 570 _____
310 _____	670 _____	999 _____	5 322 _____	1 800 000 _____

Now you will hear some of the numbers above. Indicate the numbers that you hear by placing a check next to them.

D. Encore des nombres. Fill in the number you hear, using numerals, not words.

EXEMPLE   VOUS ENTENDEZ : mille sept cent cinquante-huit
VOUS ÉCRIVEZ : **1 758**

a. _____   e. _____

b. _____   f. _____

c. _____   g. _____

d. _____   h. _____

E. Dictée. You will hear a student talk about where she lives. The first time, just listen to what she says at normal speed. Then fill in the missing words as it is repeated more slowly. Pause the recording as needed to allow enough time to fill in the words.

Moi, j'habite dans un appartement _____ **(1).**

Mon appartement est _____ **(2)** d'un grand

_____ **(3).** Il y a _____

(4) et _____ **(5).** Mon appartement

n'est pas _____ **(6)** l'université et il n'est pas

_____ **(7).** C'est très _____

(8). Ma chambre est _____ **(9)** et elle est

_____ **(10)** la salle de bains. Ma sœur habite dans une

maison _____ **(11),** mais mon frère préfère habiter

_____ **(12).**

*F. Et vous ? Answer the following questions about where you live. Pause the recording between questions to allow enough time to respond.

1. _____

2. _____

3. _____

4. _____

5. _____

COMPÉTENCE 2

Talking about your possessions

By the time you finish this **Compétence,** you should be able to talk about your belongings in French and tell where they are.

Partie écrite

A. Qu'est-ce que vous avez? Look at the illustration of the living room. First, identify the pictured items. Then say if you have each item in your home. Use **un, une,** or **des** with the noun, or change them to **de (d')** if the verb is negated.

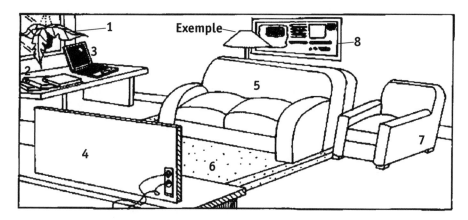

EXEMPLE   C'est **une lampe. Moi, j'ai une lampe (des lampes) / je n'ai pas de lampe** chez moi.

1. C'est _____. Moi, _____.

2. Ce sont _____. Moi, _____.

3. C'est _____. Moi, _____.

4. C'est _____. Moi, _____.

5. C'est _____. Moi, _____.

6. C'est _____. Moi, _____.

7. C'est _____. Moi, _____.

8. C'est _____. Moi, _____.

B. Dans le salon. Look at the living room pictured in **A. Qu'est-ce que vous avez?** Complete the sentences with the correct word or expression from the choices given in parentheses.

1. La lampe est _____ le canapé. (derrière / devant)

2. La table est _____. (près de la porte / dans le coin)

3. Le portable est _____ la table. (sur / sous)

4. Les livres sont _____ portable (à gauche du / à droite du)

5. La télé est _____ canapé. (en face du / à côté du)

6. Le canapé est _____ le fauteuil et la table. (entre / devant)

7. Le tapis est _____ le canapé. (sous / sur)

C. Une conversation. Complete this conversation between two friends who are thinking of sharing a house.

MARIE: Tu _____ **(1)** un appartement ici ? Écoute, moi, j'ai

(are looking for)

une maison avec deux _____ **(2)**. Elle est assez

(bedrooms)

_____ **(3)** l'université et elle n'est pas _____ **(4)**.

(near)   *(expensive)*

Tu voudrais _____ **(5)** la maison avec moi ?

(to share)

KARIMA: _____ **(6)**. Tu aimes _____ **(7)** ?

(Maybe)   *(animals)*

J'ai _____ **(8)** et _____ **(9)**.

(a cat)   *(a dog)*

Ils sont un peu _____ **(10)**. Ils aiment dormir

(annoying)

_____ **(11)** ou _____ **(12)**.

(on the chairs)   *(on the couch)*

MARIE: _____ **(13)**. J'aime beaucoup les animaux. Est-ce que tu

(No problem)

_____ **(14)** ? Parce que moi, _____ **(15)**.

(smoke)   *(I don't smoke)*

KARIMA: _____ **(16)**. Alors, ça va.

(Me neither)

D. Possessions. Philippe is talking to Thomas about what they have. Complete the following statements with the verb **avoir** and the pictured noun.

Exemple   **1**   **2**   **3**

4   **5**   **6**

EXEMPLE   Moi, j'**ai un iPod.**

1. Nous _____.

2. Claude et toi, vous _____.

3. Thomas, tu _____?

4. Claude _____.

5. Moi, j' _____.

6. Les étudiants au quatrième étage _____.

E. C'est où ? First, complete each of the phrases that follow with the correct form of **de** (**du, de la, de l', des**). Remember that **de + le = du** and **de + les = des.** Then, indicate whether the first or second italicized choice is the most logical completion of each sentence by selecting **1** or **2**.

1. Les livres sont *à côté* _____ *ordinateur / à côté* _____ *voiture.*   1. _____ 2. _____

2. Le réfrigérateur est *dans le coin* _____ *toilettes / dans le coin* _____ *cuisine.*   1. _____ 2. _____

3. L'ordinateur est *à gauche* _____ *vélo / à gauche* _____ *imprimante (printer).*   1. _____ 2. _____

4. Le cellulaire est *à côté* _____ *télé / à côté* _____ *tapis.*   1. _____ 2. _____

5. Les CD sont *à droite* _____ *lecteur CD / à droite* _____ *lecteur DVD.*   1. _____ 2. _____

6. La télé est *en face* _____ *tableaux / en face* _____ *canapé.*   1. _____ 2. _____

F. Où ? Look at the illustration of Thomas's friend Marion's living room. Complete the paragraph with the appropriate prepositions (**sous, sur,** etc.). Imagine that you have just entered the room through the door and you are standing in the doorway, facing the table. The first blank has been completed for you as an example.

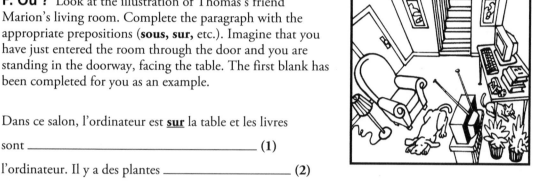

Dans ce salon, l'ordinateur est **sur** la table et les livres

sont _____ **(1)**

l'ordinateur. Il y a des plantes _____ **(2)**

la table. Le fauteuil est _____ **(3)**

la télé. Le chien est _____ **(4)** le fauteuil, _____ **(5)**

le fauteuil et la télé. Les plantes sont _____ **(6)** la télé. L'escalier est

_____ **(7)** les deux tableaux.

Look back at the picture of Marion's living room and create sentences in French telling where these objects are with respect to each other in the room. You are still standing in the doorway. Remember **de + le = du** and **de + les = des.**

EXEMPLE   the computer / the table   **L'ordinateur est sur la table.**

1. the computer / the books

_____

2. the stairway / the door

_____

3. the lamp / the armchair

_____

4. the TV / the plants

_____

5. the cat / the table

_____

*G. Colocataires. You and a new friend are thinking about sharing a house and he/she wants to know more about you. Answer the questions he/she asks.

1. Tu as beaucoup de choses?

_____

2. Quels meubles *(furniture)* as-tu pour le salon?

_____

3. Tu passes beaucoup de temps dans le salon?

_____

4. Quels appareils électroniques *(electronics)* est-ce que tu as? Tu écoutes souvent de la musique? Tu regardes souvent la télé?

_____

_____

5. Tu fumes?

_____

6. Tu aimes les animaux? Tu as des animaux?

_____

_____

---

*Journal. Create a paragraph describing where you live. Tell:
- whether you live in a house, an apartment, or a dorm room
- whether it is downtown, in town, in the suburbs, or in the country; and if it is near, far from, or on the campus
- if you like your house / apartment / dorm room, and why or why not
- what there is in the living room (**Dans le salon, il y a…**) and where each item is located (**La télé est en face du fauteuil…**)

_____

_____

_____

_____

_____

_____

_____

_____

_____

_____

_____

Partie auditive

 A. Dans le salon de Thomas. You will hear sentences saying where some of the items in Thomas's living room are located. Decide if each one is true or false according to the illustration and indicate **vrai** or **faux** as appropriate.

EXEMPLE   VOUS ENTENDEZ : **La table est dans le coin.**
VOUS MARQUEZ : **vrai** ✓   faux _____

1. vrai _____   faux _____   **3.** vrai _____   faux _____   **5.** vrai _____   faux _____   **7.** vrai _____   faux _____

2. vrai _____   faux _____   **4.** vrai _____   faux _____   **6.** vrai _____   faux _____   **8.** vrai _____   faux _____

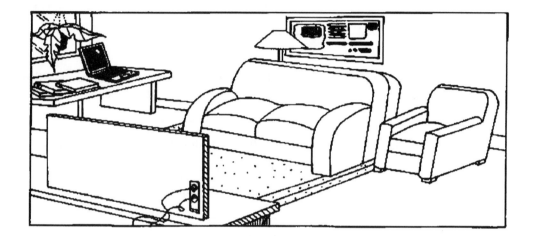

 B. Prononciation : *Avoir* et *être*. Pause the recording and review the ***Prononciation*** section on page 116 of the textbook. Then turn on the recording and repeat these forms of **avoir** and **être,** paying attention to how they are different.

être :   tu es   il est   elle est   ils sont   elles sont
avoir :   tu as   il a   elle a   ils ‿ont   elles ‿ont

Now you will hear questions about Thomas's living room. Fill in the verb form you hear in the question under the correct column and indicate **oui** or **non** to answer the question according to the illustration in *A. Dans le salon de Thomas.* Pause the recording as needed to allow enough time to respond.

EXEMPLE   VOUS ENTENDEZ : Thomas, il a un grand salon ?
VOUS ÉCRIVEZ :

	AVOIR	ÊTRE		
EXEMPLE	a	_____	oui _____	non ___✓___

	AVOIR	ÊTRE		
1.	_____	_____	oui _____	non _____
2.	_____	_____	oui _____	non _____
3.	_____	_____	oui _____	non _____
4.	_____	_____	oui _____	non _____
5.	_____	_____	oui _____	non _____
6.	_____	_____	oui _____	non _____

C. Prononciation: *De, du, des.*

Pause the recording and review the *Prononciation* section on page 118 of the textbook. Then turn on the recording and listen to the sentences, completing them with the form of the preposition **de** you hear. Look at the illustration in *A. Dans le salon de Thomas* and indicate if each sentence is true or false by indicating **vrai** or **faux.**

EXEMPLE VOUS ENTENDEZ: La table est près de la fenêtre.
VOUS COMPLÉTEZ: La table est près **de la** fenêtre.   vrai ✓   faux _____

1. La table est dans le coin _____ salon.   vrai _____   faux _____

2. Le fauteuil est à côté _____ table.   vrai _____   faux _____

3. L'ordinateur est à côté _____ livres.   vrai _____   faux _____

4. La télé est en face _____ canapé.   vrai _____   faux _____

5. La plante est à gauche _____ ordinateur.   vrai _____   faux _____

D. Un appartement.

You will hear a conversation between two prospective roommates. The first time, just listen to it at normal speed. Then fill in the missing words as it is repeated more slowly.

— Tu cherches un appartement _____ **(1)**?

Je _____ **(2)** un nouveau colocataire. Tu voudrais

_____ **(3)** mon appartement avec moi?

— Je ne sais pas. _____ **(4)** ton appartement?

— Il n'est pas très grand, mais _____ **(5)** beaucoup de choses.

— Tu _____ **(6)** ou un chat? _____ **(7)**

beaucoup d'allergies.

— Non, je n'ai pas _____ **(8).** Et _____ **(9)**

non plus. Est-ce que tu voudrais _____ **(10)** cet après-midi

pour voir l'appartement?

— Oui, j'ai cours jusqu'à deux heures, alors _____ **(11)**?

— Oui, c'est parfait!

*Now imagine that you are considering moving in with a classmate. How would you answer these questions? Answer each one *with a complete sentence.* Pause the recording between items in order to respond.

1. _____

2. _____

3. _____

4. _____

5. _____

COMPÉTENCE 3

Describing your room

By the time you finish this *Compétence*, you should be able to describe your room in French.

Partie écrite

A. Une chambre. Label the objects in Marie's bedroom. Include the indefinite article (**un, une, des**) with the noun.

1. _____
2. _____
3. _____
4. _____
5. _____
6. _____
7. _____

Now answer the following questions about the bedroom above *with complete sentences.*

1. La chambre est en ordre ou en désordre? Tout est à sa place? La chambre est propre ou un peu sale?

_____

_____

2. Où sont les vêtements? Marie laisse ses vêtements par terre?

_____

_____

3. Qu'est-ce qu'il y a devant la fenêtre? Qu'est-ce qu'il y a derrière la plante?

_____

_____

*B. Couleurs. Complete the following sentences with the name of a colour. Remember that colours agree (masculine / feminine, singular / plural) with the noun they describe. If you live in a dormitory, describe where you live when not at the university. If you do not have one of the items mentioned, imagine which colour you would like this item to be if you had one.

   EXEMPLE   Dans ma chambre, les rideaux sont **bleus.**

1. Dans ma chambre, la porte est _____ et les

   murs sont _____. Le tapis est et les rideaux sont

   _____. Ma couverture est _____.

2. Dans le salon, la porte est _____ et les murs

   sont _____. Le tapis est et les rideaux sont

   _____. Le canapé est _____. Le

   fauteuil est _____.

C. Une conversation. A student is visiting a friend's new apartment. Complete their conversation.

SOPHIE: Ton nouvel appartement te plaît?

HAHN: Oui, il me plaît beaucoup. _____ **(1)** ma chambre.
(Come see)

Elle est _____ **(2)**.
(at the end of the hallway)

SOPHIE: C'est ta chambre là, près de la salle de bains?

HAHN: Mais non! Ça, c'est _____ **(3)**. Sa
(Anne's bedroom)

chambre est toujours un peu _____ **(4)** et
(dirty)

_____ **(5)**. Elle
(in disorder)

_____ **(6)** tout _____ **(7)**.
(leaves)   *(on the floor)*

Voilà ma chambre. _____ **(8)**, chez moi
(As you see)

_____ **(9)** est _____ **(10)**.
(each thing)   *(in its place)*

SOPHIE: Ta chambre est agréable et tu as _____ **(11)**.
(a beautiful view)

J'aime beaucoup ta chambre.

D. C'est-à-dire... Sometimes in a foreign language, you have to rephrase what you want to say. Here are several ideas, each expressed two ways. Complete the first sentence with the correct form of **avoir** and the second sentence with the appropriate possessive adjective.

    EXEMPLE   Vous **avez** une très belle maison. **Votre** maison est très belle.

1. J' _____ un grand lit. _____ lit est grand.

2. J' _____ une couverture bleue. _____ couverture est bleue.

3. J' _____ une nouvelle affiche. _____ affiche est nouvelle.

4. J' _____ de jolis rideaux. _____ rideaux sont jolis.

5. Tu _____ une belle chambre. _____ chambre est belle.

6. Tu _____ un grand bureau. _____ bureau est grand.

7. Tu _____ des meubles bizarres. _____ meubles sont bizarres.

8. Marie _____ un beau tapis. _____ tapis est beau.

9. Thomas _____ une belle voiture. _____ voiture est belle.

10. Il _____ une grande étagère. _____ étagère est grande.

11. Il _____ des amis bizarres. _____ amis sont bizarres.

12. Nous _____ de grands placards. _____ placards sont grands.

13. Nous _____ une belle vue. _____ vue est belle.

14. Vous _____ des murs blancs? _____ murs sont blancs?

15. Vous _____ une belle chambre? _____ chambre est belle?

16. Mes amis _____ une belle maison. _____ maison est belle.

17. Ils _____ de beaux chiens. _____ chiens sont beaux.

E. Je préfère mes affaires.
Everyone likes his or her *own* things. Complete these sentences with the correct form of the possessive adjective (**mon, ma, mes, ton, ta, tes, son, sa, ses, notre, nos, votre, vos, leur, leurs**).

EXEMPLE   **Moi, j'aime mon portable.**
Ma sœur aime mieux **son portable**.

1. Tu aimes _____ table et _____ chaises.

   Philippe aime mieux _____ table et _____ chaises.

2. Mes amis aiment _____ vêtements.

   Moi, j'aime mieux _____ vêtements.

3. Nous aimons _____ maison.

   Nos voisins *(neighbours)* aiment mieux _____ maison.

4. J'aime _____ fauteuil.

   Ma sœur aime mieux ___ fauteuil.

*F. Et toi?
A friend is asking you about your bedroom. Complete each question with **ton, ta,** or **tes**. Then answer the question, using **mon, ma,** or **mes**.

EXEMPLE   — Quelle est **ta** couleur préférée?
                — **Ma couleur préférée, c'est le rouge.**

1. — Comment est _____ chambre?

   — _____

2. — De quelle couleur sont _____ murs? _____ rideaux? De quelle couleur est

   _____ couverture? _____ tapis?

   — _____

   _____

   _____

3. — _____ chambre est en ordre ou en désordre en général? Tu laisses _____ affaires

   partout?

   — _____

   _____

4. —Tu mets *(put)* _____ livres sur _____ étagère? Tu mets _____ vêtements dans _____ placard ou dans _____ commode? *(Answer with* **Je mets…** *or* **Je ne mets pas…***)*

— _____

_____

5. — Est-ce que _____ lit est près de la fenêtre?

— _____

6. — Tu aimes faire _____ devoirs dans _____ chambre?

— _____

G. Les adjectifs possessifs. Complete the following conversation logically with **son, sa, ses,** or **leur, leurs.**

— L'appartement de Thomas, Philippe et Claude est super, non?

— Oui, il est super. _____ **(1)** salon est très confortable et _____ **(2)** chambres sont assez grandes.

— Oui, mais la chambre de Claude est un désastre. Il laisse tous _____ **(3)** vêtements par terre!

_____ **(4)** chien aime dormir sur _____ **(5)** lit et _____ **(6)** chat aime dormir sur _____ **(7)** étagère.

— Pourtant, dans les chambres de Thomas et de Philippe, c'est le contraire. _____ **(8)** chambres sont

presque toujours en ordre. _____ **(9)** vêtements sont dans le placard, _____ **(10)** livres sont sur

l'étagère et _____ **(11)** lits sont toujours faits *(made).*

*H. Et vous? Answer the following questions about your room *with complete sentences.*

1. Est-ce que vous aimez votre chambre? Pourquoi?

_____

_____

2. Votre chambre est à quel étage?

_____

_____

3. Qu'est-ce qu'il y a dans votre chambre? Qu'est-ce que vous voudriez acheter *(to buy)* pour votre chambre?

_____

_____

4. Quelle est votre couleur préférée? Qu'est-ce que vous avez de cette couleur chez vous?

_____

_____

5. Est-ce que vous passez beaucoup de temps dans votre chambre?

_____

_____

6. Qu'est-ce que vous aimez faire dans votre chambre?

_____

_____

Partie auditive

 A. Dans la chambre. Stop the recording, look at the illustration of the bedroom, and complete the sentences that follow. When you have finished, start the recording and verify your responses. Repeat each sentence after the speaker, paying attention to your pronunciation.

EXEMPLE	VOUS COMPLÉTEZ: Il y a un chien sous **le lit.**
	VOUS ENTENDEZ: Il y a un chien sous le lit.
	VOUS RÉPÉTEZ: **Il y a un chien sous le lit.**

1. Il y a une plante devant _____.

2. Par terre, derrière la plante, il y a _____.

3. Il y a une couverture sur _____.

4. Entre la fenêtre et le lit, il y a _____.

5. Les vêtements sont dans _____.

6. _____ est à droite de la porte.

7. Par terre, il y a _____.

 B. C'est à moi ! A friend is asking if these items are yours. Identify them as yours, as in the example. After a pause for you to respond, you will hear the correct answer. Verify your response and your pronunciation and indicate the form of the possessive adjective that is used.

EXEMPLE	VOUS ENTENDEZ: C'est ta chambre?
	VOUS DITES: **Oui, c'est ma chambre.**
	VOUS ENTENDEZ: Oui, c'est ma chambre.

EXEMPLE mon _____ ma __✓__ mes _____

1. mon _____ ma _____ mes _____   5. mon _____ ma _____ mes _____

2. mon _____ ma _____ mes _____   6. mon _____ ma _____ mes _____

3. mon _____ ma _____ mes _____   7. mon _____ ma _____ mes _____

4. mon _____ ma _____ mes _____

C. Chez Thomas. Thomas exaggerates everything. How does he answer a friend's questions? Use the appropriate possessive adjective **(mon, ma, mes, ton, ta, tes, son, sa, ses, notre, nos, votre, vos, leur, leurs)** in the response. Pause the recording between items in order to respond.

EXEMPLES VOUS ENTENDEZ: La chambre de Claude est agréable?
VOUS ÉCRIVEZ: Oui, **sa chambre** est très agréable.
VOUS ENTENDEZ: Votre appartement est grand?
VOUS ÉCRIVEZ: Oui, **notre appartement** est très grand.

1. Oui, _____ est très agréable.

2. Oui, _____ est très confortable.

3. Oui, _____ sont très sympas.

4. Oui, _____ est très agréable.

5. Oui, _____ est très beau.

6. Oui, _____ sont quelquefois très embêtants.

7. Non, _____ n'est pas très cher.

8. Oui, _____ sont très spacieuses *(spacious)*.

9. Oui, _____ est très moderne.

10. Oui, _____ sont super intéressants.

D. On sort ? Didier and Philippe are going out to dinner, and Didier has arranged to pick up Philippe at his apartment. Listen to their conversation, pause the recording, and answer the questions *in English*. You may need to listen more than once.

1. Name two things Didier particularly admires about Philippe's apartment.

_____

2. What is one of the things Didier likes about where he lives?

_____

3. What are two inconveniences he mentions about where he lives?

_____

_____

4. Why does Thomas decline Didier's invitation to the restaurant?

_____

5. What is the street number on **rue Caroline** of the restaurant Philippe and Didier are going to?

_____

*E. Comment est ta chambre ? A friend is asking you questions about your room. Answer each one *with a complete sentence in French*. Pause the recording between items in order to respond.

1. _____

2. _____

3. _____

4. _____

5. _____

COMPÉTENCE 4

Giving your address and phone number

By the time you finish this **Compétence,** you should be able to give personal information about yourself, such as your address and telephone number, in French.

Partie écrite

A. Des renseignements personnels. You are working at the **Hôtel Vieux Québec.** A newly arrived guest gives you the following information. Complete what she says.

> **EXEMPLE**   **Mon nom de famille,** c'est McAlpine.

1. _____, c'est Jane.

2. _____, c'est 2081, rue Oak.

3. _____, c'est Prince George et

   _____, c'est la Colombie-Britannique.

4. Le V2L 1Z5, c'est _____.

5. Le Canada, c'est _____.

6. Le 250-826-7660, c'est _____.

7. _____, c'est jmcs123@airmail.ca.

HÔTEL VIEUX QUÉBEC
Fiche d'inscription pour voyageurs étrangers
Nom de famille :

_____

Prénom(s) :

_____

Adresse :

_____ (rue)

_____ (ville)

_____ (pays)

Numéro de téléphone : _____

Nationalité : _____

B. Quel est...? Determine what questions you would need to ask as a hotel clerk to get the following information from a newly arrived guest. Remember to use the correct form of **quel (quel, quelle, quels, quelles).**

> **EXEMPLE**   his last name :   **Quel est votre nom de famille ?**

1. his first name : _____

2. his address : _____

3. his city : _____

4. his province : _____

5. his postal code : _____

6. his phone number : _____

7. his e-mail address : _____

8. his nationality : _____

C. Une conversation. Complete this conversation between two friends.

MARION : Tu habites dans _____(1)?
(a new apartment)

ADRIEN : Oui, je _____ (2) un appartement _____ (3)
(share)   *(near)*

l'université avec un ami.

MARION : Il te plaît ?

ADRIEN : Oui, beaucoup. Il y a _____ (4) tout près
(a bus stop)

et l'appartement n'est pas _____ (5).
(too expensive)

MARION : C'est combien, _____ (6) ?
(the rent)

ADRIEN : C'est 700 dollars _____ (7), _____ (8)
(per month)   *(shared between)*

nous deux. Alors pour moi, ça fait 350 dollars.

MARION : _____ (9) de l'appartement ?
(What's the address)

ADRIEN : C'est le 38, _____ (10) Nelson.
(street)

*D. Quel mot ? Both quel and qu'est-ce que can be translated as *what*. Remember to use a form of quel directly before a noun or before the verb forms est and sont. In other cases, use qu'est-ce que. Complete the following questions with qu'est-ce que or a form of quel. Then answer each question *with a complete sentence*.

1. _____ est votre adresse ?

   _____

2. Votre chambre est à _____ étage ?

   _____

3. _____ vous avez dans votre chambre ?

   _____

4. Chez vous, dans _____ pièces est-ce que vous préférez passer votre temps ?

   _____

5. _____ vous aimez faire dans le salon ?

   _____

6. _____ sont vos passe-temps préférés ?

   _____

7. _____ vos amis préfèrent faire la fin de semaine ?

   _____

8. _____ vous voudriez faire aujourd'hui après les cours ?

   _____

E. Un immeuble. Complete these questions with **ce**, **cet**, **cette**, or **ces**, as appropriate.

1. _____ immeuble a combien d'étages?

2. Est-ce que _____ étudiants préparent les cours ou est-ce qu'ils jouent au soccer maintenant?

3. Qu'est-ce qu'il y a dans le salon de

   _____ appartement?

4. Qu'est-ce que _____ jeunes hommes aiment faire?

5. Qu'est-ce que _____ jeune femme aime faire?

6. Combien d'enfants est-ce qu'il y a dans _____ famille?

7. _____ homme est paresseux ou travailleur *(hard-working)*?

Now answer the questions above according to the illustration.

1. _____
2. _____
3. _____
4. _____
5. _____
6. _____
7. _____

F. Où est-ce que je mets ça? A friend is helping you move in. Tell your friend in which room to put these items. Use **ce**, **cet**, **cette**, or **ces** in your answers, as in the example.

Exemple   **1**   **2**   **3**

EXEMPLE   Mets *(Put)* **cette table dans la salle à manger.**

1. Mets _____.

2. Mets _____.

3. Mets _____.

4

5

6

4. Mets _____.

5. Mets _____.

6. Mets _____.

---

*Journal. Describe your bedroom. Include the following information:

- whether or not you like your bedroom and why or why not
- what furniture there is and where it is placed
- what colour the walls, rug, bed cover, and curtains are
- what floor your bedroom is on and, if it's not on the ground floor, whether there is a stairway or an elevator
- if you spend a lot of time in your room

_____

_____

_____

_____

_____

_____

_____

_____

_____

_____

_____

_____

_____

_____

_____

_____

_____

_____

_____

Partie auditive

 *A. L'inscription à l'université. You are enrolling at a university. Complete the questions you hear. Then provide the information requested. *You do not need to answer in complete sentences.* Pause the recording as needed to allow enough time to write.

1. Quel est votre _____?

   _____

2. Quel est votre _____?

   _____

3. Quelle est votre _____?

   _____

4. Vous habitez dans quelle _____?

   _____

5. Vous habitez dans quel _____?

   _____

6. Quel est votre _____?

   _____

7. Quelle est votre _____?

   _____

8. Quelle est votre _____?

   _____

 B. Prononciation : *La voyelle e de ce, cet, cette, ces.* Pause the recording and review the *Prononciation* section on page 128 of the textbook. Then turn on the recording, listen, and repeat these words.

ce	de	je	ne	que	le	me
ces	des	mes	tes	les	aller	danser
cet	cette	quel	elle	cher	frère	mère

 C. Mes préférences. A friend is asking about your preferences. Listen to his questions and indicate the form of **quel** that would be used in each one, based on the gender and number of the noun that follows.

> **EXEMPLE** VOUS ENTENDEZ : Quel est ton restaurant préféré ?
> VOUS INDIQUEZ : quel ✔   quels ____   quelle ____   quelles ____

1. quel ____   quels ____   quelle ____   quelles ____   3. quel ____   quels ____   quelle ____   quelles ____

2. quel ____   quels ____   quelle ____   quelles ____   4. quel ____   quels ____   quelle ____   quelles ____

*Now play the questions again and answer them. Pause the recording to allow enough time to respond. Remember to make the proper agreement with the adjective **préféré(e)(s).**

EXEMPLE   VOUS ENTENDEZ : Quel est ton restaurant préféré ?
                VOUS ÉCRIVEZ :   **Mon restaurant préféré, c'est Pizza Nizza.**

1. _____

2. _____

3. _____

4. _____

D. Quel appartement ? You are talking about an apartment where you are considering rooming with someone. Describe it by filling in the missing words you hear. Pause the recording as needed to allow enough time to fill in the words.

EXEMPLE   VOUS ENTENDEZ :   Cet appartement est loin de l'université.
                VOUS COMPLÉTEZ : **Cet appartement** est loin de l'université.

1. La vue de _____ est laide.

2. _____ est près du centre-ville.

3. _____ est agréable.

4. _____ sont très grandes.

5. La couleur de _____ est jolie.

6. _____ est nouveau.

7. _____ est sale.

8. _____ fume.

E. Dictée. You will hear a conversation between **l'hôtelier** (*the hotel manager*) and a newly arrived guest. The first time, just listen to what they say at normal speed. Then fill in the missing words as the conversation is repeated more slowly. Pause the recording as needed to allow enough time to fill in the words.

L'HÔTELIER : Alors, vous _____ **(1)** une chambre pour

_____ **(2)**. Nous avons une chambre

_____ **(3)** à _____ **(4)** dollars.

LE CLIENT : _____ **(5)** est calme ?

L'HÔTELIER : Oui, monsieur. Elle est _____ **(6)**, loin

_____ **(7)**.

LE CLIENT : Et elle est _____ **(8)** ?

L'HÔTELIER : Au troisième. Il y a _____ **(9)** derrière vous,

_____ **(10)**.

LE CLIENT : Il y a _____ **(11)** dans l'hôtel ?

L'HÔTELIER : Non, mais il y a un restaurant tout près, juste _____ **(12)**.

LE CLIENT : _____ **(13)** ferme _____ **(14)** ?

L'HÔTELIER : À _____ **(15)**.

LE CLIENT : Bon, je vais prendre la chambre. _____ **(16)** de la chambre ?

L'HÔTELIER : C'est la chambre _____ **(17)**.

En famille

Chapitre 4

COMPÉTENCE 1

Describing your family

By the time you finish this *Compétence,* you should be able to name family members and describe them in French.

Partie écrite

A. La famille de Claude. Claude is identifying some of his family members. Finish his statements to clarify what family member he is talking about.

> **EXEMPLE** C'est le père de mon père. C'est **mon grand-père.**

1. C'est la mère de mon père. C'est _____.
2. Ce sont les parents de ma mère. Ce sont _____.
3. C'est la sœur de mon père. C'est _____.
4. C'est le mari de ma tante. C'est _____.
5. Ce sont les enfants de ma tante. Ce sont _____.
6. C'est le fils de mon frère. C'est _____.
7. C'est la fille de mon frère. C'est _____.

B. La parenté. A friend is showing you pictures of family members. Complete each question asking your friend to clarify her relationship to each one.

> **EXEMPLE** Voilà ma grand-mère.
> C'est **la mère** de ton père ou de ta mère?

1. Voilà ma tante Marie.

   C'est _____ de ton père ou de ta mère?

2. Voilà mon oncle Antoine.

   C'est _____ de la sœur de ton père ou de la sœur de ta mère?

3. Voilà mon grand-père.

   C'est _____ de ton père ou de ta mère?

4. Voilà mon neveu.

   C'est _____ de ton frère ou de ta sœur?

5. Voilà ma nièce.

   C'est _____ de ton frère ou de ta sœur?

C. Une conversation. Claude is telling Robert about his family. Complete their conversation.

ROBERT: Vous _____ (1) dans ta famille?
(are how many)

CLAUDE: Nous _____ (2): mon père, mon frère, ma sœur et moi.
(are four)

Mon frère a l'intention de _____ (3) ici avec moi.
(spend the weekend)

ROBERT: Il est plus jeune ou _____ (4) toi?
(older than)

_____ (5)?
(How old is he)

CLAUDE: _____ (6).
(He's fourteen years old)

ROBERT: _____ (7)?
(What's his name)

CLAUDE: _____ (8) Marc.
(His name is)

D. Comment sont-ils? Complete the descriptions of Charles and Vincent by copying each sentence under the name of the person it describes. The first one has been done as an example.

Il est de taille moyenne et il est mince.

Il est un peu grand.

Il a environ quarante-cinq ans.

Il a environ soixante-cinq ans.

Il a les cheveux gris.

Il a les cheveux noirs.

Il n'a pas de moustache.

Il a une moustache mais il n'a pas de barbe.

Charles

Vincent

Il s'appelle Charles.

Il est de taille moyenne et il est mince.

_____

_____

_____

Il s'appelle Vincent.

_____

_____

_____

_____

E. Descriptions. Say how these people are feeling using an expression with **avoir**.

avoir peur / avoir chaud / avoir froid / avoir sommeil / avoir soif / avoir faim

EXEMPLE J'…   **1.** Anne…   **2.** Les enfants…   **3.** Mes amis et moi…

    EXEMPLE **J'ai froid.**

1. Anne _____.

2. Les enfants _____.

3. Mes amis et moi _____.

F. Une fête d'anniversaire (A birthday party). Complete the following statements between parents at Robert's niece's birthday party using the logical expressions with **avoir** in parentheses.

EXEMPLE (avoir l'intention de, avoir faim, avoir soif)
Si *(If)* vous, __avez soif__ il y a de l'eau minérale, du coca et de la limonade et si vous __avez faim__, il y a de la pizza et des sandwichs. Nous _____avons l'intention_____ de manger le gâteau *(cake)* plus tard.

1. (avoir faim, avoir envie de, avoir besoin de)

J' _____ servir le gâteau. Les enfants

_____ et ils _____ manger le

gâteau maintenant.

2. (avoir l'air, avoir… ans, avoir raison)

— Votre fille _____ cinq _____? Elle _____ plus âgée!

— Oui, vous _____. Elle est assez grande pour son âge.

3. (avoir envie de, avoir raison, avoir tort)

— Mon fils de neuf ans _____ un téléphone

portable pour son anniversaire mais je pense qu'il est trop jeune. Est-ce que

j' _____ de refuser un portable à mon fils?

— Non, vous _____. Il est trop jeune.

*G. Et vous? Talk about yourself by completing the following sentences. Use a verb in the infinitive.

1. Demain, j'ai l'intention de (d') _____.

2. Cette semaine, j'ai besoin de (d') _____.

3. Cette fin de semaine, j'ai envie de (d') _____.

4. Quelquefois, j'ai peur de (d') _____.

*H. Quelques questions. Answer each question *with a complete sentence in French.*

1. Vous êtes combien dans votre famille? Combien de frères et de sœurs est-ce que vous avez? Ils/Elles sont plus âgé(e)s que vous?

_____

_____

_____

_____

2. Votre famille habite dans quelle ville? Est-ce que vous passez beaucoup de temps chez vos parents?

_____

_____

_____

3. Avec quel membre de votre famille passez-vous le plus de temps *(the most time)*? Comment s'appelle-t-il/elle? Quel âge a-t-il/elle? Il/Elle a les yeux et les cheveux de quelle couleur? Il/Elle porte des lunettes ou des verres de contact *(contacts)*? Qu'est-ce que vous aimez faire ensemble?

_____

_____

_____

_____

_____

_____

4. Est-ce que vous avez l'intention de passer la fin de semaine prochaine avec votre famille? Qu'est-ce que vous avez envie de faire?

_____

_____

_____

_____

Partie auditive

 A. Qui est-ce ? Listen as Thomas points out family members and fill in the missing words.

> **EXEMPLE** VOUS ENTENDEZ : **C'est le père de mon père.**
> VOUS ÉCRIVEZ : C'est **le père** de **mon père.**

1. C'est _____ de _____.
2. C'est _____ de _____.
3. C'est _____ de _____.
4. C'est _____ de _____.
5. Ce sont _____ de _____.
6. C'est _____ de _____.

Now listen to Thomas's statements again. This time, identify the name of each relationship he describes. After a pause for you to answer, you will hear the correct response.

> **EXEMPLE** VOUS ENTENDEZ : C'est le père de mon père.
> VOUS DITES : **C'est son grand-père.**
> VOUS ENTENDEZ : C'est son grand-père.

B. Je vous présente… You will hear the first part of some introductions. For each one, repeat what you hear and complete the sentence with the corresponding female family member, as in the example. After a pause for you to respond, you will hear the correct answer. Verify your response.

> **EXEMPLE** VOUS ENTENDEZ : Voici mon père et…
> VOUS DITES : **Voici mon père et ma mère.**
> VOUS ENTENDEZ : Voici mon père et ma mère.

C. Les parents de Gisèle. You will hear Gisèle describe her parents. Repeat each sentence after her. Then pause the recording and indicate whether each statement is **vrai** or **faux** according to the illustration. Respond using **V** or **F**.

____ Mon père s'appelle Christian.

____ Il a cinquante-huit ans.

____ Il a l'air sportif.

____ Il est de taille moyenne.

____ Il a les cheveux courts et noirs.

____ Il a une moustache et une barbe.

____ Ma mère s'appelle Diane.

____ Elle a trente-deux ans.

____ Elle a l'air intellectuel.

____ Elle est assez grande.

____ Elle a les cheveux longs et noirs.

____ Elle porte des lunettes.

Paul, 48 ans et Diane, 42 ans

D. Stratégie: *Asking for clarification.* A new acquaintance is talking about her family. You should understand everything she says except one word or name. For each statement you hear, indicate the letter of the expression that you should use to ask for clarification.

a. Comment? Répétez, s'il vous plaît.　　　**b.** Qu'est-ce que ça veut dire?　　　**c.** Ça s'écrit comment?

1. _____　　**2.** _____　　**3.** _____　　**4.** _____　　**5.** _____　　**6.** _____

E. Une sortie. Thomas and Robert are spending the day with Robert's nephew and niece in Caraquet. How would Robert respond to each of Thomas's questions or statements that you hear? Indicate the logical response as you say it aloud. Then listen to the correct answer and repeat again.

> **EXEMPLE**　　VOUS VOYEZ:　　　　　　Oui, j'ai chaud.　　　　　　　Oui, j'ai froid.
> 　　　　　　　　VOUS ENTENDEZ:　　　　Tu portes un short et un tee-shirt?
> 　　　　　　　　VOUS INDIQUEZ ET VOUS DITES: _X_ **Oui, j'ai chaud.**　　　Oui, j'ai froid.
> 　　　　　　　　VOUS ENTENDEZ:　　　　Oui, j'ai chaud.
> 　　　　　　　　VOUS RÉPÉTEZ:　　　　　**Oui, j'ai chaud.**

1. ____ Oui, tu as raison. C'est un bon film.　　　____ Oui, tu as raison. Les enfants ont peur de ce film.

2. ____ Oui, nous avons sommeil.　　　　　　　____ Oui, nous avons soif.

3. ____ Oui, il a faim.　　　　　　　　　　　____ Oui, il a une barbe.

4. ____ Oui, elle a peur des chiens.　　　　　　____ Oui, il a cinq ans et elle a sept ans.

5. ____ Oui, ça a l'air intéressant.　　　　　　　____ Oui, j'ai besoin de dormir un peu.

6. ____ Oui, ils ont sommeil.　　　　　　　　　____ Oui, ils ont envie d'aller au cinéma.

F. La famille de Thomas. You will hear Thomas talk about his family. After you listen, pause the recording and complete the following sentences according to what he says.

1. Thomas a deux _____. Philippe a _____ ans et Yannick a _____ ans.

2. La sœur de Thomas est mariée et elle a _____ enfants.

3. Son père s'appelle Paul et il a deux _____ et trois _____.

4. Ses oncles s'appellent _____, _____ et _____.

5. Sa mère travaille dans _____.

6. Son père travaille pour _____.

7. Les personnes suivantes habitent avec les parents de Thomas: _____,

_____ et les _____ de Thomas.

*G. Et votre meilleur ami? Answer the questions you hear about your best male friend in French. Pause the recording in order to respond.

1. _____

2. _____

3. _____

4. _____

5. _____

6. _____

COMPÉTENCE 2

Saying where you go in your free time

By the time you finish this **Compétence,** you should be able to tell in French where you go in your free time and suggest activities to your friends.

Partie écrite

A. Où va-t-on? Say where one goes to do each of the activities. Complete the sentences using the pronoun **on** and the logical place from the list.

au parc / à la plage / au café / au centre commercial / à un concert / à la librairie / au musée

EXEMPLE   Pour écouter de la musique, **on va à un concert.**

1. Pour prendre un verre, _____.

2. Pour voir une exposition, _____.

3. Pour faire du magasinage, _____.

4. Pour acheter des livres, _____.

5. Pour jouer avec son chien, _____.

6. Pour nager et se détendre, _____.

B. Conversation.   Claude and Thomas are talking about their plans for the afternoon. Complete their conversation.

Claude : _____ **(1)** des vêtements.
　　　　　　　　　　　(I need to buy)

　　　　　_____ **(2)** au centre commercial?
　　　　　　　　　　　(How about going)

Thomas : D'accord, mais _____ **(3)** manger
　　　　　　　　　　　　　　　　(let's go)

_____ **(4)** d'abord *(first).*
　　　　　(something)

Claude : _____ **(5)**! Moi aussi, _____ **(6).**
　　　　　　　(Good idea)　　　　　　　　　　　　　　*(I'm hungry)*

_____ **(7)** au McDo?
　　　　　(How about going)

Thomas : _____ **(8)** au restaurant La Guadeloupe. C'est
　　　　　　(Let's go instead)

un nouveau restaurant où on sert de la cuisine antillaise. C'est comme la cuisine de ma mère.

_____ **(9)**?
　　　　　　　(How does that sound)

Claude : Oui. J'adore manger _____ **(10).**
　　　　　　　　　　　　　　　(at your mother's house)

C. La préposition à. Complete the following passage with the appropriate form of **à** and the definite article **le, la, l'**, or **les**. Remember that **à + le** contracts to **au** and **à + les** contracts to **aux**.

Yannick est toujours très occupé *(busy)*. En semaine, il va tous les jours **(1)** _____

école *(school)*. À midi, il va dîner **(2)** _____ café avec ses amis. Après les cours, ils

vont ensemble **(3)** _____ bibliothèque où ils font leurs devoirs. Ensuite, ils vont

(4) _____ maison de Yannick pour jouer au basketball. Le vendredi soir, Thomas

et Yannick aiment aller **(5)** _____ cinéma ou **(6)** _____ parc.

Le samedi, Yannick va **(7)** _____ centre commercial avec ses amis pour faire du

magasinage. Le dimanche matin, toute la famille va **(8)** _____ église et à midi, ils vont

(9) _____ restaurant parce que sa mère n'aime pas faire la cuisine *(to cook)* le dimanche.

D. Où vont-ils? Claude is talking about his family. Complete the following sentences telling how often the indicated people go to the places shown. Use the adverb in parentheses.

EXEMPLE Mes grands-parents…   **1.** Mes amis et moi, nous…   **2.** Moi, je…
             (rarement)   (souvent)   (rarement)

EXEMPLE Mes grands-parents **vont rarement au théâtre.**

1. Mes amis et moi, nous _____.

2. Moi, je _____.

3. Mon meilleur ami…   **4.** Ma famille…   **5.** Mes amis…
        (tous les dimanches)   (ne… jamais)   (le samedi d'habitude)

3. Mon meilleur ami _____.

4. Ma famille _____.

5. Mes amis _____.

E. Comment? Robert was not paying attention to what Claude said in **D. Où vont-ils?** and asks the following questions. Answer each one *with a complete sentence* using the pronoun **y**.

> EXEMPLE   Tes grands-parents vont souvent au théâtre?
> **Non, ils y vont rarement.**

1. Tes amis et toi, vous allez souvent à la piscine?

   _____

2. Tu vas souvent à des concerts?

   _____

3. Ton meilleur ami va souvent à l'église?

   _____

4. Ta famille et toi, vous allez souvent au centre commercial?

   _____

5. Tes amis vont souvent au parc?

   _____

*F. Où va-t-on? Where do people go in your city to do the indicated things? Create complete sentences using the pronoun **on** with a specific place, as in the example. Remember that the name of a place generally follows the type of place. For example, for *Alliance Cinema,* you say **le cinéma Alliance.**

> EXEMPLE   Pour acheter des livres, **on va à la librairie *Chapters.***

1. Pour assister à *(to attend)* un concert, _____.
2. Pour acheter des vêtements chers, _____.
3. Pour voir des expositions intéressantes, _____.
4. Pour bien manger, _____.

G. Quelle province? A French friend is going to visit both New Brunswick and Québec. Where would you tell her to do the following things? Write a **tu** form command and indicate the logical place.

> EXEMPLE   _____Mange_____ (manger) de la poutine.   au Québec _X_ au Nouveau-Brunswick ___

1. _____ (aller) au Festival acadien.   au Québec ___ au Nouveau-Brunswick ___
2. _____ (passer) quelques jours
   au Festival de jazz de Montréal.   au Québec ___ au Nouveau-Brunswick ___
3. _____ (acheter) des vêtements
   chauds *(warm)*   au Québec ___ au Nouveau-Brunswick ___
4. N' _____ (avoir) pas peur de
   pagayer sur les plus hautes marées du monde.   au Québec ___ au Nouveau-Brunswick ___

H. Suggestions. Would you tell a group of people visiting Québec to do or not do the following things? Provide logical **vous** form commands in the affirmative or negative.

> **EXEMPLE**   être timide : **Ne soyez pas timides.**

1. être à l'heure à l'aéroport : _____

2. manger de la poutine : _____

3. aller toujours manger dans des restos rapides : _____

4. écouter du jazz : _____

5. avoir peur : _____

I. Des projets. It is Friday night and you are making plans with a classmate. Answer your friend's questions by making suggestions with the **nous** form of the verb to say *Let's …*

> **EXEMPLE**   Alors, on va au cinéma ce soir ou on regarde un film à la télé?
> **Allons au cinéma ! / Regardons un film à la télé !**

1. On regarde un film français ou un film canadien?

_____

2. On invite d'autres étudiants du cours de français?

_____

3. On mange quelque chose d'abord?

_____

4. Et demain, on reste à la maison ou on va au parc?

_____

*Journal. Describe your best friend. Tell his/her name. Describe his/her physical appearance, including age, hair and eye colour, and personality. Then, using the pronoun **on** to say *we,* tell how often the two of you go different places and what you like to do there.

_____
_____
_____
_____
_____
_____
_____
_____
_____
_____

Partie auditive

A. Où vont-ils? Robert and his friends are visiting these places this week. For each picture, you will hear two places named. Identify the place that corresponds to the picture. After a pause for you to respond, you will hear the correct answer. Verify your response and your pronunciation.

EXEMPLE   VOUS ENTENDEZ : Où vont-ils? Ils vont dans les boutiques ou au café?
VOUS RÉPONDEZ : **Ils vont dans les boutiques.**
VOUS ENTENDEZ : Ils vont dans les boutiques.

EXEMPLE   **dans les boutiques**

a. _____

b. _____   c. _____   d. _____

e. _____   f. _____   g. _____

h. _____   i. _____   j. _____

Now play this section again and write where Robert and his friends are going under the corresponding illustration. Be sure to include the prepositions that are used to say *to the*. The first one has been done as an example.

B. Invitations. Suggest a logical place to do whatever your friend wants to do. Choose from the list. First make a suggestion using **on** to say *Shall we …,* then say *Let's …,* using the **nous** form of the verb in the imperative form. After a pause for you to respond, you will hear the correct answers. Verify your response and indicate the number of that question in the blank next to the name of the place.

EXEMPLE VOUS ENTENDEZ : Je voudrais aller voir une pièce.
VOUS DITES : **On va au théâtre? Allons au théâtre!**
VOUS ENTENDEZ : On va au théâtre? Allons au théâtre!
VOUS ÉCRIVEZ :

_____ au parc   **Exemple** au théâtre   _____ à la piscine   _____ au musée

_____ au café   _____ au centre commercial   _____ à la librairie

C. Qu'est-ce qu'on fait? Robert and Thomas are making plans for this evening. The first time, just listen to what they say at normal speed. Then fill in the missing words as it is repeated more slowly. Pause the recording as needed to allow enough time to write.

THOMAS : Alors, _____ (1) ce soir ou on sort?

ROBERT : _____ (2). Il y a un festival de jazz.

_____ (3) c'est toujours excellent.

THOMAS : _____ (4) quelque chose avant

d' _____ (5)?

ROBERT : Oui, il y a un restaurant où on sert de la _____ (6) tout

_____ (7). C'est un de mes restaurants préférés.

_____ (8)?

THOMAS : _____ (9)! _____ (10)

vraiment bien ici au Nouveau-Brunswick.

Now pause the recording and find all of the places where the pronoun **on** is used. For each one, indicate whether it means *we* and is used to make a suggestion *(Shall we … ?),* or whether it is used to talk about people in general and is translated as *one, they,* or *you.* List each verb with **on** according to its use. The first one has been done as an example.

Making a suggestion *(we):* <u>on reste,</u> _____

Talking about people in general *(one, they, you):* _____

D. Prononciation : Les lettres *a, au* et *ai.* Pause the recording and review the *Prononciation* section on page 152 of the textbook. Then turn on the recording and repeat the following sentences, making sure to distinguish between the vowel sounds **a, au,** and **ai.** As you listen, determine whether **a, au,** or **ai** is missing from each place's name and fill in the blank.

1. On va au cinéma G _____ *mont* samedi après-midi.

2. J'aime faire du magasinage à la boutique J _____ *cob.*

3. J'achète souvent des livres à la librairie _____ *vicenne.*

4. Aujourd'hui, je vais manger au restaurant _____ *x Lyonn* _____ *s.*

COMPÉTENCE 3

Saying what you are going to do

By the time you finish this **Compétence,** you should be able to talk about your plans for tomorrow, this weekend, and the near future in French.

Partie écrite

*A. La fin de semaine. Answer the following questions about your typical Saturday *with complete sentences in French. Use the present tense.*

>   **EXEMPLE**   Jusqu'à quelle heure est-ce que vous restez au lit le samedi généralement?
>   **Généralement le samedi, je reste au lit jusqu'à... heures.**

1. À quelle heure est-ce que vous quittez la maison le samedi?

_____

2. Est-ce que vous allez souvent boire un café avec des amis?

_____

3. Avec qui est-ce que vous passez la soirée?

_____

4. Est-ce que vous rentrez souvent tard le samedi soir?

_____

5. Est-ce que vous aimez partir pour la fin de semaine? Où est-ce que vous préférez aller?

_____

6. Est-ce que vous allez souvent voir des amis ou votre famille dans une autre ville?

_____

B. Une conversation. Robert and Thomas are making plans for the weekend. Complete their conversation.

THOMAS: Qu'est-ce qu'on fait cette fin de semaine?

ROBERT: _____ **(1)** pour
                          (I don't have plans)

vendredi. Je vais _____ **(2)** à
                          (spend the evening)

la maison et regarder des films. Samedi, on va _____ **(3)** mon père.
                                                  (go see)

_____ **(4)**, on va dîner ensemble.
            (First)

_____ **(5)**, on va _____ **(6)**
        (Next)   *(go see)*

une exposition à la Galerie des arts.

THOMAS: Et samedi soir?

ROBERT: Après l'exposition, on va rentrer _____ (7).
                                            (to my father's house)

_____ (8), on va aller à un festival de _____ (9).
     (And then)   *(Acadian music)*

THOMAS: _____ (10)!
                  (Great)

C. Projets. Robert, Claude, and Thomas are talking about what they are going to do this weekend. Fill in each blank with the correct form of **aller** followed by the logical infinitive from the list. The first one has been done as an example.

préparer / quitter / rester

Samedi matin, je _____vais quitter_____ la maison tôt mais Thomas _____ (1) au lit. Claude _____ (2) ses cours à la maison.

aller / nager

Samedi après-midi, Thomas _____ (3) à la bibliothèque et après, nous _____ (4) à la piscine.

boire / aller / rentrer

Dimanche après-midi, je _____ (5) au parc avec Claude pour jouer au frisbee. Plus tard, on _____ (6) quelque chose au café avec une amie. On _____ (7) tard.

*D. Des projets d'avenir. Create sentences in French telling what the indicated people are going to do at each of the following times. If you don't know, guess! Use the **future proche (aller + infinitive).**

1. Ce soir, je _____.

2. Demain soir, mes amis _____.

3. La fin de semaine prochaine, mes amis et moi _____.

4. Le mois prochain, je _____.

5. Le dernier jour du semestre, les étudiants _____.

6. L'année prochaine, je _____.

E. Quelle est la date? Which of the activities listed in parentheses would Robert most likely say his family members are going to do on these dates? Create sentences, spelling out the dates.

> **EXEMPLE**   25/12 – je… (sortir avec des amis, aller voir ma famille)
> **Le vingt-cinq décembre, je vais aller voir ma famille.**

1. 1/1 – mes frères… (rester à la maison, être en cours)

_____

2. 14/2 – mon père… (aller à un match de basketball avec ses amis, acheter des roses pour sa femme)

_____

3. 1/7 – on… (aller voir des feux d'artifice *[fireworks]*, voir des matchs de soccer à la télé)

_____

4. 31/10 – je… (faire une fête chez moi, aller chez des amis)

_____

5. 25/12 – nous… (passer la journée chez ma mère, aller à la plage)

_____

F. C'est quand? If today is March 15 **(le quinze mars),** when are the following dates? Create sentences with the date and the logical expression in parentheses as in the example.

> **EXEMPLE**   16/3 (la semaine prochaine, demain)
> **Le seize mars, c'est demain.**

1. 18/3 (dans trois semaines, dans trois jours)

_____

2. 23/3 (la semaine prochaine, le mois prochain)

_____

3. 1/4 (la semaine prochaine, le mois prochain)

_____

4. 15/9 (dans six mois, l'année prochaine)

_____

*G. Quelques questions. Answer each question *with a complete sentence in French.*

1. Quelle est la date aujourd'hui? Qu'est-ce que vous allez faire ce soir? Avec qui allez-vous passer la soirée?

_____

_____

_____

2. Quelle est la date samedi prochain? Qu'est-ce que vous allez faire samedi matin? samedi après-midi?
   samedi soir?

_____

_____

_____

3. Quelle est la date de votre anniversaire? Qu'est-ce que vous allez faire pour fêter *(to celebrate)* votre
   anniversaire?

_____

_____

_____

4. (Regardez la liste des fêtes dans le vocabulaire supplémentaire à la page 160 du livre.) Quelle est votre fête
   préférée? Cette fête est en quel mois? Qu'est-ce que vous allez faire cette année?

_____

_____

_____

Partie auditive

 A. Cette fin de semaine. Look at the pictures illustrating what various friends are or are not going to do this weekend. After you hear the cue, ask whether the friend is going to do the indicated activity. Then repeat the answer you hear and indicate with an **X** the ones that the friends are not going to do. Do not mark anything for those that they are going to do.

> **EXEMPLE** VOUS ENTENDEZ : quitter l'appartement tôt samedi
> VOUS DEMANDEZ : **Tu vas quitter l'appartement tôt samedi ?**
> VOUS ENTENDEZ : Non, je ne vais pas quitter l'appartement tôt samedi.
> VOUS DITES : **Non, je ne vais pas quitter l'appartement tôt samedi.**
> VOUS INDIQUEZ :

EXEMPLE _____X_____   1. _____   2. _____   3. _____

4. _____   5. _____   6. _____

 B. Les expressions qui indiquent le futur. You will hear several pairs of expressions of time. Repeat the one that is the most distant in the future. After a pause for you to answer, you will hear the correct response. Verify your answer and pronunciation.

> **EXEMPLE** VOUS ENTENDEZ : demain matin / demain soir
> VOUS RÉPÉTEZ : **demain soir**
> VOUS ENTENDEZ : demain soir

 C. Présent ou futur ? For each statement Robert's friend Christine makes, decide if she is talking about what she generally does on Saturdays **(le présent)** or what she is going to do this Saturday **(le futur).** Fill in the blank with a **P** for **le présent** and an **F** for **le futur.**

1. ___   2. ___   3. ___   4. ___   5. ___   6. ___   7. ___   8. ___   9. ___

D. Les années et les mois de l'année. Listen to the following years and months and repeat after the speaker, paying careful attention to your pronunciation. Repeat the activity until you feel comfortable saying the numbers and the months.

1789	1978	janvier	avril	juillet	octobre
1864	1999	février	mai	août	novembre
1945	2018	mars	juin	septembre	décembre

E. Dates. Say these dates in French. After a pause for you to respond, you will hear the correct answer. Verify your response and your pronunciation.

EXEMPLE   VOUS VOYEZ: le 15 mars 1951
              VOUS ENTENDEZ: Quelle est la date?
              VOUS DITES: **C'est le quinze mars mille neuf cent cinquante et un.**
              VOUS ENTENDEZ: C'est le quinze mars mille neuf cent cinquante et un.

1. le 17 septembre 1949   **3.** le 7 décembre 1945   **5.** le 14 juillet 1789

2. le 4 juillet 1776   **4.** le 1er juillet 1867   **6.** le 1er janvier 2015

F. Qu'est-ce qu'on fait? Listen as Robert and Thomas discuss their plans for this evening. Then stop the recording and select the correct answer based on what you heard. Play this section again as needed.

_____ 1. Ce soir, ils vont…   **a.** regarder la télé   **b.** regarder un film sur Netflix   **c.** aller au cinéma

_____ 2. Ils vont voir…   **a.** un film français   **b.** un film italien   **c.** un film canadien

_____ 3. C'est un…   **a.** très bon film   **b.** film amusant   **c.** film triste

_____ 4. C'est l'histoire (story)…   **a.** d'un couple   **b.** d'une petite fille   **c.** d'un jeune garçon

G. Qu'est-ce que tu vas faire? Two friends are talking about their plans for today. The first time, just listen to what they say at normal speed. Then fill in the missing words as it is repeated more slowly. Pause the recording as needed to allow enough time to complete the conversation.

— Alors, _____ **(1)** aujourd'hui?

— _____ **(2)** travailler un peu sur

l'ordinateur. _____ **(3)**, cet après-midi, _____

(4) la nouvelle exposition au musée. _____ **(5)** d'aller au musée?

— Combien de temps _____ **(6)** au musée?

— _____ **(7)** vers quatre heures.

— Alors oui, _____ **(8)** avec toi. _____ **(9)**

après ça, _____ **(10)** ce soir?

— Je n'ai pas de _____ **(11)** pour ce soir.

COMPÉTENCE 4

Planning how to get there

By the time you finish this **Compétence,** you should be able to talk about where you are going to go and how you are going to get there in French.

Partie écrite

A. Moyens de transport. This family is visiting the Atlantic provinces. The mother is talking about how they are going to get around. Complete each sentence with the means of transportation.

EXEMPLE On…

1. On…

2. Nos amis…

3. Mon fils…

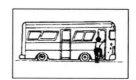

4. Moi, je…

5. Mon chéri, tu…?

EXEMPLE On va prendre la **voiture** pour aller à Moncton.

1. On va prendre l' _____ pour aller à l'Île-du-Prince-Édouard.

2. Nos amis vont prendre un _____ pour aller d'une plage à l'autre.

3. Mon fils va prendre son _____ pour aller au parc.

4. Moi, je vais prendre l' _____ pour aller en ville.

5. Mon chéri, tu vas prendre le _____ pour aller à Halifax?

B. Comment? A friend of the woman in **A. Moyens de transport** did not hear what she said and asks the following questions. Answer using the pronoun **y** and the verb **aller.**

EXEMPLE Comment est-ce que vous allez à Moncton?
On y va en voiture.

1. Comment est-ce que vous allez à l'Île-du-Prince-Édouard?

_____

2. Comment est-ce que vos amis vont à l'autre plage?

_____

3. Comment est-ce que ton fils va au parc?

_____

4. Comment est-ce que tu vas en ville?

_____

5. Comment est-ce que ton mari va à Halifax?

_____

C. Une conversation. Robert and Thomas are meeting some friends at the park. Complete their conversation.

ROBERT: _____ **(1)**, on va partir bientôt. Tu es _____ **(2)**?
                     (Listen)   *(ready)*

THOMAS: Oui. _____ **(3)**?
                           (Shall we go there by car)

ROBERT: Non, _____ **(4)**. Ce n'est pas
                      (let's go to the park on foot)

_____ **(5)**.
                           (far)

THOMAS: Ça _____ **(6)** pour
                      (takes how much time)

_____ **(7)**?
                         (to go there)

ROBERT: Ça prend _____ **(8)**, pas plus.
                      (around twenty minutes)

THOMAS: _____ **(9)** va-t-on rester au parc?
                      (How long)

ROBERT: _____ **(10)** vers cinq heures?
                      (Shall we come back)

D. Des touristes. Two tourists are returning from a trip. Answer each question *with a complete sentence* according to the illustrations.

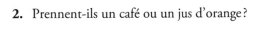

1. À quelle heure prennent-ils le déjeuner?

_____

2. Prennent-ils un café ou un jus d'orange?

_____

3. Comment vont-ils de l'hôtel à l'aéroport : en taxi, en métro ou en autobus ?

_____

4. Prennent-ils le train ou l'avion ?

_____

5. À quelle heure prennent-ils l'avion ?

_____

6. À quelle heure est-ce qu'ils prennent quelque chose à manger dans l'avion ?

_____

E. Au café. A mother is asking what everyone wants to order in a café. Complete their conversation with the verb **prendre**.

— Les enfants, vous _____ **(1)** une limonade ou un coca ?

— Nous _____ **(2)** une limonade.

— Et toi, chéri, tu _____ **(3)** une eau minérale ou un jus de fruits ?

— Je _____ **(4)** un jus de fruits. Et toi, qu'est-ce que tu vas

_____ **(5)** ?

— Je vais _____ **(6)** un café.

Now the mother is ordering for her family. Based on the previous dialogue, what does she say to the waiter? Use the verb **prendre** in the present tense.

1. Les enfants _____.

2. Mon mari _____.

3. Et moi, je _____.

F. Le verbe *venir*. A friend is talking to you on campus. Complete what she says with the correct form of the verb **venir**.

Ce trimestre, je _____ **(1)** à l'université tous les jours. D'habitude,

je _____ **(2)** à pied et ma colocataire _____ **(3)**

en autobus, mais quelquefois nous _____ **(4)** à vélo. Beaucoup

d'étudiants _____ **(5)** à l'université à vélo parce qu'il n'y a pas assez

de stationnements. Et toi ? Comment est-ce que tu _____ **(6)**

à l'université ? Tes amis et toi, vous _____ **(7)** à l'université la fin de

semaine pour étudier ou pour assister *(to attend)* aux matchs de soccer ou de basketball ?

*Now answer the questions asked in **6** and **7** *with complete sentences in French.*

6. _____

7. _____

*G. En cours de français. A classmate is asking you these questions. Complete his questions with the correct form of the verb indicated in parentheses. Then answer them *with complete sentences.*

1. Est-ce que tu _____ (venir) à l'université à pied? Combien de temps

    est-ce que ça _____ (prendre) pour venir de chez toi jusqu'à l'université:

    quinze minutes? une heure?

    _____

    _____

2. Comment est-ce que les étudiants _____ (venir) en cours en général?

    Est-ce que beaucoup d'étudiants _____ (prendre) l'autobus pour venir

    à l'université?

    _____

    _____

3. Dans quels cours est-ce que tu _____ (apprendre) beaucoup? peu?

    _____

    _____

4. Généralement, est-ce que les étudiants _____ (comprendre) bien en

    cours de français?

    _____

5. Est-ce que le cours de français _____ (devenir) difficile?

    _____

---

*Journal. Write about your plans for tomorrow. Use the immediate future and include the following information.

- where you are going to have breakfast and at what time
- what time you are going to leave your house, apartment, or dormitory
- where you are going to go, why you are going to each place, and how you are going to go there
- what time you are going to return home

_____

_____

_____

_____

_____

_____

_____

_____

Partie auditive

 A. Comment est-ce qu'on y va? The following illustrations show how Robert and his acquaintances are traveling. Answer each question affirmatively or negatively with the pronoun **y** and the correct means of transportation. Indicate whether you answered affirmatively or negatively by selecting **oui** or **non**.

EXEMPLE   VOUS ENTENDEZ :   Thomas et Claude vont à Montréal en train?

              VOUS DITES :   **Non, ils y vont en avion.**

              VOUS ENTENDEZ :   Non, ils y vont en avion.

              VOUS INDIQUEZ :

EXEMPLE oui _____ non ✓   **1.** oui _____ non _____   **2.** oui _____ non _____   **3.** oui _____ non _____

4. oui _____ non _____   **5.** oui _____ non _____   **6.** oui _____ non _____   **7.** oui _____ non _____

 B. Prononciation : Les verbes *prendre* et *venir*. Pause the recording and review the ***Prononciation*** section on page 164 of the textbook. Then turn on the recording and fill in the verb forms as you hear them pronounced.

prendre

Je _____ souvent l'autobus.

Tu _____ souvent le train?

On _____ le métro?

Nous _____ l'autobus.

Vous _____ souvent l'autobus?

Les Québécois ne _____ pas souvent le train.

venir

Je _____ à l'université à pied.

Comment _____-tu en cours?

Il _____ en cours en autobus.

Nous _____ en cours en voiture.

Vous _____ toujours en cours?

Ils _____ en cours à l'heure.

Now listen as Thomas, who is at school, talks about how some of his friends get around. Indicate whether he is talking about just one friend or about a group of friends.

1. ___ un ami   ___ un groupe   **4.** ___ un ami   ___ un groupe

2. ___ un ami   ___ un groupe   **5.** ___ un ami   ___ un groupe

3. ___ un ami   ___ un groupe   **6.** ___ un ami   ___ un groupe

Nom _____   Date _____

C. Comment est-ce que vous y allez? Restate each sentence you hear with the verb **prendre,** as in the example. You will then hear the correct answer. Verify your response and repeat again.

       EXEMPLE   VOUS ENTENDEZ: Thomas va en ville en autobus.
                 VOUS DITES: **Thomas prend l'autobus pour aller en ville.**
                 VOUS ENTENDEZ: Thomas prend l'autobus pour aller en ville.
                 VOUS RÉPÉTEZ: **Thomas prend l'autobus pour aller en ville.**

D. Comment est-ce qu'on y va? You will hear two means of transportation proposed. Suggest taking the one that is usually faster. You will then hear the correct answer. Verify your response, repeat again, and fill in the blank with the selected means of transportation.

       EXEMPLE   VOUS ENTENDEZ: On prend la voiture ou on y va à pied?
                 VOUS DITES: **Prenons la voiture!**
                 VOUS ENTENDEZ: Prenons la voiture!
                 VOUS RÉPÉTEZ: **Prenons la voiture!**
                 VOUS ÉCRIVEZ:

       EXEMPLE _____ *la voiture* _____

1. _____ 3. _____ 5. _____
2. _____ 4. _____ 6. _____

E. Un départ. Two of Thomas's friends are flying down to meet him in Halifax, and they are about to leave for the airport **(l'aéroport).** Listen to their conversation, then pause the recording and complete the following sentences.

1. Leur avion va partir à _____ heures _____.
2. Ils vont aller à l'aéroport en _____.
3. Ils ne prennent pas la voiture pour aller à l'aéroport parce qu'il n'aime pas _____ au stationnement de l'aéroport.
4. Pour aller à leur hôtel à Halifax, ils vont _____.

***F. Et vous?** Imagine that a classmate asks you these questions in class. Answer the questions *with complete sentences,* pausing the recording in order to respond.

1. _____
2. _____
3. _____
4. _____
5. _____

Les projets

Chapitre 5

Saying what you did

By the time you finish this **Compétence,** you should be able talk about what you did yesterday.

Partie écrite

A. La journée d'Alice. Alice is talking about what she did last Saturday. Complete her statements according to the illustrations. In the blank, write the verb in the past tense (**passé composé**). Then indicate the correct italicized completion. The first one has been done as an example.

 1   2   3   4   5

1. Samedi matin, j'**ai dormi** (dormir) *sur le divan /* (*dans mon lit*) *sous une tente.*

   J' _____ (dormir) jusqu'à *dix heures / midi / huit heures.*

2. J' _____ (prendre) mon déjeuner *au café / chez moi / au restaurant.*

   J' _____ (manger) *avec mon mari / avec mes enfants / seule.*

3. J' _____ (dîner) *chez moi / au parc / en ville.*

   J' _____ (dîner) *avec un ami / avec une amie / seule.*

4. Le soir, j' _____ (retrouver) une amie *au cinéma / au centre commercial / à la bibliothèque.*

   J' _____ (voir) *une pièce / un film / un DVD.*

5. Plus tard *(later)* à la maison, j' _____ (lire) *le journal / un livre / une lettre.*

B. Conversation. Reread the conversation between Léa and Edgar on page 181 of your textbook. Then, complete this conversation between two other students with the indicated words.

FLORENCE : _____ **(1)** une bonne fin de semaine ?
               *(Did you have [use **passer**])*

THÉO :   Bof, pas trop. Samedi matin, _____ **(2)**
                                   (I prepared)

        mes cours et _____ **(3)**, j'ai travaillé.
                   (Saturday afternoon)

FLORENCE: _____ (4) dimanche?
          (What did you do)

THÉO: Dimanche matin, _____ (5) et dimanche
                        (I slept)

      après-midi, _____ (6).
                   (I watched TV)

FLORENCE: Et _____ (7)?
             (last night)

THÉO: _____ (8).
      (Last night, I did nothing)

C. La journée d'Alice.
Alice is talking about her day last Sunday. Complete the following paragraph by putting the verbs in parentheses in the **passé composé.**

Dimanche dernier, j' _____ (1) (dormir) jusqu'à huit heures et demie.

Le matin, je _____ (2) (ne rien faire) de spécial. Vincent et

moi _____ (3) (prendre) le déjeuner avec les enfants et

après, Vincent et les enfants _____ (4) (faire) une promenade.

Moi, j' _____ (5) (préférer) rester à la maison. J' _____ (6)

(lire) le journal. Vers onze heures, j' _____ (7) (téléphoner)

à mon amie Sophie pour l'inviter à dîner avec Vincent et moi. Nous _____ (8)

(retrouver) Sophie et son mari en ville où nous _____ (9) (manger)

dans un excellent restaurant. Après le dîner, Vincent et moi _____ (10)

(faire) du magasinage et nous _____ (11) (prendre) l'autobus

pour rentrer à la maison. Nous _____ (12) (passer) la soirée à la

maison. Nous _____ (13) (voir) un bon film à la télé et après,

Vincent et les enfants _____ (14) (jouer) aux cartes. Moi,

j' _____ (15) (faire) de l'exercice.

D. Un peu d'histoire.
Tell a little about francophone history in Canada by putting the verbs in the following sentences in the **passé composé.**

1. En 1534, l'explorateur français, Jacques Cartier _____

   (prendre) possession du Canada (la Nouvelle-France) pour la France et en 1604, les Français

   _____ (commencer) à coloniser la Cadie (plus tard l'Acadie),

   aujourd'hui la Nouvelle-Écosse *(Nova Scotia)*, le Nouveau-Brunswick, l'Île-du-Prince-Édouard et

   Terre-Neuve-et-Labrador. En 1608, Samuel de Champlain _____

   (fonder) la ville de Québec.

2. En 1682, les Français _____ (prendre) possession de la Louisiane.

3. Les Anglais _____ (gagner) le contrôle de l'Acadie en 1713 et en 1755,

   ils _____ (commencer) à expulser *(to remove)* les Français de la région.

4. De 1756 à 1763, les Anglais et les Français _____ (faire) la guerre

(war). Les Anglais _____ (gagner) la guerre et, en 1763, la France

_____ (céder) ses territoires canadiens aux Anglais. De 1764 à 1785,

les Acadiens _____ (trouver) un nouveau pays en Louisiane.

5. En 1803, les Américains _____ (acheter) la Louisiane à la France pour

15 millions de dollars. Mais les Acadiens _____ (être) isolés pendant

plus de 100 ans dans le sud de la Louisiane. Entre 1880 et 1905, ils _____

(commencer) à avoir plus de contacts avec les anglophones avec l'arrivée du chemin de fer *(railroad)*, de

l'électricité et de l'industrie pétrolière.

E. Pour mieux lire : *Using the sequence of events to make logical guesses.* In a logical
sequence of events, what might the italicized verbs mean in these sentences describing what Léa did last
Saturday? Give the *English* equivalent of each italicized verb in the blank in parentheses.

1. À onze heures, une amie a téléphoné. Léa *a répondu* (_____) au téléphone et elle

a parlé à son amie pendant une demi-heure. Elles ont décidé d'aller faire du magasinage et elles ont terminé la

conversation. Après la conversation, Léa *a raccroché* (_____) le téléphone.

2. L'après-midi, Léa a retrouvé son amie au centre commercial où elle a acheté beaucoup de choses. À

un certain moment, elle *a perdu* (_____) sa carte de crédit. Elle l'a cherchée

partout et finalement elle a trouvé sa carte de crédit et ses lunettes par terre.

3. Son amie et elle ont pris quelque chose au café. Quand Léa a payé, elle *a reçu* (_____)

trop de monnaie, alors elle *a rendu* (_____) cinq dollars au serveur.

4. Le soir, Léa *a mis* (_____) ses nouveaux vêtements, elle a quitté la

maison, elle a retrouvé ses amis en ville et ils ont dansé toute la soirée.

5. Vers deux heures du matin, elle a pris un taxi pour rentrer à la maison. Elle est allée dans sa chambre, elle *a

enlevé* (_____) ses vêtements, elle *a mis* (_____) son

pyjama et elle a dormi jusqu'au lendemain.

F. Qu'est-ce qu'elle a fait ? Reread the story *Qu'est-ce qu'elle a fait ?* on
page 185 of the textbook. Then, for each location, say one thing Léa did and one
thing she didn't do.

> **EXEMPLE** au café :
> **Léa a commandé un coca mais elle n'a pas bu le coca.**

1. à la station de métro :

_____

_____

2. au magasin de vélos :

_____

_____

Now explain in your own words *in English* why Léa did what she did.

_____

_____

*G. Toujours des questions. Imagine that a friend wants to ask you about your activities last Saturday. Use the elements given to create his questions. Then, answer each question.

> **EXEMPLE** faire samedi dernier *(what)*
> **— Qu'est-ce que tu as fait samedi dernier?**
> **— J'ai bricolé. / Je n'ai rien fait.**

1. dormir *(until what time)*

— _____

— _____

2. passer la matinée *(where)*

— _____

— _____

3. quitter la maison *(at what time)*

— _____

— _____

4. déjeuner *(with whom)*

— _____

— _____

5. manger *(where)*

— _____

— _____

6. faire samedi après-midi *(what)*

— _____

— _____

7. passer la soirée *(where)*

— _____

— _____

Nom _____ Date _____

Partie auditive

 A. Une journée chargée. You will hear Alice say some of the things she did yesterday. Indicate the number of each sentence you hear under the corresponding picture.

a. _____

b. _____

c. _____

d. _____

e. _____

f. _____

 B. Et vous? Now you will hear several sentences in which Léa says what she did the last day she went to class. After each one, pause the recording and fill in the blank to say whether you did the same thing the last day you went to French class.

EXEMPLE	VOUS ENTENDEZ:	**J'ai téléphoné à un ami.**
	VOUS ÉCRIVEZ:	Moi, **j'ai téléphoné à un ami.**
		Moi, **je n'ai pas téléphoné** à un ami.

1. Moi, _____ jusqu'à midi.

2. Moi, _____ la matinée chez moi.

3. Moi, _____ mon déjeuner au lit.

4. Moi, _____ le journal.

5. Moi, _____ le bus.

6. Moi, _____ les mots de vocabulaire.

7. Moi, _____ mes devoirs avant les cours.

8. Moi, _____ la leçon *(the lesson)*.

9. Moi, _____ un film / de film au cinéma.

10. Moi, _____ la télé.

C. Tu as passé une bonne fin de semaine? Listen to a conversation between two students about last weekend and complete the following two sentences with things that they did.

1. Un étudiant n'a pas fait grand-chose *(not much)*. Il _____

   et il _____.

2. L'autre étudiant a retrouvé des amis en ville. Ils _____

   et ils _____.

   Le dimanche, il _____

   et il _____.

D. Dictée. You will hear two friends, Olivia and Arthur, discuss their weekend. The first time, just listen to what they say at normal speed. Then fill in the missing words as the conversation is repeated more slowly.

OLIVIA: _____ **(1)** une bonne fin de semaine?

ARTHUR: Oui, _____ **(2)**. Et toi? Qu'est-ce que

   _____ **(3)**?

OLIVIA: Samedi à midi, _____ **(4)** des amis au

   café et _____ **(5)** ensemble. Après,

   _____ **(6)** un tour de la ville

   et le soir, _____ **(7)** un film.

ARTHUR: Et dimanche?

OLIVIA: Dimanche matin, _____ **(8)** le journal et après,

   _____ **(9)** le déjeuner avec un ami.

ARTHUR: Qu'est-ce que _____ **(10)** après?

OLIVIA: _____ **(11)** une promenade.

*E. Et vous? Answer these questions about your own activities yesterday *with complete sentences in French*.

1. _____

2. _____

3. _____

4. _____

5. _____

6. _____

7. _____

8. _____

COMPÉTENCE 2

Telling where you went

By the time you finish this *Compétence,* you should be able to tell in French where you went and when you did something.

Partie écrite

*A. Mon voyage. Talk about the last time you left town. Fill in the blanks with the verbs in the **passé composé** and complete the sentences as indicated.

1. Je _____ (aller) à _____ *[quelle ville].*

2. Je _____ (partir) _____ *[quand].*

3. J'y _____ (aller) en _____ *[comment].*

4. Je _____ (arriver) _____ *[quand].*

5. Je _____ (descendre) _____ *[où].*

6. Je _____ (rentrer) _____ *[quand].*

B. Conversation. Reread the conversation between Claire and Alice on page 186 of the textbook. Then, complete this conversation between two other friends with the indicated words.

JULIE :   Qu'est-ce que tu as fait _____ **(1)** ?
                                                      (last weekend)

MARTIN :   _____ **(2)** à Ottawa.
                    (I went)

JULIE :   _____ **(3)** ! J'adore Ottawa ! Tu as pris le train ?
                (What luck)

MARTIN : Oui, _____ **(4)** samedi matin et _____ **(5)**
                        (I left)   *(I arrived)*

          vers midi. _____ **(6)** hier soir.
                            (I returned)

JULIE :   Où est-ce que tu es descendu ?

MARTIN :   _____ **(7)** dans un petit hôtel au centre-ville.
                    (I stayed)

JULIE :   Moi, j'ai visité Ottawa en juin. Je suis restée _____ **(8).**
                                                                              (with some relatives)

C. Le dernier cours. Say whether or not the following people did the things indicated in parentheses the last day you went to French class. Use the **passé composé** and don't forget the agreement of the past participle when needed.

EXEMPLE   Je **suis parti(e) / ne suis pas parti(e)** (partir) tôt de la maison.

1. Tous les étudiants _____ (aller) en cours de français.

2. Je _____ (arriver) en cours en retard *[late].*

3. Nous _____ (aller) au laboratoire de langues.

4. Le professeur _____ (sortir) de la salle de classe pendant *[during]* le cours.

5. Je _____ (rentrer) chez moi après le cours.

6. Les autres étudiants _____ (rester) dans la salle de classe après le cours.

7. Je _____ (revenir) le soir pour travailler avec d'autres étudiants à la bibliothèque.

D. La journée d'Éric.

Complete the following passage about what Éric and his family did yesterday by supplying the correct form of the appropriate auxiliary verb **avoir** or **être**.

Éric _____ **(1)** commencé sa journée à 7 h 30. D'abord, il _____ **(2)** fait du jogging dans le quartier et après, il _____ **(3)** rentré à la maison où il _____ **(4)** pris son déjeuner. Ensuite, il _____ **(5)** allé en ville. L'après-midi, il _____ **(6)** joué au soccer avec des amis. Éric _____ **(7)** parti à 5 h 30 pour rentrer à la maison. Hier soir, une amie _____ **(8)** invité Éric à souper chez elle. Alors Vincent, Alice et les autres enfants _____ **(9)** soupé en ville et ils _____ **(10)** allés au cinéma. Toute la famille _____ **(11)** rentrée très fatiguée à 11 h du soir.

E. Qui?

Based on the illustrations, write a sentence to say who did each of the indicated things. Make sure you choose the correct auxiliary, **avoir** or **être**.

Alice	Vincent	Vincent et Alice	Vincent et Alice

EXEMPLE **Vincent est resté** (rester) à la maison pendant la journée.

1. _____ (travailler) sur l'ordinateur.

2. _____ (sortir) vers 7 h 30.

3. _____ (faire) une promenade.

4. _____ (passer) la soirée chez des amis.

5. _____ (prendre) un verre avec leurs amis.

6. _____ (beaucoup parler) avec leurs amis.

7. _____ (rentrer) assez tard.

8. _____ (monter) à leur appartement vers minuit.

F. Quand? Translate these expressions into French, then number them from the closest to now (1) to the furthest from now (8). The first one has been done as an example.

a few minutes ago	**il y a quelques minutes**	**1**
last month	_____	_____
yesterday morning	_____	_____
last year	_____	_____
yesterday afternoon	_____	_____
two hours ago	_____	_____
last week	_____	_____
last night	_____	_____

G. Déjà? Say whether you have *already* done these things or whether you have *not yet* done them. Use **déjà** or **ne... pas encore.**

EXEMPLE   prendre le déjeuner aujourd'hui:
J'ai déjà pris le déjeuner aujourd'hui. /
Je n'ai pas encore pris le déjeuner aujourd'hui.

1. dîner aujourd'hui: _____ aujourd'hui.

2. faire tous les devoirs pour mon prochain cours: _____

   tous les devoirs pour mon prochain cours.

3. sortir de chez moi aujourd'hui: _____ de chez moi

   aujourd'hui.

4. être en cours cette semaine: _____ en cours cette semaine.

H. Tu as passé une bonne fin de semaine? Two men are talking about the weekend. Complete their conversation by putting the verbs in parentheses into the **passé composé** and supplying the missing expressions of past time. Be careful to distinguish which verbs take **avoir** as their auxiliary verb and which ones require **être.**

— Je _____ **(1)** de Charlottetown _____ **(2).**
       (rentrer)   *[last night]*

Et toi, tu _____ **(3)** _____ **(4)**?
            (voyager)   *[recently]*

— Je (J') _____ **(5)** aux chutes Niagara avec ma petite amie et ses
          (aller)

parents _____ **(6).**
        [two months ago]

— Quand est-ce que vous _____ **(7)**?
                         (partir)

— Nous _____ **(8)** Gatineau le vendredi 6 mars.
       (quitter)

— Vous _____ (9) à Niagara
        (rester)

_____ (10)?
        [for how long]

— Nous y _____ (11) _____ (12).
        (rester)   *[for five days]*

— Vous _____ (13) à l'hôtel?
        (descendre)

— Non, nous _____ (14) chez des amis.
        (rester)

---

*Journal. Write a paragraph about a trip you took to another city. Tell the following:

- where you went, when you left, how you went there
- who you travelled with, how long you stayed, and where you stayed
- a few things you did
- when you came back

_____

_____

_____

_____

_____

_____

_____

_____

_____

_____

_____

_____

_____

_____

_____

_____

_____

_____

Nom _____ Date _____

Partie auditive

A. Alice a fait un voyage. Listen as Alice talks about a weekend trip she took. Then pause the recording and complete these statements based on what she says. When you have finished, turn on the recording and check your work. Repeat the sentences after the speaker to correct your pronunciation.

Elle est allée à Québec. Elle n'y est pas allée en train, elle y est allée _____ **(1)**.

Elle est partie le _____ **(2)** et elle

est arrivée vers _____ **(3)**. Elle est descendue dans un charmant

petit _____ **(4)**. Dimanche, elle est allée _____ **(5)**

Jacques-Cartier. Elle est rentrée tard le _____ **(6)**.

B. Prononciation : Les verbes auxiliaires *avoir* et *être*. Pause the recording and review the *Prononciation* section on page 188 of the textbook. Then start the recording and repeat the following forms of the verbs **avoir** and **être** after the speaker, being careful to pronounce them distinctly.

1. tu as ____   tu es ____   **3.** il a ____   il est ____

2. tu as ____   tu es ____   **4.** ils ont ____   ils sont ____

Now you will hear a friend's questions about the last time you went away on vacation (**la dernière fois que tu es parti[e] en vacances),** with either **avoir** or **être** as the auxiliary verb. Indicate the auxiliary verb that you hear in items 1–4 above.

*Now play the questions again. This time, *answer* the questions *with complete sentences.*

1. _____

2. _____

3. _____

4. _____

C. Claire décrit sa fin de semaine. Claire has spent a weekend in Québec. Listen as she describes her weekend to Alice. The first time, simply listen to the conversation at normal speed. It will then be repeated at a slower speed with pauses for you to fill in the missing words in the sentences.

ALICE :   Alors, Claire, raconte-moi ta fin de semaine à Québec!

CLAIRE :   D'abord, _____ **(1)** le train et

_____ **(2)** dans un charmant petit hôtel.

Le premier soir, _____ **(3)** dans un très bon restaurant

où nous avons goûté *(tasted)* des spécialités de la région. C'était *(It was)* très bon! Dimanche,

_____ **(4)** la journée à la plage.

Nom _____ Date _____

ALICE: Est-ce que _____ (5) au casino?

CLAIRE: Oui, dimanche soir, mais _____ (6).

Mon mari n'aime pas jouer pour de l'argent. Après, _____ (7)

à un concert de jazz au centre culturel. _____ (8) la

musique. _____ (9) à l'hôtel à trois heures du matin!

D. Les expressions qui désignent le passé. Pause the recording and match each phrase expressing present time on the left with a parallel expression of past time from the lettered list on the right. The first one has been done as an example. Afterward, turn on the recording and correct your work. Repeat each time expression after the speaker to practise pronunciation.

__g__ 1. aujourd'hui   **a.** la semaine dernière

_____ 2. ce matin   **b.** hier soir

_____ 3. cet après-midi   **c.** le mois dernier

_____ 4. ce soir   **d.** hier après-midi

_____ 5. cette fin de semaine **e.** la fin de semaine dernière

_____ 6. cette semaine   **f.** l'année dernière

_____ 7. ce mois-ci   **g.** hier

_____ 8. cette année   **h.** hier matin

E. Léa est occupée (busy). Listen as Léa talks about her recent activities. Then replay the passage and pause the recording as needed to list, *in English*, two things Léa did at each of the indicated times.

1. *last month:* _____

_____

2. *last week:* _____

_____

3. *last weekend:* _____

_____

4. *yesterday morning:* _____

_____

5. *yesterday afternoon:* _____

_____

6. *last night:* _____

_____

COMPÉTENCE 3

Discussing the weather and your activities

By the time you finish this **Compétence**, you should be able to describe the weather and say what people do in different seasons.

Partie écrite

A. Quel temps fait-il ? Say two things about what the weather is like in each of these four scenes. Use the *present* tense.

EXEMPLE   **Il fait chaud et il fait soleil.**

    Exemple   **1**   **2**   **3**

1. _____

2. _____

3. _____

*Now say two things about what the weather is like in your region in these seasons.

EXEMPLE   été : **En été ici, il fait beau et il fait soleil.**

1. hiver : _____

2. automne : _____

3. printemps : _____

4. été : _____

B. Conversation. Reread the vocabulary and the conversation between Alice and Léa on page 193 of the textbook. Then, complete this conversation between two friends.

CHLOÉ :   En _____ **(1)** préfères-tu voyager ?
                        (what season)

OLIVIA :   J'aime voyager _____ **(2)** parce que j'aime
                              (in summer)

           _____ **(3)** et
                        (to go boating)

           _____ **(4).**
                        (to waterski)

CHLOÉ : Moi, je préfère voyager _____ (5) parce

qu'_____ (6). J'aime aller
　　　　　　(it's cool)

_____ (7)
　　　　(to the mountains)

pour _____ (8) et pour
　　　　　　　(to go camping)

_____ (9). _____ (10)
　　(to go all-terrain biking)　　　　　　　　　*(If it's sunny)*

cette fin de semaine, j' _____ (11) faire du camping à la campagne.
　　　　　　　　　　　　　　　(intend to)

C. Un après-midi. Complete the following conversation between Alice and Vincent by filling in each blank with the correct form of **faire** in the *present* tense or in the *infinitive.*

— Où sont les enfants ? Qu'est-ce qu'ils _____ (1) cet après-midi ?

— Léa _____ (2) du magasinage avec son amie et les garçons

_____ (3) du vélo.

— Et toi, qu'est-ce que tu _____ (4) ?

— Je ne _____ (5) rien de spécial. Et ton ami et toi, vous

_____ (6) du vélo, comme d'habitude ?

— Non, je n'ai pas l'intention de _____ (7) du vélo aujourd'hui.

— Alors, on _____ (8) quelque chose ensemble ?

— Nous ne _____ (9) pas assez d'exercice en ce moment.

Allons au parc pour _____ (10) une promenade.

D. Des photos. Alice is looking at various photos and saying what the weather was like and what everyone did the day each photo was taken. Complete her sentences with the illustrated weather condition and a verb in the **passé composé.**

Exemple　　　　　**1**　　　　　**2**　　　　　**3**

EXEMPLE Ce jour-là *(That day),* il **a fait froid** et Vincent **a fait une promenade.**

1. Ce jour-là, il _____ et Éric _____.

2. Ce jour-là, il _____ et moi, j' _____.

3. Ce jour-là, il _____ et les enfants _____.

E. Suggestions. Review how to form commands on page 154 in *Chapitre 4* of the textbook. Imagine that you are trying to get a friend to have some fun with you, rather than doing what he should around the house. Tell him not to do what he is supposed to and suggest doing the other activity with you.

    EXEMPLE   faire les courses / faire du jogging
                 Ne fais pas les courses! Faisons du jogging!

1. faire du bateau / faire le lavage

_____

2. faire la vaisselle / faire une promenade

_____

3. faire du vélo / faire le ménage

_____

4. faire la cuisine / faire du ski

_____

F. Hier. Alice is talking about what happened yesterday. One of the things listed in parentheses did not happen, but the other two did. Compose sentences in the **passé composé,** putting the logical verb in the negative form.

    EXEMPLE   Hier matin, Alice **n'est pas restée** (rester) à la maison. Elle **est sortie** (sortir) à huit heures et elle **a fait** (faire) des courses.

1. Vincent _____ (passer) la matinée à la maison et il

_____ (faire) le ménage. Il _____

(jouer) au golf avec ses amis.

2. Léa et Michel _____ (aider *[to help]*) avec le ménage.

Ils _____ (aller) au centre commercial et ils _____

(faire) du magasinage.

3. Hier après-midi, il _____ (faire) beau. Il

_____ (pleuvoir). Il _____ (faire) soleil.

4. Alice et Vincent _____ (aller) au cinéma. Ils _____

(aller) au parc et ils _____ (faire) une promenade.

5. Hier soir, Alice et Vincent _____ (faire) la cuisine et ils

_____ (manger) à la maison. Ils _____

(souper) au restaurant.

6. Après le souper, Léa _____ (regarder) la télé avec ses parents.

Elle _____ (rester) dans la cuisine et elle

_____ (faire) la vaisselle.

Nom _____   Date _____

*G. Et toi? A friend is asking you questions. Answer his questions *in complete sentences in French.*

1. Quelle saison préfères-tu? Qu'est-ce que tu aimes faire pendant cette saison?

   _____

   _____

   _____

2. Quel temps fait-il aujourd'hui?

   _____

   _____

3. Qu'est-ce que tu aimes faire quand il fait très froid? et quand il fait très chaud?

   _____

   _____

   _____

4. Quel temps va-t-il probablement faire la fin de semaine prochaine? Qu'est-ce que tu as l'intention de faire s'il fait beau samedi? Et s'il fait mauvais?

   _____

   _____

   _____

   _____

5. Quel temps a-t-il fait samedi dernier? Qu'est-ce que tu as fait?

   _____

   _____

   _____

6. Est-ce que tu aimes mieux faire le lavage ou le ménage? faire la cuisine ou la vaisselle? faire des courses ou du jardinage?

   _____

   _____

   _____

7. Qu'est-ce que tu fais d'habitude la fin de semaine? Qu'est-ce que tu as besoin de faire cette fin de semaine? Qu'est-ce que tu as envie de faire?

   _____

   _____

   _____

   _____

Nom _____ Date _____

Partie auditive

 A. Quel temps fait-il? For each illustration, you will be asked what the weather is like. After a pause for you to respond, you will hear the correct answer.

EXEMPLE   VOUS ENTENDEZ: Quel temps fait-il?
   VOUS DITES: **Il fait chaud.**
   VOUS ENTENDEZ: Il fait chaud.

Exemple   1   2

   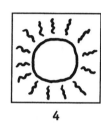   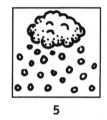   

3   4   5   6

 B. La météo. You will hear a weather report for Canada. The first time, just listen as it is read at normal speed. Then, complete the sentences as you hear it again more slowly with pauses for you to fill in the missing words.

Voici le bulletin météorologique pour demain: _____ **(1)**

sur l'ensemble du pays, sauf en Colombie-Britannique où _____ **(2)**

le matin et _____ **(3)** dans le courant de l'après-midi.

Les températures vont varier de _____ **(4)** à _____ **(5)**

degrés dans les Prairies et en Ontario. Mais _____ **(6)**

au Québec, où les températures vont atteindre _____ **(7)** degrés. À Terre-Neuve,

sur la côte est, sortez vos skis: _____ **(8)**!

 C. Le verbe *faire*. Pause the recording and fill in the blanks with the correct form of the verb **faire**.

— Qu'est-ce que tu _____ **(1)** samedi?

— Je ne _____ **(2)** rien.

— Alors, on _____ **(3)** quelque chose ensemble?

— Mes amis et moi, nous _____ **(4)** souvent du sport le samedi.
   Tes amis et toi, vous _____ **(5)** souvent de l'exercice?

— Mes amis _____ **(6)** souvent du jogging et moi, je _____ **(7)** du yoga.

Now listen to the recording and repeat each sentence of the preceding conversation after the speakers, paying attention to the pronunciation of the forms of the verb **faire**. Listen carefully. In only one of the forms, the letter combination **ai** is pronounced irregularly like the **e** of **je**. Which form is it?

The **ai** is pronounced like the **e** of **je** in the form _____.

Nom _____ Date _____

D. Préférences. You will hear Éric say which of each pair of activities he prefers. For each pair, indicate the illustration of the activity he prefers.

1

a. _____   b. _____

2

a. _____   b. _____

3

a. _____   b. _____

4

a. _____   b. _____

5

a. _____   b. _____

*Now you will hear a friend ask which activities you prefer. Fill in the blank with your preference.

1. Pendant mon temps libre, je préfère _____.

2. Comme exercice, je préfère _____.

3. J'aime mieux _____.

4. J'aime mieux _____.

5. Je préfère _____.

6. Quand je fais un voyage, je préfère _____.

7. J'aime mieux _____.

*E. Et vous? Answer the questions you hear *in complete sentences in French.*

1. _____

2. _____

3. _____

4. _____

5. _____

6. _____

COMPÉTENCE 4

Deciding what to wear and buying clothes

By the time you finish this *Compétence*, you should be able to talk about your clothing and buy clothes in a store.

Partie écrite

*A. C'est logique. Fill in the blanks logically with the name of a clothing item or an accessory.

1. Quand il fait chaud, on met _____ et _____.

2. Quand il fait froid, on met _____ et _____.

3. Quand il pleut, il est bon d'avoir _____ ou _____.

4. Pour aller travailler dans une banque, un homme met _____ et

   _____ et une femme met _____ et

   _____.

5. On met son argent dans _____ ou dans _____.

*B. Conversation. Reread the conversation at the clothing store on page 199 of the textbook. Now imagine that you want to buy a new bathing suit. Complete the following conversation with the salesperson in a logical way.

La vendeuse : Bonjour, monsieur / madame / mademoiselle. Je peux vous aider ?

Vous : _____.

La vendeuse : Vous faites quelle taille ?

Vous : _____.

La vendeuse : Quelle couleur est-ce que vous préférez ?

Vous : Je préfère quelque chose en _____.

La vendeuse : Nous avons ces maillots-ci et ils sont tous en solde.

Vous : J'aime bien ce maillot-ci. Est-ce que je peux _____?

La vendeuse : Mais bien sûr ! Voilà la cabine d'essayage.

La vendeuse : Alors, qu'en pensez-vous ?

Vous : _____.

C. Léa fait du magasinage. Léa is shopping and is taking everything she likes. According to the indications for each item pictured, complete the first sentence to say whether or not she likes it. Then write a second sentence to say whether or not she is taking it. Use a direct object pronoun in each of your answers.

EXEMPLE 1   Elle n'aime pas **ce jean.**
Elle **ne le prend pas.**

EXEMPLE 2   Elle aime bien **cette jupe.**
Elle **la prend.**

Example 1   **Example 2**

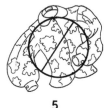

1   **2**   **3**   **4**   **5**   **6**

1. Elle n'aime pas _____. Elle _____.
2. Elle aime bien _____. Elle _____.
3. Elle aime bien _____. Elle _____.
4. Elle n'aime pas _____. Elle _____.
5. Elle n'aime pas _____. Elle _____.
6. Elle aime bien _____. Elle _____.

D. Que faites-vous? Say whether you often do these things. Use the appropriate direct object pronoun each time.

EXEMPLE   prendre *votre déjeuner* chez vous
Je **le prends** souvent chez moi. / Je **ne le prends pas** souvent chez moi.

1. faire *vos devoirs* à la bibliothèque

   Je _____ souvent à la bibliothèque.

2. regarder *la télé* dans votre chambre

   Je _____ souvent dans ma chambre.

3. prendre *votre déjeuner* au café

   Je _____ souvent au café.

4. écouter *la radio* dans le salon

   Je _____ souvent dans le salon.

5. passer *votre temps libre* chez des amis

   Je _____ souvent chez des amis.

Review the placement of the direct object pronouns with infinitives on page 200 of the textbook. Then, say whether or not you are going to do these things on Saturday. Use a direct object pronoun and the immediate future in your answer.

EXEMPLE   faire *les devoirs* samedi matin
Je **vais les faire** samedi matin. **/** Je **ne vais pas les faire** samedi matin.

1. prendre *votre déjeuner* au café

Je _____ au café.

2. passer *la journée* chez vous

Je _____ chez moi.

3. inviter *votre meilleur(e) ami(e)* au restaurant

Je _____ au restaurant.

4. passer *l'après-midi* avec des amis

Je _____ avec des amis.

5. regarder *la télé* samedi après-midi

Je _____ samedi après-midi.

Review the placement of object pronouns and the agreement of the past participle on page 200 of the textbook. Then, say whether or not you did these things last Saturday. Use a direct object pronoun and the **passé composé** in your answer.

EXEMPLE   faire *les devoirs* samedi matin.
Je **les ai faits** samedi matin. **/** Je **ne les ai pas faits** samedi matin.

1. faire *votre lit* avant de prendre le déjeuner

Je _____ avant de prendre le déjeuner.

2. prendre *votre parapluie* avant de sortir

Je _____ avant de sortir.

3. quitter *votre chambre* avant 9 h du matin

Je _____ avant 9 h du matin.

4. faire *vos devoirs* à la bibliothèque

Je _____ à la bibliothèque.

5. passer *la matinée* chez vous

Je _____ chez moi.

*E. Encore des pronoms! Answer the following questions, replacing the italicized direct objects with a pronoun.

> **EXEMPLE** Où est-ce que vous retrouvez *vos amis* pour prendre un café?
> **Je les retrouve chez *Tim Hortons* pour prendre un café.**

1. Est-ce que vous invitez souvent *vos amis* chez vous? Est-ce que vous allez inviter *vos amis* chez vous ce soir?

   _____

   _____

2. Est-ce que vous préférez passer *votre temps libre* chez vous ou chez des amis?

   _____

3. Est-ce que vous avez passé *la journée* chez vous samedi dernier?

   _____

4. Est-ce que vous préparez toujours *le souper* chez vous? Est-ce que vous avez préparé *le souper* hier soir?

   _____

5. Vous aimez regarder *la télé*? Vous allez regarder *la télé* ce soir? Vous avez regardé *la télé* pendant le souper hier?

   _____

   _____

   _____

---

*Journal. Write a paragraph describing your day yesterday. Include the following information.

- until what time you slept
- what clothes you put on (use *mettre*)
- what time you left your house
- where you went
- what you did yesterday morning, afternoon, and evening
- what time you returned home

   _____

   _____

   _____

   _____

   _____

   _____

   _____

   _____

   _____

Partie auditive

 A. Quels vêtements? You will hear several short conversations. Indicate the illustrations of all the clothing and accessories you hear mentioned.

 B. Je les prends. Alice is buying clothes only for herself today, and none for her husband. As the salesclerk names an item, pause the recording and complete Alice's statements saying whether she is or is not taking it, using the appropriate direct object pronoun. Turn on the recording after each item to check your work as you hear the correct response.

EXEMPLE VOUS ENTENDEZ : Cette jupe?
VOUS ÉCRIVEZ : Je **la prends.**
VOUS ENTENDEZ : Je la prends.

1. Je _____.

2. Je _____.

3. Je _____.

4. Je _____.

5. Je _____.

6. Je _____.

C. Qu'est-ce qu'elle va mettre? Look at both illustrations. You will hear a piece of clothing named. Pause the recording and indicate when in the next two days Alice is going to wear it, or that she is not going to wear it. Use direct object pronouns *in complete sentences.* Turn on the recording and check your work as you hear the correct answer.

EXEMPLES VOUS ENTENDEZ : Sa blouse blanche ?
VOUS ÉCRIVEZ : Elle **va la mettre samedi.**
VOUS ENTENDEZ : Elle va la mettre samedi.

VOUS ENTENDEZ : Sa nouvelle robe ?
VOUS ÉCRIVEZ : Elle **ne va pas la mettre.**
VOUS ENTENDEZ : Elle ne va pas la mettre.

samedi   **dimanche**

1. Elle _____.
2. Elle _____.
3. Elle _____.
4. Elle _____.
5. Elle _____.
6. Elle _____.

D. Une cliente exigeante. You will hear a scene in which a young woman is shopping. Listen to the conversation, then pause the recording and complete these statements.

1. La jeune femme cherche _____.

2. Comme taille, elle fait du _____.

3. Elle ne prend pas le premier article suggéré par la vendeuse parce qu'elle n'aime pas le style. Elle n'aime pas le deuxième non plus parce qu'elle cherche quelque chose en _____.

4. Elle ne prend pas le troisième non plus parce qu'il est trop _____.

5. Le quatrième bikini est bleu et il est aussi en _____.

*E. Et vous? Answer the questions you hear *in complete sentences in French.*

1. _____
2. _____
3. _____
4. _____
5. _____

Les sorties
Chapitre 6

Inviting someone to go out

By the time you finish this *Compétence,* you should be able to make plans with friends and accept or refuse invitations.

Partie écrite

A. Invitons des amis ! Use **Tu veux…** or **Vous voulez…** and one of the following expressions given to invite the indicated people to do the pictured activity.

étudier   **aller prendre un verre**   **aller danser**   **faire du magasinage**

1   2   3   4

1. à votre petit(e) ami(e) : _____ samedi soir ?

2. à votre mère : _____ cet après-midi ?

3. à des camarades de classe : _____ avec moi ce soir ?

4. à des amis : _____ plus tard ?

Indicate which of the following expressions could be used instead of **tu veux** or **vous voulez** in the preceding invitations.

1. Je vous invite à… ____   Je t'invite à…. ____

2. Vous voudriez… ____   Tu voudrais… ____

3. Vous voudriez… ____   Je t'invite à… ____

4. Je vous invite à… ____   Tu voudrais… ____

*B. On vous invite à… Imagine that a close friend invites you to do the following things. Accept or refuse each invitation. Use a variety of expressions.

Oui, je veux bien. Quelle bonne idée ! Avec plaisir !	Je regrette mais… je ne suis pas libre. je ne peux vraiment pas. je dois travailler.	Je préfère… J'aime mieux… Allons plutôt à…

EXEMPLE   Tu veux aller au centre commercial avec moi cet après-midi?
Oui, je veux bien. / Non, je regrette, mais je ne peux vraiment pas. Je dois travailler aujourd'hui. / Allons plutôt au cinéma.

1. Tu as envie d'aller prendre un café?

_____

2. Est-ce que tu voudrais faire la cuisine ce soir?

_____

3. On va voir le nouveau film avec Ryan Gosling?

_____

4. Tu veux aller à la plage avec ma famille cette fin de semaine?

_____

5. Tu es libre jeudi matin? Tu voudrais aller au musée?

_____

C. Les séances. The university film club is having a classic French film festival. Convert the show times from official time to conversational time, as in the following example.

À bout de souffle	lun. / mer. / vend.	12 h 15	14 h 45	17 h 15
Les quatre cents coups	mar. / jeu.	11 h 20	13 h 30	15 h 45
La Belle et la Bête	sam. / dim.	18 h 05	20 h 15	22 h 25

EXEMPLE   *À bout de souffle:* 12 h 15 = **midi et quart**
14 h 45 = **trois heures moins le quart de l'après-midi**
17 h 15 = **cinq heures et quart de l'après-midi**

1. *Les quatre cents coups:*

11 h 20 = _____

13 h 30 = _____

15 h 45 = _____

2. *La Belle et la Bête:*

18 h 05 = _____

20 h 15 = _____

22 h 25 = _____

D. Conversation. Reread the conversation between Michèle and Éric on page 225 of the textbook. Then, complete this phone conversation between two other friends with the indicated words.

Aurélie: _____ **(1)**?
                         (Hello)

Didier: Salut, Aurélie. _____ **(2)**, Didier. Ça va?
                                      (It's me)

AURÉLIE : Oui, très bien. Et toi ?

DIDIER : Moi, ça va. Écoute, tu es _____ **(3)** ce soir ? Tu voudrais sortir ?
(free)

AURÉLIE : _____ **(4)**, mais ce soir _____ **(5)**.
(I'm sorry)   *(I can't)*

Je suis libre demain soir.

DIDIER : Alors, qu'est-ce que tu _____ **(6)** ?
(feel like doing)

Tu veux aller voir ce film avec Ellen Page ?

AURÉLIE : Oui, je veux bien. À quelle heure ?

DIDIER : Il y a _____ **(7)** à dix-neuf heures.
(a showing)

AURÉLIE : Veux-tu _____ **(8)** six heures et quart ?
(come by my house around)

DIDIER : _____ **(9)**. À demain, Aurélie.
(Okay)

AURÉLIE : Au revoir, Didier.

E. Encore une invitation.
Éric is inviting Michèle to go out again. Complete the following invitation with the present tense of the verbs in parentheses.

ÉRIC :   Tu es libre samedi après-midi ? Tu _____ **(1)** (vouloir) faire quelque chose avec moi ?

MICHÈLE : Je ne _____ **(2)** (pouvoir) vraiment pas, parce que je _____ **(3)** (devoir)

rester à la maison avec mes deux petits frères.

ÉRIC :   Ils _____ **(4)** (pouvoir) venir avec nous si tu _____ **(5)** (vouloir).

Nous _____ **(6)** (pouvoir) aller au parc.

MICHÈLE : Bon, d'accord, mais nous _____ **(7)** (devoir) rentrer avant cinq heures.

Now complete these questions about Éric and Michèle's conversation with the correct forms of the indicated verbs. Then answer each question *with a complete sentence.*

1. Quand est-ce qu'Éric _____ (vouloir) faire quelque chose avec Michèle ?

   _____

2. Pourquoi est-ce qu'elle _____ (ne pas pouvoir) ?

   _____

   _____

3. Où est-ce qu'ils _____ (pouvoir) aller tous *(all)* ensemble ?

   _____

4. À quelle heure est-ce qu'ils _____ (devoir) rentrer ?

   _____

F. Pourquoi pas? Alice is explaining that the following people want to do the activity in the first illustration, but they cannot because they have to do the second. Complete her sentences using the verbs **vouloir, pouvoir,** and **devoir.**

EXEMPLE Vincent et moi **voulons aller à la plage, mais nous ne pouvons pas parce que nous devons aller au centre commercial.**

1. Éric _____

_____

_____

_____ .

2. Vincent et moi _____

_____

_____

_____ .

3. Les enfants _____

_____

_____

_____ .

*G. Et vous? Complete the following questions about yourself and your friends with the present tense of the verb in parentheses. Then answer each question *with a complete sentence.*

1. Qu'est-ce que vos amis _____ (vouloir) faire la fin de semaine, en général?

_____

2. Qu'est-ce que vous _____ (vouloir) faire ce soir?

_____

3. Quels soirs est-ce que vous _____ (pouvoir) sortir avec vos amis?

_____

4. Généralement, est-ce que vous _____ (devoir) travailler la fin de semaine?

_____

5. Où est-ce qu'on _____ (pouvoir) aller près du campus pour prendre

un verre avec des amis?

_____

Partie auditive

A. Tu veux bien...? Éric's friend Dominique loves to go out with friends, but is not at all athletic. You will hear friends invite her to do various things. In each case, indicate her probable response.

1. Avec plaisir! ____   Je regrette, mais je dois partir maintenant ! ____

2. Oui, je veux bien! ____   Je regrette, mais je ne suis pas libre. ____

3. Mais oui! Avec plaisir! ____ Je regrette, mais je suis occupée *(busy).* ____

4. D'accord! ____   Je voudrais bien, mais je dois travailler. ____

5. Quelle bonne idée! ____   Je regrette, mais je ne peux vraiment pas! ____

B. Prononciation : Les verbes *vouloir, pouvoir* et *devoir*. Repeat the phrases after the speaker, paying attention to the pronunciation of the forms of **vouloir, pouvoir,** and **devoir.**

Je veux aller au cinéma, mais je ne peux pas. Je dois travailler.
Tu veux sortir ce soir, mais tu ne peux pas. Tu dois préparer tes cours.
Éric veut aller au musée, mais il ne peut pas. Il doit rester avec son petit frère.
Nous voulons partir pour la fin de semaine, mais nous ne pouvons pas. Nous devons travailler.
Vous voulez aller à la plage, mais vous ne pouvez pas. Vous devez faire le ménage.
Ils veulent aller au café, mais ils ne peuvent pas. Ils doivent aller en classe.

Notice the difference between the pronunciation of the third-person singular and plural forms of these verbs. Listen and repeat.

Elle veut aller au cinéma. Elles veulent aller au cinéma.
Elle ne peut pas. Elles ne peuvent pas.
Elle doit rester à la maison. Elles doivent rester à la maison.

Now, listen to Alice talk about Vincent and Éric. For each statement, indicate whether she is just talking about Vincent or whether she is talking about both Vincent and Éric.

1. Vincent ____   Vincent et Éric ____   4. Vincent ____   Vincent et Éric ____

2. Vincent ____   Vincent et Éric ____   5. Vincent ____   Vincent et Éric ____

3. Vincent ____   Vincent et Éric ____   6. Vincent ____   Vincent et Éric ____

Now you will hear these sentences again. Complete each sentence with the missing words.

1. _____ cet après-midi.

2. _____ avec moi ce soir.

3. _____

   parce qu'_____.

4. _____ à Winnipeg cette fin de semaine.

5. _____ cette fin de semaine.

6. _____ à la maison aujourd'hui.

C. Pour mieux comprendre: *Noting the important information.* It's Monday afternoon and Alice is listening to messages on her voicemail. After each message, pause the recording and fill in the requested information in the chart.

	Qui parle ?	Quelle est l'activité proposée ?	Quel jour ?	À quelle heure ?
Message 1				
Message 2				
Message 3				
Message 4				

D. Au cinéma. Alice and Vincent have just arrived at the movie theatre. Listen to their conversation. Then pause the recording and indicate if these statements are true or false by selecting **vrai** or **faux.**

1. Alice n'a jamais vu *Les quatre cents coups.*   vrai _____   faux _____
2. Vincent a envie de voir un autre film.   vrai _____   faux _____
3. Les séances des deux films sont à des heures différentes.   vrai _____   faux _____
4. Alice va voir un film de Steven Spielberg avec Vincent.   vrai _____   faux _____

Now play this section again and answer these questions with *a few words* in French.

1. Combien de fois est-ce que Vincent a déjà vu le film qu'Alice voudrait voir ?

_____

2. Pourquoi est-ce qu'Alice a aimé le film ? Donnez une des raisons.

_____

3. Qu'est-ce qu'Alice voudrait faire après le film ?

_____

COMPÉTENCE 2

Talking about how you spend and used to spend your time

By the time you finish this **Compétence,** you should be able to compare how things are now with how they used to be in the past.

Partie écrite

*A. Ici ou en France? A high school student has just moved from France to Canada, and is comparing his new school here with his former school in France. Write sentences in the present tense that he would probably say about how things are at his high school compared to how things used to be at his **lycée** in France.

EXEMPLES En France, j'avais cours du lundi au samedi.
Ici, j'**ai cours du lundi au vendredi.**

En France, j'avais une spécialisation en maths.
Ici, je **n'ai pas de spécialisation.**

1. En France, on étudiait deux ou trois langues étrangères généralement.

   Ici, on _____ généralement.

2. En France, la langue étrangère la plus populaire était l'anglais.

   Ici, la langue étrangère la plus populaire _____ .

3. En France, les élèves *(pupils, students)* avaient de neuf à douze cours.

   Ici, les étudiants _____ cours.

4. En France, j'étais avec le même groupe d'élèves dans presque tous mes cours.

   Ici, je _____ dans tous mes cours.

5. En France, je ne pouvais pas participer à beaucoup d'activités parascolaires *(extracurricular)*.

   Ici, je _____ .

6. En France, le sport n'était pas très important.

   Ici, le sport _____ .

7. En France, l'école n'avait pas d'orchestre.

   Ici, l'école _____ .

8. En France, nous avions deux semaines de vacances d'hiver en février entre les vacances de Noël et les vacances de printemps.

   Ici, nous _____ en février.

9. En France, les vacances d'été commençaient en juillet.

   Ici, les vacances d'été _____ .

10. En France, on avait deux mois de vacances en été.

    Ici, on _____ .

B. Conversation. Reread the conversation between Michèle and Éric on page 225 of the textbook. Then, complete this conversation in which they talk about when Éric was a little boy.

MICHÈLE: _____ **(1)**
(What did you used to like to do)

la fin de semaine quand tu étais petit?

ÉRIC: Le samedi matin, _____ **(2)** des dessins animés à la télé.
(I liked to watch)

MICHÈLE: Et le samedi après-midi, qu'est-ce que tu faisais généralement?

ÉRIC: J'aimais jouer avec _____ **(3)** du quartier.
(my pals)

On _____ **(4)** ou on jouait à des jeux vidéo.
(skateboarded)

MICHÈLE: Et qu'est-ce que tu faisais le dimanche?

ÉRIC: Le dimanche matin, on _____ **(5)** à l'église et
(went)

l'après-midi _____ **(6)**.
(I didn't do anything special)

C. M. Monotone. One of Michèle's professors, poor **M. Monotone**, has done the same thing for years. Here is a description of his day yesterday. It is exactly the same as what he did years ago. Complete the second paragraph in the imperfect describing his daily routine when he first began teaching.

Avant de quitter la maison hier matin, M. Monotone **a pris** un café avec sa femme et ils **ont mangé** un croissant. Il **a quitté** la maison à 7 h 45 et il **a pris** l'autobus à 7 h 52 à l'arrêt d'autobus devant son immeuble. Quand il **est arrivé** sur le campus, il **est entré** dans son bureau et il **a commencé** à travailler. Il **est resté** à l'université toute la journée jusqu'à 16 h 55, et il **a quitté** son bureau pour rentrer à la maison. Quand il **est arrivé** à la maison, sa femme **a préparé** le souper et ils **ont mangé**. Après le souper, sa femme **a pris** un bain et M. Monotone **a fait** la vaisselle. Ensuite, ils **ont regardé** la télé pendant une heure avant d'aller se coucher *(going to bed)*.

Avant de quitter la maison tous les matins, M. Monotone **prenait** un café avec sa femme et ils

_____ **(1)** un croissant. Il _____ **(2)** la maison à 7 h 45 et il

_____ **(3)** l'autobus à 7 h 52 à l'arrêt d'autobus devant son immeuble. Quand il

_____ **(4)** sur le campus, il _____ **(5)** dans son bureau et il

_____ **(6)** à travailler. Il _____ **(7)** à l'université toute la journée

jusqu'à 16 h 55, et il _____ **(8)** son bureau pour rentrer à la maison. Quand il

_____ **(9)** à la maison, sa femme _____ **(10)** le souper et ils

_____ **(11)**. Après le souper, sa femme _____ **(12)** un bain et

M. Monotone _____ **(13)** la vaisselle. Ensuite, ils _____ **(14)**

la télé pendant une heure avant d'aller se coucher.

D. La routine de Michèle. Talk about Michèle's habits by filling in the blanks with the correct *present tense* form of the verb in parentheses. The first one has been done as an example.

Michèle ____a____ (avoir) cours tous les jours. Pendant la semaine, elle _____ **(1)** (dormir) jusqu'à sept heures et elle _____ **(2)** (partir) pour l'université vers huit heures. À midi, elle _____ **(3)** (dîner) à la cafétéria. Elle _____ **(4)** (sortir) de ses cours à quatre heures et elle _____ **(5)** (rentrer) à la maison. Elle _____ **(6)** (être) souvent fatiguée et elle _____ **(7)** (dormir) un peu. La fin de semaine, elle _____ **(8)** (sortir) souvent avec ses copains. Ils _____ **(9)** (faire) de la planche à roulettes ou ils _____ **(10)** (jouer) au tennis. Le samedi soir, ils _____ **(11)** (sortir) ensemble. Ils _____ **(12)** (rentrer) tard et ils _____ **(13)** (dormir) tard le dimanche. Ils _____ **(14)** (aimer) aussi voyager et ils _____ **(15)** (partir) souvent en voyage ensemble en été.

*Now imagine that a friend is asking about your routine. Complete his questions with the correct *present tense* form of the verb given. Then, answer his questions.

EXEMPLE Quels jours de la semaine est-ce que tu **as** (avoir) cours?
J'ai cours le mardi et le jeudi.

1. Le premier jour de la semaine où tu as cours, tu _____ (dormir) jusqu'à quelle heure?
_____

2. À quelle heure est-ce que tu _____ (partir) de chez toi pour aller en cours?
_____

3. Est-ce que des étudiants _____ (dormir) quelquefois dans tes cours ou à la bibliothèque?
_____

4. À quelle heure est-ce que tu _____ (sortir) de ton dernier cours?
_____

5. D'habitude, qu'est-ce que tu _____ (vouloir) faire après les cours?
_____

6. Est-ce que tu _____ (pouvoir) faire une sieste *(take a nap)* après les cours si tu _____ (vouloir)?
_____

7. Tes copains (copines) et toi, est-ce que vous _____ (sortir) souvent la fin de semaine?
_____

8. Quand tu _____ (sortir) avec tes copains (copines), est-ce que tu _____ (pouvoir) rentrer quand tu _____ (vouloir) ou est-ce que tu _____ (devoir) rentrer avant une certaine heure?
_____

*E. Et à l'école secondaire ? Using the answers to the questions in the second part of **D. La routine de Michèle** as a guide, write a paragraph describing your life when you were in high school. Use the imperfect.

> **EXEMPLE** Quand j'étais à l'école secondaire, j'avais cours tous les jours sauf la fin de semaine.

_____

_____

_____

_____

_____

_____

_____

_____

*Journal. Write three paragraphs describing your Saturdays. In the first paragraph, use the *present* tense to say four things you generally do on Saturdays now. In the second paragraph, use the *passé composé* to state four things you did last Saturday. Finally, in the third paragraph, use the *imperfect* to talk about four things you used to do on Saturdays in high school. Mention different things in each paragraph.

Le samedi, _____

_____

_____

_____

_____

Samedi dernier, _____

_____

_____

_____

_____

Quand j'étais à l'école secondaire, le samedi, _____

_____

_____

_____

_____

_____

Nom _____ Date _____

Partie auditive

A. À l'université ou à l'école secondaire ? Michèle is comparing her life now with how things were in high school. Listen to what she says. Pause the recording after each sentence and fill in the missing word or words.

1. Maintenant, _____.

   À l'âge de quinze ans, _____.

2. Maintenant, _____ du lundi au vendredi.

   À l'école secondaire, _____ le samedi matin aussi.

3. _____ à l'université,

   mais quand j'étais jeune, _____.

4. La fin de semaine, _____ et _____

   beaucoup. Quand _____,

   _____ aussi.

5. La fin de semaine, _____ avec _____ et le

   samedi, on joue au tennis. Quand _____, je sortais avec des

   copains et le samedi, _____.

B. Prononciation : Les terminaisons de l'imparfait. Pause the recording and review the *Prononciation* section on page 226 of the textbook. Then turn on the recording. Listen and repeat to practise the pronunciation of the endings of the imperfect tense. Complete the last clause of each sentence with the missing verb.

Quand j'étais jeune, j' _____ avec ma famille.

Quand tu étais jeune, où _____ -tu ?

Nous habitions à la campagne. Nous _____ souvent en ville.

Vous habitiez en ville ? Vous _____ une jolie maison ?

Il y avait beaucoup de jeunes dans le village. On _____ l'autocar pour aller en ville.

Mes amis aimaient sortir. Ils _____ souvent au cinéma.

C. La jeunesse de Michèle. Michèle's life has changed very little from when she was young. Listen to statements about her present situation and say that they were also true when she was young. Use the imperfect. Verify your response and fill in the missing words as you hear the correct answer.

EXEMPLE	VOUS ENTENDEZ :	Ses parents travaillent beaucoup.
	VOUS DITES :	**Ses parents travaillaient beaucoup quand elle était jeune.**
	VOUS ENTENDEZ :	Ses parents travaillaient beaucoup quand elle était jeune.
	VOUS COMPLÉTEZ :	Ses parents **travaillaient beaucoup** quand elle était jeune.

1. Elle _____ quand elle était jeune.

2. Ils _____ quand elle était jeune.

3. Leur appartement _____ quand elle était jeune.

4. Elle _____ quand elle était jeune.

5. Ses parents _____ quand elle était jeune.

6. Son père _____ quand elle était jeune.

7. Sa mère _____ quand elle était jeune.

D. Prononciation : Les verbes *sortir, partir* et *dormir*. Pause the recording and review the
Prononciation section on page 228 of the textbook. Then turn on the recording and repeat these verb forms
after the speaker. As you repeat the forms of **partir** and **sortir,** fill in the missing ending, using **dormir** as a
model.

dormir *(to sleep)*	**partir** *(to leave)*	**sortir** *(to go out, to leave)*
je dors	je par____	je sor____
tu dors	tu par____	tu sor____
il dort	il par____	il sor____
elle dort	elle par____	elle sor____
on dort	on par____	on sor____
nous dormons	nous par____	nous sor____
vous dormez	vous par____	vous sor____
ils dorment	ils par____	ils sor____
elles dorment	elles par____	elles sor____

*E. Chez vous ? A friend is asking you about your habits. Answer her questions *with complete sentences.*

1. _____

2. _____

3. _____

4. _____

5. _____

6. _____

COMPÉTENCE 3

Talking about the past

By the time you finish this **Compétence,** you should be able to tell what happened in the past and describe the circumstances.

Partie écrite

*A. Une sortie. Answer the following questions about the last time you got together with friends at a restaurant for dinner. Use the same tenses as in the questions in each clause of your answer.

1. Est-ce que vos amis étaient déjà au restaurant quand vous êtes arrivé(e)?

   _____

   _____

2. Quelle heure était-il quand vous êtes arrivé(e) au restaurant?

   _____

   _____

3. Est-ce que vous aviez faim quand vous êtes arrivé(e) au restaurant?

   _____

   _____

4. Après le repas, êtes-vous parti(e) tout de suite parce que vous étiez fatigué(e) ou est-ce que vous êtes resté(e) au restaurant parce que vous vouliez parler avec vos amis?

   _____

   _____

5. Quelle heure était-il quand vous avez quitté le restaurant?

   _____

   _____

B. Conversation. Reread the conversation between Micheline and Léa on page 231 of the textbook. Then, complete this conversation between Léa and another friend about a date she had.

Léa: Tu _____ **(1)** avec Didier la fin de semaine dernière?
                              (went out)

Aurélie: Oui, nous _____ **(2)** un film avec Ellen Page.
                              (went to see)

Léa: _____ **(3)**?
              (Did you like it)

Aurélie: Beaucoup. _____ **(4).**
                              (It was really good)

Léa: _____ **(5)** avec Didier après?
              (What did you do)

Aurélie: _____ **(6).** J'étais _____ **(7)** et je suis rentrée.
           (Nothing at all)   *(tired)*

C. Leur journée. Complete the following sentences in the past. Put the verb stating what happened in the **passé composé** and the verb describing the circumstances in the imperfect. Be careful, the first clause is not always in the **passé composé**.

EXEMPLE Alice **est allée** (aller) au bureau parce qu'elle **avait** (avoir) beaucoup de choses à faire.

1. Il _____ (pleuvoir) quand Vincent _____ (aller) au parc.

2. Éric _____ (beaucoup manger) au déjeuner parce qu'il

   _____ (avoir) très faim.

3. Vincent _____ (vouloir) aller voir un film ; alors il

   _____ (chercher) un film sur Internet.

4. Vincent et les enfants _____ (aller) au cinéma Odéon parce qu'il y

   _____ (avoir) un bon film d'aventure.

5. Alice _____ (rester) à la maison parce qu'elle

   _____ (être) fatiguée après sa longue journée au bureau.

D. Situations. Vincent is describing the people in each picture when these snapshots were taken. Complete each sentence, using the logical verb in parentheses.

EXEMPLE (porter, être, faire)
Alice **était** en ville. Elle **faisait** des courses.
Elle **portait** une robe.

1. (être, faire, porter)

   Éric et moi _____ du jogging.

   Nous _____ au parc.

   Nous _____ des survêtements.

2. (être, faire, porter)

   Moi, je _____ un tee-shirt et un jean.

   J' _____ à la maison.

   Je _____ le lavage.

3. (aller, vouloir, porter)

   Éric et son ami _____ à la piscine.

   Ils _____ des maillots de bain.

   Ils _____ nager.

E. Une panne d'électricité. Say what the following people were doing at the Li household yesterday when the electricity went out.

EXEMPLE Louise et son amie Audrey **mangeaient quelque chose.**

1. Madame Li _____ sur Internet.
2. Monsieur Li _____ la télé.
3. Étienne _____ de la musique.
4. Dominique _____ et son petit ami Georges _____ du piano.

Now say who was doing these things when the electricity went off. Use the imperfect.

EXEMPLE **Monsieur Li voulait** (vouloir) voir un match de football.

5. _____ (être) dans la cuisine.
6. _____ (avoir) l'iPod de sa sœur Dominique.
7. _____ (faire) des recherches sur Internet.
8. _____ (dormir) devant la télé.
9. _____ (vouloir) danser avec son petit ami dans le salon.

F. Beaucoup de problèmes. Éric is telling why they weren't able to do what they were going to in one of his classes today. Use the imperfect of the verb **aller** followed by the logical infinitive in parentheses to say what they were going to do. Put the other verb in parentheses in the imperfect to explain the circumstances that didn't allow them to do so.

EXEMPLE **J'allais faire mes devoirs,** mais je **ne comprenais pas les exercices.**
(ne pas comprendre les exercices, faire mes devoirs)

1. J' _____, mais je _____.
_____ (apprendre le vocabulaire, ne pas pouvoir trouver mon livre)

2. Nous _____, mais le lecteur DVD
_____. (voir un film en cours, ne pas marcher *[to work]*).

3. Des étudiants _____, mais ils
_____. (ne pas être prêts, faire une présentation)

4. J' _____, mais il
_____. (pleuvoir, rentrer chez moi à pied)

Nom _____ Date _____

G. Une soirée. Éric is talking about an outing with his girlfriend last night. Combine the sentences from the two columns, changing the verbs from the present to the past. Put the italicized verbs saying how people felt or describing the circumstances in the imperfect. Put the italicized verbs stating the sequence of actions in the **passé composé.** The first one has been done as an example.

HOW PEOPLE FELT / CIRCUMSTANCES

Ma petite amie Michèle *veut* sortir, alors…
Il *est* six heures et demie quand…
Le film *est* un peu bête et il y *a* beaucoup
de violence, alors…
Je *veux* partir aussi, mais…
Après le film, nous *avons* faim, alors…
Le souper *est* excellent et…
Nous ne *voulons* pas rentrer, alors…
Il *est* minuit quand…

SEQUENCE OF ACTIONS

nous *allons* au cinéma.
je *retrouve* Michèle au cinéma.
beaucoup de gens *partent* avant
     la fin *(the end)*.
nous *restons*.
nous *soupons* dans un petit restaurant.
je *mange* bien.
nous *prenons* un dessert.
nous *rentrons*.

EXEMPLE

Hier soir, ma petite amie Michèle voulait sortir, alors nous sommes allés au cinéma
_____
_____
_____
_____
_____
_____
_____
_____

*H. Et vous? Answer the following questions about the last time you went to the movies with someone.

1. Avec qui êtes-vous allé(e) au cinéma? C'était en fin de semaine ou pendant la semaine?

_____
_____

2. Quel était le titre du film? Quels acteurs jouaient dans le film? Comment était le film?

_____
_____

3. Est-ce qu'il y avait beaucoup de monde *(a big crowd)* au cinéma? Est-ce que vous aviez une bonne place *(seat)*? Pouviez-vous voir le film sans problème?

_____
_____

4. Quelle heure était-il et quel temps faisait-il quand vous êtes sorti(e) du cinéma?

_____
_____

Partie auditive

 A. Des vacances. Two of Alice's friends, Catherine and David, came to visit her in Vancouver. Repeat each question about the day they went to the airport (**l'aéroport**) to leave for their trip and match the number of the question with its correct answer.

EXEMPLE   VOUS ENTENDEZ : Où était Catherine quand David est sorti pour faire du jogging?
              VOUS RÉPÉTEZ : **Où était Catherine quand David est sorti pour faire du jogging?**
              VOUS INDIQUEZ :

_____ Non, il ne pleuvait pas.

_____ Elle était déjà dans le taxi.

_____ Il était six heures et demie.

_____ Il était onze heures moins le quart.

_____ Il était midi.

_____ Non, ils n'avaient pas beaucoup de temps.

_____ Oui, il était encore à l'aéroport.

_____*Exemple*_____ Elle était encore au lit.

_____ Non, elle ne dormait pas.

 B. Prononciation : Le passé composé et l'imparfait. Pause the recording and review the *Prononciation* section on page 232 of the textbook. Then turn on the recording. Listen and repeat to practise distinguishing the present, the imperfect, and the **passé composé.**

___ je parle ___ tu regardes ___ il est ___ nous arrivons ___ vous mangez ___ ils dansent

___ je parlais ___ tu regardais ___ il était ___ nous arrivions ___ vous mangiez ___ ils dansaient

___ j'ai parlé ___ tu as regardé ___ il a été ___ nous sommes arrivés ___ vous avez mangé ___ ils ont dansé

Now you will hear one of the verb forms from each column above. Identify the form that you hear.

 ***C. Passé composé ou imparfait?** Listen to a series of questions about your high school years. Select **PC** for **passé composé** if you are being asked about a single event that happened or **IMP** for **imparfait** if being asked about how things used to be in general. Then, listen again and answer each question with *a complete sentence.*

1. PC ___ IMP ___ _____

2. PC ___ IMP ___ _____

3. PC ___ IMP ___ _____

4. PC ___ IMP ___ _____

5. PC ___ IMP ___ _____

6. PC ___ IMP ___ _____

Nom _____ Date _____

 D. La journée d'Alice. Listen as Alice describes her day. Each sentence has one verb in the **imparfait** to describe what was already in progress or the circumstances and one in the **passé composé** to tell what happened. Pause the recording after each sentence and put the two verbs and their subjects in the appropriate column.

> **EXEMPLE**   VOUS ENTENDEZ :   Il faisait beau quand je suis
> sortie de l'appartement.
>
> VOUS AJOUTEZ :

WHAT WAS IN PROGRESS / CIRCUMSTANCES   WHAT HAPPENED

     EXEMPLE   **il faisait**   **je suis sortie**

1. _____   _____

2. _____   _____

3. _____   _____

4. _____   _____

5. _____   _____

6. _____   _____

 E. Une sortie. Listen as Alice talks about the last time she and Vincent went to a restaurant. The first time, simply listen to the conversation at normal speed. It will then be repeated at a slower speed with pauses for you to complete the paragraph with the missing words. Pause the recording as needed to have sufficient time to respond. Play this section again to correct your work.

On _____ **(1)** ensemble au restaurant samedi soir. On _____ **(2)**

la maison vers sept heures. Comme *(Since)* il _____ **(3)** beau, on

_____ **(4)** au restaurant à pied. Il _____ **(5)** environ sept

heures et demie quand on _____ **(6)**. Je _____ **(7)** très

faim et on _____ **(8)** tout de suite. On _____ **(9)**

un verre de vin avant. Le repas _____ **(10)** délicieux et

j' _____ **(11)**. Après, nous _____ **(12)** trop fatigués ;

alors nous _____ **(13)** une promenade. Il _____ **(14)**

environ dix heures quand nous _____ **(15)** et nous

_____ **(16)** directement au lit. Le lendemain, c' _____ **(17)**

dimanche et j' _____ **(18)** jusqu'à onze heures.

Date

COMPÉTENCE 4

Narrating in the past

By the time you finish this **Compétence,** you should be able to recount a story in the past.

Partie écrite

A. Le Magicien d'Oz. Éric is telling Michèle the beginning of his favourite childhood movie when he was growing up, *The Wizard of Oz.* Complete the following sentences by putting the verb describing what was already in progress in the imperfect and the verb saying what happened next or what changed in the **passé composé.**

1. Une jeune fille appelée Dorothy _____ (habiter) chez son oncle et sa tante au Kansas quand une violente tornade _____ (arriver).

2. La tornade _____ (transporter) la maison où Dorothy _____ (dormir) dans un pays imaginaire.

3. Quand elle _____ (sortir) de la maison après la tornade, elle n' _____ (être) plus *(no longer)* au Kansas.

4. Après quelques minutes dans ce pays fabuleux, elle _____ (rencontrer) les Microsiens *(Munchkins),* les petites personnes qui y _____ (habiter).

5. Les Microsiens _____ (poser) des questions à Dorothy quand Glinda, la bonne sorcière du Nord *(witch of the North),* _____ (arriver).

6. Dorothy _____ (parler) à Glinda quand elle _____ (voir) une mauvaise sorcière morte sous sa maison.

7. Glinda _____ (donner) à Dorothy les chaussures de rubis que la sorcière morte _____ (porter).

8. Ensuite, une autre mauvaise sorcière, la sœur de la sorcière morte, _____ (venir) chercher les chaussures de rubis parce qu'elles _____ (être) magiques.

9. Avant de partir, elle _____ (avertir *[to warn]*) Dorothy qu'elle _____ (aller) se venger *(to get her revenge).*

10. La bonne sorcière _____ (recommander) à Dorothy de suivre un chemin *(road)* de briques jaunes pour aller voir le Magicien d'Oz à la cité d'Émeraude si elle _____ (vouloir) rentrer au Kansas.

11. Sur le chemin de briques jaunes, Dorothy _____ (rencontrer) un épouvantail *(scarecrow)* sans cervelle *(brain),* un homme en fer blanc *(tin)* sans cœur *(heart)* et un lion qui _____ (avoir) peur de tout.

12. Ils _____ (décider) d'accompagner Dorothy à la cité d'Émeraude pour voir si le magicien _____ (pouvoir) les aider aussi.

B. Conversation. Reread the conversation where Léa asks Éric about his weekend on page 236 of the textbook. Then, complete this conversation where Éric asks Léa *about her weekend.*

ÉRIC :   Tu _____ **(1)** samedi soir ?
                               (stayed home)

LÉA :   Oui, _____ **(2)**, alors _____ **(3)**
                    (I was tired)   *(I watched)*

       le film *Capitaine America* sur Netflix.

ÉRIC :   J'adore ce film ! C'est un bon film d'action avec un peu d'humour. _____ **(4)** ?
                                                            (Did you like it)

LÉA :   Oui, _____ **(5)**. C'était excellent.
                    (I liked it a lot)

       Les acteurs, les dialogues et _____ **(6)** vraiment super,
                                          (the special effects were)

       mais _____ **(7)**.
                      (there was a little too much violence)

C. Un entretien *(interview)*. Alice is telling about an interview with an applicant for a position with her company. First read a version in English. As you read, identify in English the six verbs indicating something that happened in the sequence of events of the interview.

1. _____   4. _____

2. _____   5. _____

3. _____   6. _____

When I *arrived* at the office, she *was* already there. She *was* a pleasant young woman, but she *looked* very nervous. She *was wearing* a very nice dress and it *was* evident that she really *wanted* to have this position. We *went* into my office and we *began* to talk. She *was* Acadian and she *was going* to finish her studies in Regina soon, where she *wanted* to work in our new office. She *spoke* not only French, but also English, Dutch, and a little German. We *did* part of the interview in English and her accent *was* excellent. We *spoke* for more than an hour. When she *left*, I *was* almost sure that I *was going* to hire her, but I *could* not say anything because there *were* still two other candidates.

Below, put the preceding paragraph into French by conjugating the six verbs indicating something that happened in the sequence of events in the **passé composé**.

Remember that the rest of the verbs, which indicate something that was already true or in progress when something else happened, will be in the imperfect.

Quand je (j') _____ **(1)** (arriver) au bureau, elle _____ **(2)** (être) déjà là. C' _____ **(3)** (être) une jeune femme agréable, mais elle _____ **(4)** (avoir) l'air très nerveuse. Elle _____ **(5)** (porter) une très belle robe et c' _____ **(6)** (être) évident qu'elle _____ **(7)** (vouloir) vraiment avoir ce poste. Nous _____ **(8)** (aller) dans mon bureau et nous _____ **(9)** (commencer) à parler. Elle _____ **(10)** (être) acadienne et elle _____ **(11)** (aller) bientôt terminer ses études à Regina où elle _____ **(12)** (vouloir) travailler dans notre nouveau bureau. Elle _____ **(13)** (parler) non seulement français, mais aussi anglais, néerlandais et un peu allemand. Nous _____ **(14)** (faire) une partie de l'entretien en anglais et son accent _____ **(15)** (être) excellent. Nous _____ **(16)** (parler) plus d'une heure. Quand elle

_____ **(17)** (partir), je (j') _____ **(18)** (être) presque

certaine que je (j') _____ **(19)** (aller) l'embaucher, mais je ne (n') _____ **(20)**

(pouvoir) rien dire parce qu'il y _____ **(21)** (avoir) encore deux autres candidats.

D. Le Petit Chaperon rouge. Retell the story of *Little Red Riding Hood* by putting the verbs in parentheses in the **passé composé** or the imperfect.

Une petite fille _____ **(1)** (habiter) avec sa mère dans une grande

forêt. Elle _____ **(2)** (ne pas avoir) de père mais sa grand-mère

_____ **(3)** (habiter) dans une petite maison de l'autre côté de la forêt. On

appelait cette petite fille le Petit Chaperon rouge parce qu'elle _____ **(4)**

(porter) toujours un chaperon rouge. Un jour, sa mère _____ **(5)** (demander) au Petit

Chaperon rouge d'apporter un panier *(to take a basket)* de bonnes choses à manger à sa grand-mère et la petite

fille _____ **(6)** (partir) tout de suite. Elle _____ **(7)** (traverser

[to cross]) la forêt quand un grand loup *(wolf)* _____ **(8)** (sortir) de derrière un arbre.

Il _____ **(9)** (avoir) très faim et il _____ **(10)** (vouloir) savoir

(to know) où le Petit Chaperon rouge _____ **(11)** (aller) avec toutes ces choses à manger.

Le Petit Chaperon rouge _____ **(12)** (expliquer *[to explain]*) qu'elle les _____ **(13)**

(apporter) chez sa grand-mère. Le loup _____ **(14)** (partir) dans la forêt et la

petite fille _____ **(15)** (continuer) son chemin *(way).* Mais le loup

_____ **(16)** (prendre) un chemin plus court pour aller chez la grand-mère et il

_____ **(17)** (arriver) le premier. Comme la porte _____ **(18)**

(ne pas être) fermée, il _____ **(19)** (entrer) dans la maison. Il _____ **(20)**

(manger) la grand-mère tout entière *(whole)* et _____ **(21)** (prendre) sa place.

Quelques minutes plus tard, sa petite-fille _____ **(22)** (entrer) dans la chambre.

Il y _____ **(23)** (avoir) très peu de lumière *(light)* et le Petit Chaperon rouge

_____ **(24)** (ne pas pouvoir) très bien voir. La petite fille _____ **(25)**

(commencer) à parler à sa grand-mère. À ce moment-là, le loup _____ **(26)**

(sauter *[to jump]*) du lit, il _____ **(27)** (manger) le Petit Chaperon rouge tout

entier et il _____ **(28)** (sortir) de la maison. Par hasard *(By chance),* un chasseur

(hunter) _____ **(29)** (passer) devant la maison à ce moment-là. Il _____ **(30)**

(voir) le loup et il le (l') _____ **(31)** (tuer *[to kill]*). Quand il a ouvert le ventre *(belly)* du

loup, la petite fille et sa grand-mère _____ **(32)** (sortir) vivantes *(alive)* parce

que le loup les avait mangées tout entières.

E. Leur départ. David and Catherine, two of Alice's Quebecker friends, went to visit her in Vancouver. Say what happened the day they left by putting the verbs in the **passé composé** or the imperfect.

Le jour de leur départ, David et Catherine ___pouvaient___ (pouvoir) prendre leur temps parce que leur avion _____ **(1)** (aller) partir à onze heures et demie. Alors David _____ **(2)** (sortir) faire du jogging à six heures et demie parce qu'il _____ **(3)** (vouloir) faire un peu d'exercice. Catherine _____ **(4)** (vouloir) rester au lit et elle _____ **(5)** (dormir) encore un peu. Quand David _____ **(6)** (rentrer) du parc, ils _____ **(7)** (prendre) un bain et ils _____ **(8)** (faire) leurs bagages. Ils _____ **(9)** (prendre) tranquillement leur déjeuner quand soudainement David _____ **(10)** (remarquer) qu'il _____ **(11)** (être) déjà dix heures. Ils _____ **(12)** (devoir) être à l'aéroport au moins une heure avant leur vol, alors ils _____ **(13)** (ne pas avoir) beaucoup de temps. Ils _____ **(14)** (sortir) rapidement de la cuisine pour aller chercher leurs bagages et Catherine _____ **(15)** (aller) dans le salon pour appeler un taxi. Le taxi _____ **(16)** (arriver) vingt minutes plus tard et ils _____ **(17)** (partir) pour l'aéroport à onze heures moins le quart. Heureusement, ils _____ **(18)** (arriver) à temps parce que l'avion _____ **(19)** (partir) à midi, avec trente minutes de retard. Catherine _____ **(20)** (être) très fatiguée et elle _____ **(21)** (dormir) pendant le vol.

*Journal. Write a paragraph in French recounting a recent outing or a trip with friends. Set the scene and give the background information using the imperfect and name as many things as you can that happened using the **passé composé.** Include such details as what day it was, what the weather was like, and who was with you. Then tell when you got there, what it was like, and what happened or what you did.

_____

_____

_____

_____

_____

_____

_____

_____

_____

Nom _____ Date _____

Partie auditive

A. La Belle et la Bête. Listen as the narrator recounts the summary of the story of *Beauty and the Beast* from page 236 of the textbook. You will then hear a series of questions. Indicate the answer to each one.

1. deux ___   trois ___

2. plus jeune ___   plus âgée ___

3. horrible et féroce ___   jolie et douce ___

4. horrible et féroce ___   jolie et douce ___

5. elle a pris sa place ___   elle l'a emprisonné ___

6. de prendre sa place ___   de l'emprisonner ___

7. tout de suite ___   petit à petit ___

8. Belle ___   la Bête ___

9. à apprécier la Bête ___   à aimer ___

B. Leur arrivée à Vancouver. Alice's friends David and Catherine came to visit her in Vancouver. Listen to the description of their arrival and complete it with the missing verbs.

Quand David et Catherine _____ (1) à Vancouver, ils _____ (2) très

fatigués et le premier soir, ils _____ (3) se reposer *(to rest)* un peu avant de téléphoner

à Alice. Ils _____ (4) un taxi pour aller à leur hôtel qui _____ (5)

loin du jardin botanique. À l'hôtel, il y _____ (6) un petit problème parce que leur réservation

_____ (7) pour la semaine suivante. Comme *(Since)* il n'y _____ (8)

pas d'autres chambres disponibles *(available)*, ils _____ (9) chercher un autre hôtel.

Le réceptionniste de l'hôtel _____ (10) à d'autres hôtels pour trouver une autre chambre

quand tout à coup, il y _____ (11) une annulation *(cancellation)* à l'hôtel. David

et Catherine _____ (12) rester là où ils _____ (13). Ils

_____ (14) tout de suite dans leur chambre. C' _____ (15) une très

belle chambre avec une vue magnifique du jardin botanique. Comme ils _____ (16)

fatigués, ils _____ (17) quelques heures avant de sortir.

Now pause the recording and answer these questions *with complete sentences.*

1. Pourquoi est-ce que David et Catherine n'ont pas téléphoné à Alice tout de suite?

_____

_____

2. Comment sont-ils allés à leur hôtel?

_____

3. Comment était leur chambre?

_____

C. Pourquoi? Indicate the logical circumstances explaining why David and Catherine did each thing you hear mentioned. Then as you hear the correct response, check your work.

> **EXEMPLE** VOUS VOYEZ: **Ils cherchaient du travail. / Ils voulaient voir Alice.**
> VOUS ENTENDEZ: Pourquoi est-ce que David et Catherine ont fait un voyage à Vancouver?
> VOUS INDIQUEZ: **Ils voulaient voir Alice.**
> VOUS ENTENDEZ: Ils ont fait un voyage à Vancouver parce qu'ils voulaient voir Alice.

1. Ils voulaient dormir un peu. ____   Ils ne voulaient pas voir Alice. ____

2. Ils trouvaient Vancouver ennuyeux. ____   Ils étaient fatigués. ____

3. Ils avaient une réservation pour la semaine suivante. ____   Ils avaient une jolie chambre. ____

4. Ils avaient une vue magnifique du jardin botanique. ____   Ils n'avaient pas de fenêtres. ____

5. Ils aimaient beaucoup leur chambre d'hôtel. ____   Ils voulaient voir Vancouver. ____

6. Ils n'avaient pas faim. ____   Ils aimaient la cuisine locale. ____

7. Ils parlaient anglais. ____   Ils ne parlaient pas anglais. ____

*D. Et vous? Answer the following questions about the last time you went out with someone.

1. _____

2. _____

3. _____

4. _____

5. _____

6. _____

La vie quotidienne Chapitre 7

COMPÉTENCE 1

Describing your daily routine

By the time you finish this **Compétence,** you should be able to describe your daily routine.

Partie écrite

A. Ma routine. Complete each sentence by putting each verb in parentheses in the logical blank.

> **EXEMPLE** **Je m'endors** facilement tous les soirs, mais le matin, **je me réveille** avec difficulté. (je me réveille, je m'endors)

1. _____ vers sept heures et demie et d'habitude

   _____ tout de suite, mais quelquefois je reste au lit une

   demi-heure si je suis fatigué(e). (je me réveille, je me lève)

2. Généralement, le matin, je n'ai pas beaucoup de temps, alors, _____

   parce que c'est plus rapide. Quelquefois le soir, _____ moussant

   (bubble) et j'écoute de la musique douce. (je prends un bain, je prends une douche)

3. _____ presque toujours avant de prendre le déjeuner.

   Généralement, _____ une jupe et un chandail pour aller en

   cours. (je m'habille, je mets)

4. Après le déjeuner, _____ les dents et

   _____ la figure. (je me lave, je me brosse)

5. Ensuite, _____ et _____

   les cheveux. (je me maquille, je me brosse)

6. _____ dans tous mes cours parce que je suis avec des amis et mes profs

   sont intéressants, sauf mon prof de maths. _____ dans son

   cours. C'est tellement ennuyeux que je m'endors de temps en temps. (je m'ennuie, je m'amuse).

7. Le soir, je prépare mes cours et après, _____ un peu. Vers

   dix heures, _____ et je mets mon pyjama. (je me déshabille, je me repose)

8. _____ vers onze heures et _____

   rapidement. (je m'endors, je me couche)

B. Conversation. Reread the conversation between Rosalie and Rose on page 255 of the textbook. Then, complete this paragraph in which Rose's cousin Patricia describes her routine.

D'habitude, _____ **(1)** vers 7 heures et je fais _____ **(2)**
              (I get up)   *(quickly)*

ma toilette. Je passe _____ **(3)** dans la salle de bains.
                           (a half hour)

_____ **(4)** et _____ **(5)**.
    (I put on make-up)   *(I get dressed)*

Je suis _____ **(6)** en moins d' _____ **(7)**.
          (ready)   *(one hour)*

Je dois _____ **(8)** mon mari parce qu'on quitte la maison ensemble.
        (to wait for)

C. Que font-ils ? Complete the following sentences in French saying what these people are doing.

1. Marcel _____

2. Francine _____

3. Christine _____

4. Lin _____

5. Monique _____

6. Patricia _____

7. Sophie _____

8. Bernard _____

D. Chez Rose. Rose is talking about her family's routine back at home in Vancouver. Complete what she says by conjugating the verbs in parentheses in the present tense.

Le matin, je _____ **(1)** (se réveiller) vers 6 h 30 et ma mère et moi, nous

_____ **(2)** (se lever) vers 6 h 45. Mes deux frères _____ **(3)** (se lever)

bien après, vers 8 h 30. Quelquefois, mon frère Alain _____ **(4)** (se recoucher) parce qu'il

_____ **(5)** (se coucher) très tard le soir et il est fatigué. Je _____ **(6)**

(prendre) mon bain le soir, alors, le matin je _____ **(7)** (se laver) la figure et

les mains, je _____ **(8)** (se maquiller) et je _____ **(9)**

(s'habiller). Ma mère _____ **(10)** (ne pas se maquiller). Mes deux frères font

leur toilette et ils _____ **(11)** (s'habiller). Et vous ? À quelle heure est-ce que vous

_____ **(12)** (se lever) ?

E. Pour mieux lire : *Using word families.* Skim the paragraph on the right and find the verb from the same word family as each of the following nouns.

EXEMPLE   un habitant   **habite**

1. un passage   _____

2. une plante   _____

3. un arrêt d'autobus _____

4. un regard   _____

5. l'admiration   _____

6. la ressemblance   _____

7. la vie   _____

> André Dupont habite depuis toujours à Genève. Il passe des heures dans son jardin où il plante des rosiers ravissants. Tous les gens du quartier s'arrêtent pour regarder son beau jardin. Un jour, une jeune fille admire son jardin. Elle ressemble à quelqu'un qu'André aimait quand il était jeune, une fille qui est partie vivre au Canada.

F. André et Rosalie.   Reread the story **Il n'est jamais trop tard !** on pages 260–261 of the textbook and select the correct completion for each sentence.

1. André est *célibataire / marié / divorcé / veuf.*

2. Rosalie est *célibataire / mariée / divorcée / veuve.*

3. André est tombé amoureux de Rosalie *il y a longtemps / récemment.*

4. Rosalie s'est mariée avec *un Canadien / un Américain / un Français.*

5. Rosalie a quitté *Genève / Paris* pour aller vivre *à Hamilton / à Vancouver.*

6. Rosalie est revenue en Suisse pour voir *son frère / son ami André / ses parents.*

7. Rosalie est venue en Suisse avec *sa fille / son mari / sa petite-fille.*

*G. Et votre journée ? Answer the following questions *with complete sentences.*

1. Est-ce que vous vous réveillez facilement le matin ?

   _____

   _____

2. Est-ce que vous vous levez tout de suite ?

   _____

   _____

3. Quel jour est-ce que vous vous levez le plus tôt *(the earliest)* ?

   _____

   _____

4. Préférez-vous prendre un bain ou une douche ?

   _____

   _____

5. Est-ce que vous vous lavez les cheveux tous les jours ?

   _____

   _____

6. Combien de fois par jour est-ce que vous vous brossez les dents ?

   _____

   _____

7. Est-ce que vous vous habillez avant le déjeuner ou après ?

   _____

   _____

8. Avec qui est-ce que vous vous amusez le plus *(the most)* ?

   _____

   _____

9. Est-ce que vous vous ennuyez quand vous êtes seul(e) ?

   _____

   _____

10. Est-ce que vous vous reposez ou est-ce que vous travaillez la fin de semaine ?

    _____

    _____

11. À quelle heure est-ce que vous vous couchez le samedi soir ?

    _____

    _____

12. Est-ce que vous vous endormez facilement ou avec difficulté en général ?

    _____

    _____

Partie auditive

A. Chez Henri et Patricia. You will hear several statements about the daily lives of Patricia and Henri. Label each drawing with the number of the statement describing it.

a. _____

b. _____

c. _____

d. _____

e. _____

f. _____

B. Ma routine quotidienne. You will hear the start of a sentence. Two of the completions below for each sentence are logical, but one is not. Pause the recording and indicate the ending that is not logical. Then, listen, check your work, and repeat after the speaker as you hear the correct sentences.

EXEMPLE
VOUS ENTENDEZ : **Je me réveille…**
VOUS INDIQUEZ : **avec difficulté / ~~la figure et les mains~~ / et je me lève tout de suite**
VOUS ENTENDEZ : **Je me réveille avec difficulté. / Je me réveille et je me lève tout de suite.**
VOUS RÉPÉTEZ : **Je me réveille avec difficulté. / Je me réveille et je me lève tout de suite.**

1. une douche / après la douche tous les jours / vite pour sortir le matin

2. les cheveux / les mains / un bain

3. dans la salle de bains / un bain / une douche

4. je n'ai rien à faire / je m'amuse avec mes amis / je suis seul(e) la fin de semaine

5. les cheveux / les mains / les dents

6. la figure et les mains / sur le divan / en cours

7. je prends ma douche / je sors / je me couche

8. je n'ai rien à faire / je suis fatigué(e) / je me réveille

C. La routine chez Patricia. You will hear Patricia talk about her daily routine. The first time, just listen to what she says at normal speed. Then fill in the missing words as it is repeated more slowly.

Le matin, _____ **(1)** en premier. Henri

_____ **(2)** facilement et _____ **(3)**

un peu après moi. Ensuite, les enfants _____ **(4)** et

nous mangeons. Après, Henri et moi, _____ **(5)** et

_____ **(6)**. Henri _____ **(7)**

et _____ **(8)**. Les enfants

_____ **(9)** et _____ **(10)**.

Le soir, Henri et les enfants _____ **(11)** ensemble, mais

_____ **(12)** le plus souvent. _____ **(13)**

et _____ **(14)** vers 10 heures. Et toi, à quelle heure est-ce que

_____ **(15)**? _____ **(16)**

facilement?

D. Les enfants de Patricia et Henri. Rose is going to babysit the children of her cousin, Patricia, for the weekend. Listen to their conversation, then complete the following statements.

1. Le samedi, les enfants se lèvent vers _____ heures

   d'habitude, mais quelquefois Philippe se réveille vers _____ heures.

2. Ils mangent et après ils _____ .

3. Pour s'amuser quand il pleut, ils aiment _____ .

4. En semaine, ils _____ à neuf heures, mais le samedi,

   ils _____ un peu plus tard.

5. Avant de se coucher, ils _____ .

*E. Et vous? Answer the questions you hear *in complete sentences in French.*

1. _____
2. _____
3. _____
4. _____
5. _____
6. _____
7. _____

COMPÉTENCE 2

Talking about relationships

By the time you finish this *Compétence*, you should be able to talk about personal relationships.

Partie écrite

A. André et Rosalie se retrouvent. Tell what happens between André and Rosalie, using the indicated verbs in the present tense.

se disputer   s'embrasser   se parler   se quitter   se regarder   se retrouver

| 1 | 2 | 3 | 4 | 5 | 6 |

1. André et Rosalie _____ .

2. Ils _____ .

3. Ils _____ pendant des heures.

4. Ils _____ vers 7 heures.

5. Ils _____ au café presque tous les jours.

6. Ils _____ rarement.

B. Conversation. Reread the conversation between Rose and Rosalie on page 262 of the textbook. Then, complete this conversation between Rose and Isabelle with the indicated words.

ISABELLE : Ton petit ami et toi, vous _____ **(1)** en général ?

(get along well)

ROSE : Non, nous _____ **(2)** très bien. Nous

(don't get along)

_____ **(3)** souvent. Nous passons beaucoup de temps

(argue)

ensemble mais nous _____ **(4)** de choses importantes.

(don't talk to each other)

ISABELLE : _____ **(5)** ! Et comment est _____ **(6)**

(That's too bad)   (the relationship)

entre Rosalie et André ?

ROSE : Moi, je _____ **(7)** d'une telle relation. Ils _____ **(8)**

(dream)   (meet each other)

tous les jours et ils _____ **(9)** bien

(get along)

_____ **(10)**. Tu sais, ils vont _____ **(11)**
(most of the time) *(to marry)*

et ils vont _____ **(12)** à Genève. Je suis certaine qu'ils vont être très
(to settle)

_____ **(13)** ensemble.
(happy)

*C. Entre amis. A classmate is asking you about you and your best friend. Complete his questions with the correct form of the indicated verb, then answer them *with complete sentences.*

1. Où est-ce que vous _____ (se retrouver) le plus souvent *(the most often)*

quand vous sortez ensemble ?

_____

2. Est-ce que vous _____ (se parler) de tout ?

_____

3. Vous _____ (s'entendre) toujours bien ?

_____

4. Vous _____ (se disputer) quelquefois ?

_____

5. Quand vous _____ (se disputer), est-ce que vous

_____ (se réconcilier) facilement ?

_____

D. Préférences. Say whether or not these people like to do the indicated things. Then say whether they are or are not going to do them tomorrow.

> **EXEMPLE** se lever tôt
> Moi, je/j'**aime (n'aime pas)** me lever tôt.
> Demain, je **vais (ne vais pas)** me lever tôt.

1. se lever tout de suite

Moi, je/j' _____.

Demain matin, je _____.

2. s'amuser ensemble

Mes amis et moi, nous _____.

Demain soir, nous _____.

3. s'habiller en noir

Mon meilleur ami (Ma meilleure amie) _____.

Demain, il/elle _____.

4. se retrouver chez moi

Mes amis _____.

Demain soir, ils _____.

E. Les verbes en -re. Review the *-re* verbs on page 268 of the textbook. Then, complete the following description of Rosalie's date with André with an appropriate **-re** verb as indicated. Remember to use the present tense to say someone is doing something (*I am waiting* = **j'attends**).

Rosalie _____ **(1)** *(hears)* son cellulaire sonner.

Elle _____ **(2)** *(answers)* et c'est André qui veut

lui _____ **(3)** *(to visit)* chez son

frère. Rosalie préfère aller au café en ville. À l'arrêt d'autobus, elle rencontre deux

vieilles amies d'enfance *(childhood)* qui _____ **(4)** *(are waiting for)*

l'autobus. En ville, ses amies _____ **(5)** *(get off)* de l'autobus au même

arrêt que Rosalie et elles parlent pendant presque une heure. Quand Rosalie arrive au café, elle est très en

retard *(late)*, mais André _____ **(6)** *(is waiting)* patiemment parce qu'il ne

_____ **(7)** *(loses)* presque jamais patience.

Now tell the preceding story in the past, putting each verb in the **passé composé** or the imperfect. Remember to use the **passé composé** to list the sequence of events that took place and the imperfect to set the scene and describe something that was already in progress when something else happened.

Rosalie _____ **(1)** (entendre) son cellulaire sonner. Elle

_____ **(2)** (répondre) et c' _____ **(3)**

(être) André qui _____ **(4)** (vouloir) lui rendre visite

chez son frère. Rosalie _____ **(5)** (préférer) aller au café en ville.

Quand elle _____ **(6)** (arriver) à l'arrêt d'autobus

pour aller retrouver André en ville, elle _____ **(7)**

(rencontrer) deux vieilles amies d'enfance qui _____ **(8)**

(attendre) l'autobus. En ville, ses amies _____ **(9)** (descendre) de

l'autobus au même arrêt que Rosalie et elles _____ **(10)** (parler)

pendant presque une heure. Quand Rosalie _____ **(11)**

(arriver) au café, elle _____ **(12)** (être) très en retard, mais André

_____ **(13)** (attendre) patiemment parce qu'il ne perd presque jamais

patience.

*F. Et toi? Your friend is asking you about your travel habits. Complete his questions with the correct form of the given verb in the present tense. Then, answer his questions *with complete sentences.*

1. Avec qui préfères-tu voyager? Est-ce que tu _____ (s'entendre) toujours bien

   avec cette personne?

   _____

   _____

2. Tu _____ (rendre souvent visite) à des amis ou à des parents

   qui habitent dans une autre ville?

   _____

   _____

3. Si tu voyages en avion et que la compagnie aérienne _____ (perdre)

   tes bagages, est-ce que tu _____ (perdre) patience ou est-ce que tu

   _____ (attendre) patiemment?

   _____

   _____

4. Tu _____ (descendre) souvent dans un hôtel ou dans une auberge de jeunesse?

   _____

5. Tu _____ (se perdre) facilement dans une nouvelle ville?

   _____

---

*Journal. Describe an ideal relationship between a happy couple. How often do they talk to each other? phone each other? get together? What do they do for each other? Do they talk to each other about everything? How do they get along? Do they argue?

Dans un couple heureux, on…

_____

_____

_____

_____

_____

_____

_____

_____

_____

_____

_____

_____

Partie auditive

A. Rosalie et André. You will hear a series of statements about Rosalie and André's interactions. Transform each statement to restate what they do to or for each other. After a pause for you to respond, you will hear the correct answer. Verify your response.

EXEMPLE   VOUS ENTENDEZ : André rencontre Rosalie et Rosalie rencontre André.
VOUS DITES : **Ils se rencontrent.**
VOUS ENTENDEZ : Ils se rencontrent.

B. La grande nouvelle ! Listen as Rosalie makes an important announcement to Rose. Then pause the recording and explain *in complete sentences* how often Rosalie and André do these things, according to what is said in the conversation.

toujours / souvent / quelquefois / rarement / ne… jamais

1. se quitter : _____

2. se disputer : _____

3. s'entendre bien : _____

C. Qui ? Patricia is talking about what she and Henri and André and Rosalie are going to do tomorrow. Pause the recording, and for each question you hear, look at the picture and answer as she would *with a complete sentence*. Turn on the recording and check your work and repeat as you hear the answer.

Henri et moi, nous… / Henri… / Moi, je… / André et Rosalie…

EXEMPLE   VOUS ENTENDEZ : Qui va se lever à six heures ?
VOUS RÉPONDEZ : **Henri et moi, nous allons nous lever à six heures.**
VOUS ENTENDEZ : Henri et moi, nous allons nous lever à six heures.
VOUS RÉPÉTEZ : **Henri et moi, nous allons nous lever à six heures.**

Exemple   1   2   3   4   5

1. _____ avec les enfants.

2. _____ à la maison.

3. _____ à minuit.

4. _____ au café.

5. _____ en ville.

D. Prononciation : Les verbes en -re. Some students are talking about their French class. Pause the recording and complete each sentence or question with the correct form of the **-re** verb given. Then turn on the recording and repeat the sentences after the speaker.

1. Nous _____ (répondre) bien.

2. Les étudiants _____ (s'entendre) bien.

3. Le professeur _____ (attendre) ta réponse.

4. Je _____ (rendre) mes devoirs.

5. Tu _____ (entendre) toujours bien le prof en cours ?

E. La routine de Rose. Rose is describing her daily routine at home in Vancouver. The first time, just listen to what she says. Then, fill in the missing words as it is repeated more slowly with pauses.

Le matin, j' _____ (1) l'autobus devant mon appartement. Quelquefois,

le bus est en retard *(late)* et je _____ (2) patience. Je n'aime pas

_____ (3) ! Quand le bus arrive, je monte dedans *(inside)* et je

_____ (4) à l'université. En cours, les étudiants ne _____ (5)

pas toujours correctement, mais le prof ne _____ (6) jamais patience avec

nous. Nous ne _____ (7) pas notre temps en cours — nous travaillons

bien ! Après les cours, je vais souvent à mon magasin préféré où on _____ (8)

des livres et des CD. Quelquefois, je _____ (9) à mon ami Jérôme. Nous

_____ (10) très bien.

*F. Et toi ? Answer each question a friend asks about your French class *with a complete sentence.*

1. _____

2. _____

3. _____

4. _____

5. _____

COMPÉTENCE 3

Talking about what you did and used to do

By the time you finish this *Compétence*, you should be able to talk about your daily routine or a relationship in the past.

Partie écrite

A. Le matin chez Rose. Complete Rose's sentences about this morning using the **passé composé.**

> **EXEMPLE**   Le réveil a sonné et je **me suis réveillée.**

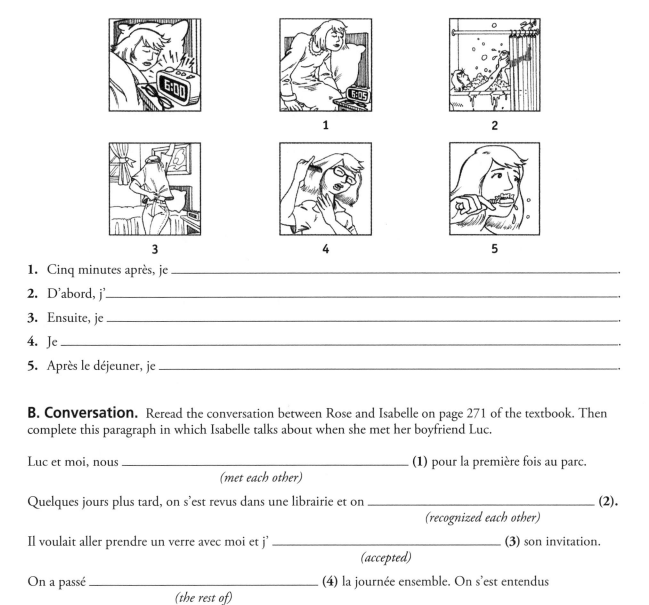

1. Cinq minutes après, je _____.

2. D'abord, j'_____.

3. Ensuite, je _____.

4. Je _____.

5. Après le déjeuner, je _____.

B. Conversation. Reread the conversation between Rose and Isabelle on page 271 of the textbook. Then complete this paragraph in which Isabelle talks about when she met her boyfriend Luc.

Luc et moi, nous _____ **(1)** pour la première fois au parc.

         (met each other)

Quelques jours plus tard, on s'est revus dans une librairie et on _____ **(2).**

                  (recognized each other)

Il voulait aller prendre un verre avec moi et j' _____ **(3)** son invitation.

            (accepted)

On a passé _____ **(4)** la journée ensemble. On s'est entendus

     (the rest of)

_____ **(5).** _____ **(6),** on passe beaucoup de temps ensemble.

 (perfectly)   *(Since then)*

C. La rencontre. Tell the story of how Rosalie and André met again after all of these years, using the words given. Remember that **se parler** does not require agreement of the past participle.

se quitter   se regarder   se rencontrer   se promener   s'embrasser   se parler

EXEMPLE   Rosalie et André **se sont rencontrés** chez le frère de Rosalie pour la première fois depuis des années. Ils **se sont regardés.**

| Exemple | 1 | 2 | 3 | 4 |

1. Ils _____ tendrement.

2. Ils _____ pendant des heures.

3. Ils _____ ensemble en ville.

4. Ils _____ vers 7 heures.

D. Qui a fait ça? Patricia is talking about what happened yesterday. Using the **passé composé,** tell who she says did each of the following things. Note that the verbs with an asterisk do not require agreement of the past participle.

EXEMPLE   s'amuser ensemble : Mes amis se sont amusés ensemble.

| Exemple   mes amis | Henri | André et Rosalie | mon frère et son amie |

| moi, je | mon amie et moi, nous | mon frère | Henri et moi, nous |

1. s'endormir sur le canapé : _____ sur le canapé.

2. *se parler au téléphone : _____ au téléphone.

3. se promener au parc : _____ au parc.

4. *s'écrire des courriels : _____ des courriels.

5. s'embrasser : _____.

6. se reposer dans son fauteuil : _____ dans son fauteuil.

7. se coucher tard : _____ tard.

E. Ce matin. Complete Rosalie's description of her day by putting the verbs in the **passé composé.**

Je _____ **(1)** (se réveiller) vers sept heures

ce matin et Rose _____ **(2)** (se lever)

un peu plus tard. J' _____ **(3)** (faire) ma

toilette et Rose _____ **(4)** (se laver) les

cheveux et _____ **(5)** (se maquiller) avant

de sortir. Nous _____ **(6)** (aller) en ville

et nous _____ **(7)** (bien s'amuser). Nous

_____ **(8)** (faire) du magasinage, puis nous

_____ **(9)** (aller) dans un café où nous

_____ **(10)** (prendre) un verre et nous

_____ **(11)** (se reposer) un peu. Après le café,

nous _____ **(12)** (se quitter). Rose et ses amis

_____ **(13)** (se retrouver) pour aller au cinéma. Moi,

je _____ **(14)** (se promener) un peu en ville, puis je

_____ **(15)** (rentrer) à la maison.

F. Chez vous. Say whether or not you did each of these things yesterday. Then, say whether you used to do each of them when you were 15. Use the **passé composé** and the imperfect as appropriate.

> **EXEMPLE** (se réveiller facilement)
> **Hier, je (ne) me suis (pas) réveillé(e) facilement.**
> **À l'âge de 15 ans, je (ne) me réveillais (pas) facilement.**

1. (se lever tout de suite)

Hier, je _____ tout de suite.

À l'âge de 15 ans, je _____ tout de suite.

2. (s'habiller en noir pour aller en cours)

Hier, je _____ en noir pour aller en cours.

À l'âge de 15 ans, je _____ en noir pour aller en cours.

3. (se brosser les dents après le déjeuner)

Hier, je _____ après le déjeuner.

À l'âge de 15 ans, je _____ après le déjeuner.

4. (s'amuser avec des copains [copines])

Hier soir, je _____ avec des copains (copines).

À l'âge de 15 ans, le soir, je _____ souvent avec des copains (copines).

G. Un souvenir du passé. Complete what André says about the past by putting the verbs in the **passé composé** or the imperfect.

Quand j' _____ **(1)** (avoir) dix-huit ans, je (j') _____ **(2)**

(vouloir) dire à Rosalie combien je l' _____ **(3)** (aimer), mais

j' _____ **(4)** (être) très timide. Un beau jour, je (j') _____ **(5)**

(décider) de déclarer mon amour à Rosalie. Je (J') _____ **(6)** (prendre) mon vélo et

je (j') _____ **(7)** (aller) chez Rosalie. Mais quand je (j') _____ **(8)**

(arriver) chez elle, je (j') _____ **(9)** (trouver) Rosalie en compagnie d'un jeune

Canadien et ils _____ **(10)** (se regarder) comme des amoureux.

Alors, je _____ **(11)** (rentrer) chez moi. Peu après, Rosalie et son Canadien

_____ **(12)** (se marier) et ils _____ **(13)** (s'installer)

au Canada.

*H. Ce matin. Answer these questions about your routine this morning.

1. À quelle heure est-ce que vous vous êtes réveillé(e) ?

_____

2. Étiez-vous fatigué(e) quand vous vous êtes levé(e) ?

_____

3. Vous avez pris un bain ou une douche ce matin ?

_____

4. Vous vous êtes brossé les cheveux ou vous vous êtes peigné(e) ?

_____

5. Vous vous êtes habillé(e) avant ou après le déjeuner ?

_____

6. À quelle heure avez-vous quitté la maison ?

_____

7. Votre meilleur(e) ami(e) et vous, vous vous êtes vu(e)s ce matin ? Vous vous êtes parlé au téléphone ?

_____

_____

8. La dernière fois que vous étiez ensemble, vous vous êtes bien amusé(e)s ? Vous vous êtes disputé(e)s ?

_____

_____

Partie auditive

 A. Hier matin. You will hear pairs of sentences in which people state two things that happened yesterday. Indicate which activity most logically came *first,* **a** or **b.** Then repeat the correct answer after the speaker.

EXEMPLE VOUS ENTENDEZ : **a. Le réveil a sonné. / b. Je me suis réveillé.**
VOUS INDIQUEZ : **a**
VOUS ENTENDEZ : **a. Le réveil a sonné.**
VOUS RÉPÉTEZ : **a. Le réveil a sonné.**

1. _____ **2.** _____ **3.** _____ **4.** _____ **5.** _____ **6.** _____

 B. Une rencontre. Listen as Rosalie describes how she accidentally ran into André at the café yesterday and how they ended up spending the day together. Label each illustration with the number of the sentence describing it.

a. _____ **b.** _____ **c.** _____ **d.** _____ **e.** _____

Play this section again, then pause the recording and answer the following questions.

1. Est-ce qu'André et Rosalie se sont vus tout de suite au café ?

_____

2. Qu'est-ce qu'ils ont fait quand ils se sont vus ?

_____

3. Après le dîner, qu'est-ce qu'ils ont fait ?

_____

4. Vers quelle heure est-ce qu'André et Rosalie se sont quittés ?

_____

 *C. Au passé composé. The best way to learn the word order of reflexive and reciprocal verbs in the **passé composé** is to practise saying them until they sound right. As you practise saying each pair of sentences, indicate the sentence that is true for you.

Je me suis levé(e) tôt ce matin. / Je ne me suis pas levé(e) tôt ce matin.

Je me suis perdu(e) en ville récemment. / Je ne me suis pas perdu(e) en ville récemment.

Je me suis endormi(e) en cours récemment. / Je ne me suis pas endormi(e) en cours récemment.

Je me suis ennuyé(e) la fin de semaine dernière. / Je ne me suis pas ennuyé(e) la fin de semaine dernière.

Mes parents et moi, nous nous sommes disputés récemment. / Nous ne nous sommes pas disputés récemment.

Mes parents se sont mariés très jeunes. / Mes parents ne se sont pas mariés très jeunes.

D. Hier chez Henri. Henri is talking about what he did yesterday. The first time, just listen to what he says. Then, fill in the missing words as it is repeated more slowly with pauses.

Hier matin, _____ **(1)** vers 7 heures

mais _____ **(2)** tout de suite parce que

_____ **(3)** sommeil. _____ **(4)**

mon bain, _____ **(5)** et _____ **(6)**.

Après le déjeuner, _____ **(7)** les dents et

les cheveux et _____ **(8)** la maison. Hier soir,

_____ **(9)** vers 7 heures. Les

enfants et moi _____ **(10)** à des jeux vidéo et _____

_____ **(11)**. Patricia _____ **(12)**

parce qu'elle _____ **(13)** fatiguée. Après le souper, elle

_____ **(14)**. Les enfants _____ **(15)**

vers 9 heures et _____ **(16)** tout de suite.

*E. Et toi ? Answer a friend's questions about your day yesterday *with complete sentences in French*.

1. _____
_____

2. _____
_____

3. _____
_____

4. _____
_____

5. _____
_____

COMPÉTENCE 4

Describing traits and characteristics

By the time you finish this *Compétence*, you should be able to talk about a relationship.

Partie écrite

A. Synonymes. Add the synonym from the list in the blank before the following words. Then, give your reaction to these characteristics in a potential partner by indicating **a, b,** or **c.**

   a. C'est un trait que j'apprécie chez un(e) partenaire.
   b. C'est un trait qui ne m'importe pas beaucoup chez un(e) partenaire.
   c. C'est un trait que je ne supporte pas chez un(e) partenaire.

    la passion   la vanité   l'indifférence   la beauté   la violence   l'infidélité   la compréhension
                            la jalousie   l'hésitation

1. _____, l'apathie, la nonchalance   a. ____ b. ____ c. ____

2. _____, l'envie, la rivalité   a. ____ b. ____ c. ____

3. _____, l'indécision, l'irrésolution   a. ____ b. ____ c. ____

4. _____, l'amour intense, l'adoration   a. ____ b. ____ c. ____

5. _____, la prétention, l'égotisme   a. ____ b. ____ c. ____

6. _____, l'élégance, le charme   a. ____ b. ____ c. ____

7. _____, la brutalité, l'agression   a. ____ b. ____ c. ____

8. _____, l'adultère, la déloyauté   a. ____ b. ____ c. ____

9. _____, la sympathie, l'indulgence   a. ____ b. ____ c. ____

B. Traits. Complete each sentence with the logical ending from the list.

a un bon sens de l'humour   cultive son esprit
cultive sa spiritualité   s'intéresse à la nature
veut réussir sa vie professionnelle   s'intéresse aux arts
prend soin de son corps

1. Quelqu'un qui passe beaucoup de temps au club de gym _____.

2. Quelqu'un qui aime faire des randonnées _____.

3. Quelqu'un qui raconte souvent des histoires amusantes _____

   _____.

4. Quelqu'un qui travaille beaucoup _____.

5. Quelqu'un qui apprend quelque chose tous les jours _____.

6. Quelqu'un pour qui la religion est très importante _____.

7. Quelqu'un qui aime la musique et le ballet _____

   _____.

C. Conversation.
C. Conversation. Reread the conversation between Rose and Isabelle on page 279 of the textbook. Then complete the following conversation as indicated.

ROSE : Alors, tu as trouvé _____ **(1)** avec Luc?
(happiness)

ISABELLE : Oui et non. Il est un peu _____ **(2)** et ça,
(jealous)

_____ **(3)**. En plus, moi, je suis
(I don't tolerate)

_____ **(4)** et lui, il est plutôt _____ **(5)**.
(liberal)   *(conservative)*

Et ton petit ami et toi, _____ **(6)**?
(you are interested in the same things)

ROSE : Pas du tout. _____ **(7)** et
(I am interested in the arts)

_____ **(8)** sport. _____ **(9)** son corps
(he is interested in)   *(He takes care of)*

et je préfère _____ **(10)**.
(to cultivate my mind)

D. Pronoms relatifs.
D. Pronoms relatifs. Combine each pair of sentences to form one sentence by removing the italicized words from the second sentence and linking the two sentences with the indicated relative pronoun, **qui, que,** or **dont.** The first sentence in each set has been done as an example.

QUE (QU')

1. André est un vieil ami. Rosalie retrouve *ce vieil ami* tous les jours en ville.

   André est un vieil ami **que Rosalie retrouve tous les jours en ville.**

2. Rosalie est une femme. André aime beaucoup *cette femme*.

   Rosalie est une femme _____.

3. Rosalie est une personne. Rose admire *cette personne*.

   Rosalie est une personne _____.

4. Le mari de Rosalie était un Canadien. Rosalie a accompagné *cet homme* à Vancouver.

   Le mari de Rosalie était un Canadien _____.

QUI

1. Le mari de Rosalie était un homme. *Cet homme* aimait beaucoup Rosalie.

   Le mari de Rosalie était un homme **qui aimait beaucoup Rosalie**.

2. Le mari de Rosalie était un homme. *Cet homme* est mort récemment.

   Le mari de Rosalie était un homme _____.

3. André est un ami d'enfance. *Cet ami d'enfance* a passé toute sa vie à Genève.

   André est un ami d'enfance _____.

4. Rosalie est une vieille amie d'André. *Cette vieille amie d'André* s'est installée à Vancouver.

   Rosalie est une vieille amie d'André _____.

DONT

1. Rosalie est une femme. André était amoureux *de cette femme* quand il était jeune.

   Rosalie est une femme **dont André était amoureux quand il était jeune**.

2. Le jeune Canadien était un homme. Rosalie est tombée amoureuse *de cet homme*.

   Le jeune Canadien était un homme _____.

3. Rosalie est une femme. André rêve toujours *de cette femme*.

   Rosalie est une femme _____.

4. André est un ami. Rosalie a fait la connaissance *de cet ami* il y a longtemps.

   André est un ami _____.

E. Et vous ? Complete the following sentences with **qui, que (qu')**, or **dont.** Then indicate whether each statement is **vrai** *(true)* or **faux** *(false)* for you.

1. Je préfère un(e) partenaire _____ n'est pas jaloux (jalouse).   V ____ F ____

2. J'ai beaucoup d'ami(e)s _____ s'intéressent à la politique.   V ____ F ____

3. J'ai beaucoup d'ami(e)s _____ je suis jaloux (jalouse).   V ____ F ____

4. L'infidélité est une chose _____ je ne supporte pas du tout.   V ____ F ____

5. Je préfère un(e) partenaire _____ cultive son esprit plutôt que

   de prendre soin de son corps.   V ____ F ____

6. La beauté est un trait _____ j'apprécie chez un(e) partenaire.   V ____ F ____

7. Je préfère passer mon temps avec des amis _____ j'ai fait la connaissance récemment.   V ____ F ____

8. Je préfère passer mon temps avec des amis _____ je connais *(I know)* depuis longtemps.   V ____ F ____

9. J'aimerais mieux *(I would prefer)* sortir avec quelqu'un _____ je trouve beau mais un

   peu bête qu'avec quelqu'un _____ je trouve intelligent mais pas très beau.   V ____ F ____

F. Lequel des deux ? Complete the following sentences in two ways, using the appropriate relative pronouns. Then select the completion that best describes your feelings or situation.

EXEMPLE   Je préfère me marier avec quelqu'un…
   dont je suis amoureux (amoureuse).
   qui a beaucoup d'argent.

1. L'amour est quelque chose…

   _____ je cherche dans la vie.

   _____ j'ai peur.

2. La beauté d'un(e) partenaire est un trait…

   _____ je suis facilement jaloux (jalouse).

   _____ je préfère.

   _____ n'a pas beaucoup d'importance pour moi.

3. Mon/Ma partenaire idéal(e) est quelqu'un…

   _____ je connais *(know)* déjà.

   _____ je n'ai pas encore fait la connaissance.

4. La politique est un sujet de conversation…

_____ je trouve intéressant.

_____ je n'aime pas parler.

5. Le grand amour est un sentiment…

_____ arrive comme un coup de foudre.

_____ il faut *(it is necessary)* cultiver.

6. Le grand amour est quelque chose…

_____ on peut avoir avec plusieurs partenaires.

_____ arrive une fois dans la vie.

7. La relation parfaite est quelque chose…

_____ je rêve encore.

_____ j'ai déjà trouvé.

---

*Journal. Write a description of your ideal partner. Discuss what traits you prefer and which ones you do not like. Also discuss your interests, what aspects of a relationship are important to you, and what you will not put up with in a relationship.

_____

_____

_____

_____

_____

_____

_____

_____

_____

_____

_____

_____

_____

_____

_____

_____

_____

_____

_____

_____

Partie auditive

A. Qualités. You will hear a series of personality traits. Decide if each one is a desirable trait or not and list it in the appropriate column.

<table>
<tr><td align="center">OUI</td><td></td><td align="center">NON</td></tr>
<tr><td>_____</td><td></td><td>_____</td></tr>
<tr><td>_____</td><td></td><td>_____</td></tr>
<tr><td>_____</td><td></td><td>_____</td></tr>
<tr><td>_____</td><td></td><td>_____</td></tr>
</table>

B. Citations. As you listen, fill in the missing words in these quotations. At the end, pause the recording, reread each one, and indicate whether or not you agree.

OUI NON **1.** Les privilèges de _____ sont immenses.

(Jean Cocteau, cinéaste)

OUI NON **2.** La fin *(end)* des _____, c'est

_____. (Yves Navarre, écrivain)

OUI NON **3.** _____ de la femme est dans ses charmes.

(Jean-Jacques Rousseau, écrivain et philosophe)

OUI NON **4.** Il y a dans _____ plus d'amour-propre *(self-love)* que d'_____. (François, duc de la Rochefoucauld,

écrivain et moraliste)

OUI NON **5.** _____ ruine plus de femmes que

_____. (Marie de Chichy-Chamrond, femme de lettres)

OUI NON **6.** _____ est un

_____ à deux. (Madame de Staël, femme de lettres)

C. Luc. Rose is telling her grandmother about her cousin Isabelle's new boyfriend, Luc. Pause the recording and complete what Rose says with **qui, que,** or **dont.** When you are done, turn on the recording and repeat the correct answers after the speaker, verifying your responses.

1. Luc est un ami _____ a un bon sens de l'humour.

2. C'est un ami _____ Isabelle retrouve tous les jours.

3. C'est un homme _____ Isabelle parle beaucoup.

4. C'est un ami _____ les autres amis d'Isabelle sont quelquefois jaloux.

5. Luc est un homme _____ comprend bien les femmes.

6. C'est un homme _____ nous trouvons très amusant.

7. C'est l'homme _____ Isabelle aime.

8. C'est l'homme _____ Isabelle est amoureuse.

D. Vrai ou faux? You will hear the beginning of a sentence and you will see two possible endings. Select the ending that fits the sentence grammatically. You will then hear the correct answer. Indicate whether or not the completed sentence is true for you.

EXEMPLE	VOUS VOYEZ:	… j'aime beaucoup. / … je suis très amoureux (amoureuse). VRAI FAUX
	VOUS ENTENDEZ:	Il y a une personne dont…
	VOUS SÉLECTIONNEZ:	**…je suis très amoureux (amoureuse).**
	VOUS DITES:	**Il y a une personne dont je suis très amoureux (amoureuse).**
	VOUS ENTENDEZ:	Il y a une personne dont je suis très amoureux (amoureuse).
	VOUS INDIQUEZ:	VRAI / FAUX

1. … a beaucoup d'importance pour moi. / … je trouve très important.   VRAI FAUX

2. … je parle peu avec mes amis. / … je n'aime pas.   VRAI FAUX

3. … n'est pas très agréable. / … je ne supporte pas.   VRAI FAUX

4. … on veut dans une relation. / … on a besoin dans une relation.   VRAI FAUX

5. … n'a pas de sens de l'humour. / … je trouve ennuyeux.   VRAI FAUX

E. Une nouvelle relation. Listen to a conversation in which two friends talk about the new girlfriend of a third friend. Then, fill in the missing words as it is repeated more slowly with pauses.

— Alors, Bernard a trouvé la femme _____ **(1)**? Qui est

cette femme, Nathalie, _____ **(2)**?

— C'est une femme qu'il a rencontrée à la piscine près de son appartement. Ils habitent dans le même

immeuble. Bernard a eu _____ **(3).**

— Tu as fait sa connaissance? Elle est comment?

— Oui, j'ai parlé avec elle l'autre jour chez Bernard. C'est une femme

_____ **(4)** et

_____ **(5),** mais je pense

qu'_____ **(6)** Bernard parce que sa famille est riche.

— Alors, c'est une relation qui est basée sur _____ **(7)** et

_____ **(8)**? Il va y avoir des problèmes, non?

— Je ne sais pas, mais tu connais Bernard. C'est un homme

_____ **(9)** et je pense

qu'_____ **(10)** de Bernard plutôt qu'à lui.

_____ **(11),** c'est quelque chose que Bernard ne supporte pas.

La bonne cuisine Chapitre 8

COMPÉTENCE 1

Ordering at a restaurant

By the time you finish this **Compétence,** you should be able to describe and order a meal at a restaurant.

Partie écrite

A. Un souper. Indicate whether each of the following foods is an **entrée, légume(s), volaille(s), viande(s), fruit(s) de mer,** or **dessert(s).**

crudités   soupe   pommes de terre   huîtres   rosbif   petits pois   poulet   dinde
tarte   moules   bifteck   côtes   haricots verts   crème   glacée   homard   crevettes

EXEMPLE **Les crudités** sont une **entrée.**

EXEMPLE

1   **2**   **3**

1. La _____ à l'oignon est une _____ .

2. Le _____ , le _____ et les
   _____ de porc sont des _____ .

3. Les _____ , les _____ et les
   _____ sont des _____ .

4   **5**   **6**

4. Le _____ et le _____ sont des _____ .

5. La _____ aux pommes et la _____ à la vanille
   sont des _____ .

6. Le _____ , les _____ ,
   les _____ et les _____ sont des
   _____ .

B. Dans quel ordre? Number the following food items from 1 to 6 to indicate in what order the French would most commonly have them at a meal.

_____ de la salade   _____ du pâté   _____ de la viande avec des légumes

_____ du café   _____ du fromage   _____ de la tarte aux cerises

C. Qu'est-ce que c'est? Ask someone to pass you the following things. Since you are referring to specific items, use the definite article with each one.

EXEMPLE   1   2   3

4   5   6   7

EXEMPLE   Pouvez-vous me passer la soupe, s'il vous plaît?

1. Pouvez-vous me passer _____, s'il vous plaît?

2. Pouvez-vous me passer _____, s'il vous plaît?

3. Pouvez-vous me passer _____, s'il vous plaît?

4. Pouvez-vous me passer _____, s'il vous plaît?

5. Pouvez-vous me passer _____, s'il vous plaît?

6. Pouvez-vous me passer _____, s'il vous plaît?

7. Pouvez-vous me passer _____, s'il vous plaît?

D. Conversation. Reread the conversation between Alexandre, Gabrielle, and the server at a restaurant on page 298 of the textbook. Then, complete this conversation where Patricia and Henri order a meal.

LE SERVEUR : Bonsoir, monsieur. Bonsoir, madame. Aimeriez-vous _____ (1)?
(a pre-dinner drink)

PATRICIA : Non, merci, pas ce soir.

HENRI : Pour _____ (2).
(me neither)

LE SERVEUR : Et pour souper? _____ (3)?
(Have you decided)

HENRI : Nous allons prendre _____ (4).
(the 24 dollar menu)

Le serveur : Très bien, monsieur. Et qu'est-ce que vous désirez _____ (5) ?
(as an appetizer)

Henri : La _____ (6) pour nous deux.
(onion soup)

Le serveur : Et comme _____ (7) ?
(main dish)

Patricia : Pour moi, le _____ (8), s'il vous plaît.
(tuna)

Henri : Et pour moi, le _____ (9).
(lobster)

Le serveur : Bien, monsieur. Et comme _____ (10) ?
(drink)

Henri : _____ (11) d'eau minérale.
(A bottle)

E. Au restaurant.

You are ordering the following things at a restaurant. Answer the waiter's questions. The first item has been done for you.

Le serveur : Que voulez-vous comme entrée ?

Vous : **La salade César, s'il vous plaît.**

Le serveur : Et comme plat principal ?

Vous : _____ (1)

Le serveur : Et avec ça, des pommes de terre ou du riz ?

Vous : _____ (2)

Le serveur : Et comme boisson ?

Vous : _____ (3)

Plus tard :

Le serveur : Est-ce que vous allez prendre un dessert ce soir ?

Vous : _____ (4)

F. Choix. Complete each blank with the logical noun in parentheses, including the appropriate article (**du, de la, de l', des, de [d']**). Remember to use **de (d')** after a negative expression or an expression of quantity.

> **EXEMPLE** **Je prends du thé** à la fin des repas généralement.
> Je **ne** prends **jamais de gâteau** parce que je suis diabétique. (fromage, gâteau)

1. Mon ami est végétarien. Il mange toujours _____ à chaque repas mais

   il ne mange pas _____. (viande, légumes)

2. Je mange _____ tous les jours. Je la préfère sans trop

   _____. (sel, soupe)

3. Au restaurant, je commande souvent _____. Je ne commande jamais

   _____ parce que je n'aime pas les fruits de mer. (rosbif, crevettes)

4. Ma femme ne mange pas _____ ni *(nor)* d'autres viandes rouges, mais

   elle mange souvent _____. (poisson, bifteck)

5. J'adore la cuisine japonaise. Je mange beaucoup _____ teriyaki avec

   _____. (riz, poulet)

6. Si tu veux être plus mince, prends _____ sans beaucoup

   _____. (sucre, desserts)

*G. Qu'est-ce que vous mangez? Complete the following questions with **du, de la, de l', des,** or **de (d')**. Then answer each question to describe your eating habits.

1. Est-ce que vous mangez _____ viande à chaque repas? Mangez-vous assez _____ légumes?

   _____

2. Faites-vous la cuisine avec beaucoup _____ sel et beaucoup _____ poivre?

   _____

3. Au déjeuner, prenez-vous _____ café, _____ jus de fruit, _____ lait ou _____ eau?

   _____

4. Mangez-vous beaucoup _____ poisson ou beaucoup _____ fruits de mer?

   _____

5. Avez-vous déjà mangé _____ escargots ou _____ fromage français tel que *(such as)* le brie?

   _____

6. Pour un repas léger *(light)*, préférez-vous manger _____ soupe ou _____ salade?

   _____

7. Mangez-vous plus souvent _____ gâteau, _____ tarte ou _____ crème glacée comme dessert?

   _____

Partie auditive

A. Bon appétit! Listen to the list of dishes for each category and fill in the missing words.

Une entrée ou un hors-d'œuvre:

_____, de la soupe, de la salade de tomates,

_____, _____

Un plat principal:

de la viande: _____, du bifteck, _____

de la volaille: _____, du poulet

du poisson: du saumon, _____

des fruits de mer: des moules, _____, des huîtres, _____

Un légume:

_____, des pommes de terre, _____

Pour finir le repas:

_____, du café, _____

de la crème glacée, _____

B. Prononciation: Le _h_ aspiré. Pause the recording and review the _**Prononciation**_ section on page 297 of the textbook. Then turn on the recording. Listen and repeat the following words and indicate whether the **h** is aspirate.

les huîtres / des huîtres / beaucoup d'huîtres	_____ H ASPIRÉ	_____ H NON ASPIRÉ
les hors-d'œuvre / des hors-d'œuvre / beaucoup de hors-d'œuvre	_____ H ASPIRÉ	_____ H NON ASPIRÉ
l'huile (oil) / de l'huile / pas d'huile	_____ H ASPIRÉ	_____ H NON ASPIRÉ
le homard / du homard / pas de homard	_____ H ASPIRÉ	_____ H NON ASPIRÉ
les hamburgers / des hamburgers / trop de hamburgers	_____ H ASPIRÉ	_____ H NON ASPIRÉ
les hot-dogs / des hot-dogs / pas de hot-dogs	_____ H ASPIRÉ	_____ H NON ASPIRÉ

Nom _____   Date _____

C. Pour mieux comprendre: *Planning and predicting.* Pause the recording and look over the different dishes you can order as an **entrée, plat principal,** or **dessert** from this menu. Then turn on the recording, listen to a scene at the restaurant, and indicate what the woman and the man order.

La femme:

Entrée: _____

Plat principal: _____

Dessert: _____

Boisson: _____

L'homme:

Entrée: _____

Plat principal: _____

Dessert: _____

Boisson: _____

Le Bistrot – 24 $

| entrée |
– soupe du jour
– salade de tomates et basilic frais

| plat principal |
– pavé de saumon avec asperges
– linguinis Alfredo aux crevettes
– pizza aux tomates, asperges, feta et herbes fraîches
– moules au vin blanc

| dessert |
– gâteau au fromage et caramel
– tarte aux pommes et crème glacée à la vanille
– salade de fruits exotiques

D. Qu'est-ce qu'il y a au menu? You are working at a restaurant. Answer each question, telling what there is on the menu. Use the correct forms of the partitive article. You will then hear the correct response. Check your answer and fill in the blank with the form of the partitive article in the answer: **du, de la, de l', des,** or **de.**

EXEMPLE   VOUS ENTENDEZ: Est-ce qu'il y a de la salade César?
              VOUS DITES: **Non, il n'y a pas de salade César.**
              VOUS ENTENDEZ: Non, il n'y a pas de salade César.
              VOUS INDIQUEZ: **de**

Comme entrée:

Comme plat principal:

Comme légume:

Comme dessert:

1. _____   3. _____   5. _____   7. _____

2. _____   4. _____   6. _____   8. _____

*E. Et vous? Answer the questions you hear *with complete sentences.*

1. _____

2. _____

3. _____

4. _____

COMPÉTENCE 2

Buying food

By the time you finish this **_Compétence,_** you should be able to talk about buying groceries.

Partie écrite

A. Qu'est-ce qu'on peut y acheter? List each of the items given with the store where you can buy it. The first one has been done as an example.

des saucisses, des crevettes, des conserves, des petits pois, une baguette, du bœuf, du poulet, du saucisson, du raisin, des pommes de terre, du porc, du poisson, du homard, un pain à grains entiers, des huîtres, un pain au chocolat, de la dinde, des plats préparés, une tarte aux cerises, du jambon

1. _____

_____

_____

_____

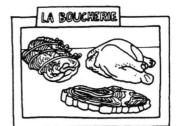

2. des saucisses, _____

_____

_____

_____

3. _____

_____

_____

_____

4. _____

_____

_____

_____

5. _____

_____

_____

_____

B. Qu'est-ce qu'il faut ? Which ingredients from the list are required to make the following dishes? Remember to use the partitive.

tomates, raisin, oignons, œufs, fromage, smoked meat, petits pois, pommes de terre, pommes, oranges, jambon, fraises, pain, carottes

EXEMPLE Pour faire un sandwich au fromage, il faut **du pain** et **du fromage.**

1. Pour faire une omelette au jambon, il faut _____ et

_____ .

2. Pour faire une salade de fruits, il faut _____ ,

_____ , _____ et

_____ .

3. Pour faire un sandwich au smoked meat, il faut _____ et

_____ .

4. Pour faire une soupe de légumes, il faut _____ ,

_____ , _____ ,

_____ et _____ .

C. Conversation. Reread the conversation in which Gabrielle is buying fruit and vegetables at the market on page 306 of the textbook. Then, complete this conversation she has at the **charcuterie** with the indicated words.

GABRIELLE :   Bonjour, monsieur.

LE MARCHAND : Bonjour, madame. _____ **(1)** ?
                                                      (What do you need today)

GABRIELLE :   Euh… _____ **(2),** une livre de jambon et
                                        (let's see)

_____ **(3).**
                     (a kilo of sausages)

LE MARCHAND : Alors, qu'est-ce que je peux vous proposer d'autre ?

GABRIELLE :   Donnez-moi aussi 500 _____ **(4).**
                                                              (grams of ham)

LE MARCHAND : Et voilà, 500 grammes. Et avec ça ?

GABRIELLE :   _____ **(5),** merci. Ça fait combien ?
                            (That's all)

LE MARCHAND : Alors, ça fait _____ **(6).**
                                            ($15.75)

D. Les quantités. You are buying groceries. Complete the following sentences with the logical item in parentheses for each quantity given.

> **EXEMPLE** Je voudrais un kilo **de pommes de terre,** s'il vous plaît. (pommes de terre, vin)

1. Il me faut une douzaine _____, s'il vous plaît. (œufs, rosbif)

2. Donnez-moi cinq tranches _____, s'il vous plaît. (riz, jambon)

3. J'ai besoin d'une bouteille _____, s'il vous plaît. (oignons, eau minérale)

4. Je voudrais aussi une livre _____, s'il vous plaît. (raisin, baguette)

5. Et donnez-moi un morceau _____ aussi, s'il vous plaît. (fromage, conserves)

6. Et avec ça, un kilo _____, s'il vous plaît. (tartelettes aux fraises, oranges)

E. Dans quel magasin ? Complete each sentence with the appropriate article (**du, de la, de l', un, une, des**) and the name of the store (besides the supermarket) where you can buy each item.

> **EXEMPLE** **On peut acheter du** pain **à la boulangerie.**

1. On peut acheter _____ conserves _____.

2. On peut acheter _____ rosbif _____.

3. On peut acheter _____ plats préparés _____.

4. On peut acheter _____ petits pois surgelés _____.

5. On peut acheter _____ tarte aux fraises _____.

6. On peut acheter _____ saumon _____.

7. On peut acheter _____ poires _____.

8. On peut acheter _____ baguette _____.

---

*Journal. Write a paragraph describing the last time you bought several things at the supermarket. Name as many things as you can that you bought, including at least three quantity expressions explaining how much you bought of different items.

_____

_____

_____

_____

_____

_____

_____

_____

_____

_____

Partie auditive

 A. Où sont-ils? You will hear five conversations in which people are buying food items in small shops. Match the number of each conversation with the store where it takes place.

a. _____

b. _____

c. _____

d. _____

e. _____

Now repeat this section and listen to the conversations again. Pause the recording and, for each conversation, indicate what the customer buys and how much he or she pays.

1. _____ _____

2. _____ _____

3. _____ _____

4. _____ _____

_____ _____

5. _____ _____

 B. Fruits et légumes. As you hear an item named, identify it as a fruit or a vegetable. After a pause for you to respond, you will hear the correct answer. Verify your response.

EXEMPLE   VOUS ENTENDEZ: Une carotte, c'est un fruit ou un légume?

                VOUS DITES: **Une carotte, c'est un légume.**

                VOUS ENTENDEZ: Une carotte, c'est un légume.

C. Quantités. Listen to the following items and fill in each expression of quantity that you hear.

1. Je voudrais _____ lait.

2. Je voudrais _____ vin.

3. Je voudrais _____ jambon.

4. Je voudrais _____ pommes de terre.

5. Je voudrais _____ confiture.

6. Je voudrais _____ sucre.

7. Je voudrais _____ œufs.

8. Je voudrais _____ fromage.

D. Quel article? Repeat each question you hear. After each one, pause the recording and identify the article used in the question.

EXEMPLE   VOUS ENTENDEZ :   Est-ce que vous mangez beaucoup de viande?
            VOUS RÉPÉTEZ :   **Est-ce que vous mangez beaucoup de viande?**
            VOUS INDIQUEZ :

	for likes and preferences				for some or any				for none and after a quantity
EXEMPLE	le ___	la ___	l' ___	les ___	du ___	de la ___	de l' ___	des ___	de ✓
1.	le ___	la ___	l' ___	les ___	du ___	de la ___	de l' ___	des ___	de ___
2.	le ___	la ___	l' ___	les ___	du ___	de la ___	de l' ___	des ___	de ___
3.	le ___	la ___	l' ___	les ___	du ___	de la ___	de l' ___	des ___	de ___
4.	le ___	la ___	l' ___	les ___	du ___	de la ___	de l' ___	des ___	de ___
5.	le ___	la ___	l' ___	les ___	du ___	de la ___	de l' ___	des ___	de ___
6.	le ___	la ___	l' ___	les ___	du ___	de la ___	de l' ___	des ___	de ___
7.	le ___	la ___	l' ___	les ___	du ___	de la ___	de l' ___	des ___	de ___

*Now play this section again and answer each question *with a complete sentence*. Pause the recording as needed in order to have time to answer.

1. _____

2. _____

3. _____

4. _____

5. _____

6. _____

7. _____

COMPÉTENCE 3

Talking about meals

By the time you finish this **Compétence,** you should be able to describe your typical meals.

Partie écrite

A. Le déjeuner. Identify the foods and drinks shown. Use the partitive article with each item: **du, de la, de l',** or **des.**

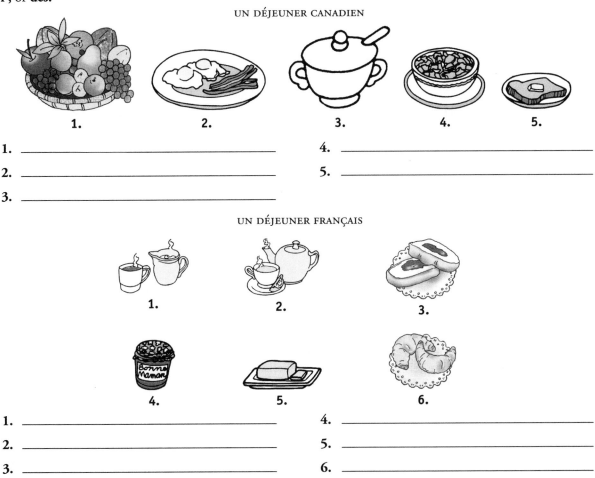

UN DÉJEUNER CANADIEN

1. 2. 3. 4. 5.

1. _____   4. _____

2. _____   5. _____

3. _____

UN DÉJEUNER FRANÇAIS

1. 2. 3.

4. 5. 6.

1. _____   4. _____

2. _____   5. _____

3. _____   6. _____

B. Un repas rapide. Complete these descriptions of things people eat as a quick meal with the appropriate partitive or indefinite article **(du, de la, de l', un, une, des).** Then, in the last blank, give the name of the dish that is described.

> **EXEMPLE** C'est **une** tranche de pain avec **du** beurre et **de la** confiture. On en mange souvent le matin. C'est **un toast.**

1. C'est _____ sandwich avec _____ viande de bœuf, _____ laitue, _____ tomate, des cornichons

   (pickles) et de la mayonnaise ou de la moutarde. On en mange beaucoup dans les restos rapides avec

   _____ frites. C'est un _____.

2. C'est _____ spécialité italienne avec de la sauce tomate, _____ fromage et souvent

avec _____ jambon, du pepperoni et des champignons *(mushrooms)*. C'est une _____.

3. C'est _____ plat avec _____ œufs, _____ sel et _____ poivre. On le prépare aussi avec _____

fromage, _____ jambon ou des champignons. C'est une _____.

C. Conversation.
Reread the conversation between Rose and her cousin on page 313 of the textbook. Then, complete this conversation between two friends with the indicated words.

MARION: _____ **(1)**? Il y a des céréales ou je peux faire
(Are you hungry)

_____ **(2)** si tu préfères.
(some toast)

SOPHIE: Non, merci. _____ **(3)** le matin.
(I'm never very hungry)

_____ **(4)**, je prendrais _____ **(5)**
(However) *(gladly)*

du café s'il y en a.

MARION: Oui, il y a du café, mais _____ **(6)**, il n'y a plus de crème.
(I'm sorry)

SOPHIE: Ça ne fait rien *(That doesn't matter)*. Je préfère le café au lait. Qu'est-ce que tu vas prendre?

MARION: Le matin, _____ **(7)** toujours du thé et quelquefois, je
(I drink)

prends des toasts.

*D. Préférences.
Say whether the following people like the specified drink **beaucoup, assez,** or **pas du tout.** Remember to use the definite article **(le, la, l', les)** with nouns after verbs indicating likes or preferences. Then say how often they drink it, using **en** with **souvent, quelquefois,** or **ne… jamais.**

EXEMPLE   mon meilleur ami (ma meilleure amie) / le coca
          Mon meilleur ami (Ma meilleure amie) aime beaucoup le coca.
          Il (Elle) en boit souvent.

1. mes parents / le vin: _____

_____

2. moi, je / le jus d'orange: _____

_____

3. les Français / le café: _____

_____

4. mes amis et moi / l'eau minérale: _____

_____

5. mon meilleur ami (ma meilleure amie) / la bière: _____

_____

6. le professeur de français / le café: _____

_____

E. Quantités. Answer the following questions about your morning eating habits, replacing the italicized words with **en**.

> **EXEMPLE** Buvez-vous beaucoup *de jus d'orange* le matin?
> **Oui, j'en bois beaucoup. / Non, je n'en bois pas beaucoup.**

1. Buvez-vous souvent *du café* le matin?

   _____

2. Avez-vous pris *un café* ce matin?

   _____

3. Est-ce que vous allez prendre *du café* plus tard aujourd'hui?

   _____

4. Prenez-vous beaucoup *de sucre* quand vous mangez des céréales?

   _____

5. Mangez-vous souvent *des œufs*?

   _____

6. Avez-vous mangé *des œufs* ce matin?

   _____

F. Citations. Complete the following quotes by famous French and Belgian writers, journalists, philosophers, and artists by conjugating the **-ir** verbs in parentheses. Then number the quotes from 1 (your favourite) to 12 (your least favourite) to indicate which ones you prefer.

1. ____ Lire, c'est boire et manger. L'esprit qui ne lit pas _____ (maigrir) comme le

   corps qui ne mange pas. (Victor Hugo)

2. ____ Les écrivains *(writers)* ne _____ (se nourrir) pas de

   viandes ou de poulet, mais exclusivement d'éloges *(praise)*. (Henry de Montherlant)

3. ____ La difficulté de trouver l'aliment *(food)* _____ (grandir)

   en fonction de la pureté *(depending on the purity)* de la faim. / L'âme *(soul)*, à la différence du corps,

   _____ (se nourrir) de sa faim. (Gustave Thibon)

4. ____ La peur _____ (nourrir) l'imagination. (Joseph Joubert)

5. ____ L'esclave *(slave)* qui _____ (obéir),

   _____ (choisir) d'obéir. (Simone de Beauvoir)

6. ____ On ne _____ (choisir) pas ses parents, on ne

   _____ (choisir) pas sa famille. On ne

   _____ (se choisir) même pas soi-même *(oneself)*. (Philippe

   Geluck)

7. ____ La vie est faite d'illusions. Parmi *(Among)* ces illusions, certaines _____

   (réussir). Ce sont elles qui constituent la réalité. (Jacques Audiberti)

8. ____ Le plus souvent on _____ (réussir) non par *(not by)* ce qu'on fait, mais par ce qu'on ne fait pas. (Jules Tellier)

9. ____ L'important, ce n'est pas ce qu'on _____ (réussir), c'est ce qu'on essaie. (Marcel Achard)

10. ____ Tout l'univers _____ (obéir) à l'amour ; Aimez, aimez, tout le reste n'est rien. (Jean de La Fontaine)

11. ____ Un intellectuel, c'est d'abord quelqu'un qui _____ (réfléchir) avant d'écrire et de parler, qui _____ (réfléchir) avant de réfléchir, et qui _____ (réfléchir) même sur l'utilité de la réflexion avant la réflexion proprement dite *(as such)*. (Bernard Pivot)

12. ____ Nous _____ (réfléchir) bien plus à l'emploi *(use)* de notre argent renouvelable *(renewable)*, qu'à celui de *(that of)* notre temps irremplaçable *(irreplaceable)*. (Jean-Louis Servan-Schreiber)

*G. Questions. Complete the following questions with the correct form of the logical verb in parentheses. Then answer each question *with a complete sentence.*

1. Quand vous allez souper au restaurant avec votre meilleur(e) ami(e), qui _____ (finir, choisir) le restaurant généralement ?

    _____

2. Généralement, est-ce que vous _____ (finir, maigrir) le repas avec un dessert ?

    _____

3. Si vous louez un film, est-ce que vous _____ (grossir, choisir) le plus souvent un film d'amour, une comédie ou un film d'aventure ?

    _____

4. Et vos amis ? Est-ce qu'ils _____ (grossir, choisir) un film étranger quelquefois ?

    _____

5. Est-ce que vous _____ (obéir, réussir) à comprendre certaines phrases quand vous regardez un film français en version originale ?

    _____

Partie auditive

 A. Au déjeuner. When asked, say that you would like some of each of the items pictured, using the correct form of the partitive: **du, de la, de l'**, or **des**. After a pause for you to respond, you will hear the correct answer. Verify your response and your pronunciation and repeat.

EXEMPLE	VOUS ENTENDEZ:	Qu'est-ce que vous voulez?
	VOUS DITES:	**Je voudrais du café au lait.**
	VOUS ENTENDEZ:	Je voudrais du café au lait.
	VOUS RÉPÉTEZ:	**Je voudrais du café au lait.**

 1

 2

 3

 4

 5

 6

 7

 8

Now listen to a brief passage about French eating habits. Identify three things that the French often eat in the morning and one thing they do not.

Le matin, les Français prennent souvent:

1. _____

2. _____

3. _____

Le matin, ils ne prennent pas:

1. _____

 B. Prononciation: Le verbe *boire*. Listen to a short passage comparing the types of drinks popular with Canadians to those popular with the French. Then pause the recording. Imagine that a French person is speaking to a Canadian. Complete each question or statement logically by selecting the appropriate choice in italics. Then, turn on the recording and verify your responses by repeating each sentence after the speaker. Pay particular attention to the pronunciation of the verb **boire**.

1. Le matin, je bois *du vin / du café*.

2. Est-ce que tu bois *du vin / du lait* le matin?

3. En France, on ne boit jamais *d'eau minérale / de lait* avec les repas.

4. Nous buvons souvent *du coca / du vin* avec un bon repas.

5. Vous buvez aussi *du vin / du coca* avec vos repas?

6. Les Français boivent quelquefois un café *avant / après* le souper.

C. La bonne santé. Would people who pay attention to their health say that they eat or drink the things you hear mentioned? Answer affirmatively or negatively as a health-conscious person would, using the pronoun **en.** Then, as you hear the correct answer, select OUI or NON to indicate whether the response was affirmative or negative.

> **EXEMPLE** VOUS ENTENDEZ : Mangez-vous beaucoup de sucre?
> VOUS DITES : **Non, je n'en mange pas beaucoup.**
> VOUS INDIQUEZ : OUI ____ NON ___✓___

1. OUI ____ NON ____ 3. OUI ____ NON ____ 5. OUI ____ NON ____ 7. OUI ____ NON ____

2. OUI ____ NON ____ 4. OUI ____ NON ____ 6. OUI ____ NON ____ 8. OUI ____ NON ____

D. Prononciation : La lettre *s* et les verbes en *-ir*. Pause the recording and review the *Prononciation* section on page 316 of the textbook. Indicate how the **s**'s in these sentences are pronounced by writing **s** or **z** in each blank below them. Then turn on the recording. Listen and repeat these words.

cousin / coussin   poison / poisson   désert / dessert

___   ___   ___

je choisis / je réussis   j'ai choisi / j'ai réussi   ils choisissent / ils réussissent

___   ___   ___   ___   ___ ___   ___ ___

il choisit / ils choisissent   il obéit / ils obéissent   elle réussit / elles réussissent

___ ___   ___   ___ ___

elle grandit / elles grandissent   il maigrit / ils maigrissent   elle réfléchit / elles réfléchissent

___   ___   ___

E. Les verbes en *-ir*. Rosalie is talking with Rose about her evenings out with André. Complete their conversation by filling in each blank with the verb that you hear.

ROSALIE : Quand nous sortons le soir, André _____ **(1)** le restaurant et moi, je

_____ **(2)** le film. Au restaurant, nous

_____ **(3)** un hors-d'œuvre et un plat principal. Après,

André _____ **(4)** son repas avec du fromage, mais moi je

préfère _____ **(5)** mon repas avec un dessert.

ROSE : Pourquoi ne _____ **(6)**-tu pas ton repas avec du fromage?

ROSALIE : Mon médecin préfère que je ne mange pas trop de matières grasses et je suis *(follow)* ses conseils

(advice). De toute façon, j' _____ **(7)** un peu depuis que je

suis en Suisse.

ROSE : Mais toi, tu _____ **(8)** toujours à rester en forme!

ROSALIE : Oui, je ne _____ **(9)** pas facilement, mais je

_____ **(10)** tout de même à rester en forme. D'abord, je fais

souvent de l'exercice et aussi je _____ **(11)** à ce que je mange.

Nom _____ Date _____

Choosing a healthy lifestyle

By the time you finish this **Compétence,** you should be able to say what you would change, if you could, to have a healthier lifestyle.

Partie écrite

A. Qu'est-ce qu'on devrait faire ? What should one do or not do to accomplish the following goals?
Complete each sentence with the logical action from the list.

manger peu de viande rouge   faire de la musculation

faire de l'aérobique   se promener à la campagne

choisir des plats sains   faire du yoga ou de la méditation

arrêter de fumer   boire beaucoup d'alcool

EXEMPLE   Pour contrôler le stress, on devrait **faire du yoga ou de la méditation.**

1. Pour éviter les effets du tabac, on devrait _____.
2. Pour faire une randonnée, on devrait _____.
3. Pour améliorer l'endurance cardiovasculaire, on devrait _____.
4. Pour devenir plus fort, on devrait _____.
5. Pour manger des aliments *(foods)* avec beaucoup de vitamines, on devrait

   _____

6. Pour éviter les matières grasses, on devrait _____.
7. Pour oublier ses problèmes, on ne devrait pas _____.

*B. Une bonne santé. Answer the following questions about health *with complete sentences.*

1. À votre avis, que devrait-on faire pour être en bonne santé ?

   _____

   _____

2. Quels aliments *(foods)* devrait-on éviter ?

   _____

   _____

3. Mangez-vous souvent des plats sains et légers ? des produits bios ?

   _____

   _____

4. Est-ce que vous évitez le tabac et l'alcool ?

   _____

   _____

5. Que faites-vous pour contrôler le stress ? Faites-vous du yoga ou de la méditation ?

_____

_____

6. Est-ce que vous vous sentez souvent fatigué(e) ? Dormez-vous assez ?

_____

_____

C. Conversation.
Reread the conversation between Patricia and Gabrielle on page 318 of the textbook. Then, complete this conversation between two co-workers with the indicated words.

NICOLAS : Tu as l'air _____ **(1)**.
(tired)

LUCIEN : Oui, _____ **(2)** très bien. J'ai _____ **(3)**
(I don't feel)   *(without a doubt)*

mangé quelque chose que je digère mal.

NICOLAS : Tu as mangé _____ **(4)** à midi, non ? C'était peut-
(some shellfish)

être ça. _____ **(5)** qu' _____ **(6)**
(Don't forget)   *(one should avoid)*

les huîtres en cette saison.

LUCIEN : Je mange des huîtres toute l'année, mais tu as sûrement raison.

NICOLAS : Tu _____ **(7)** rentrer à la maison.
(would do better to)

D. Que feriez-vous ?
If you wanted to improve your health, would you do the following things ? Put the verbs in the conditional.

EXEMPLE   dormir toute la journée
Non, je ne dormirais pas toute la journée.

1. faire plus d'exercice : _____

2. éviter le stress : _____

3. boire beaucoup d'alcool : _____

4. aller à un club de gym : _____

5. choisir des plats sains : _____

6. prendre des vitamines : _____

7. se coucher plus tôt : _____

8. manger beaucoup de sucre : _____

E. Soyons polis! You are eating with friends at a restaurant. Rewrite the following questions in the conditional so that they sound more polite.

1. Voulez-vous une table à l'intérieur ou sur la terrasse?

   _____

2. Avez-vous une autre table? _____

3. Est-ce que nous pouvons voir le menu? _____

4. Veux-tu manger des escargots? _____

5. Quel vin est bon avec ce plat? _____

6. Peux-tu me passer le sel? _____

F. Résultats. Would one have the indicated results if one ate or drank a lot of the illustrated items? Use a **si** *(if)* clause with the imperfect followed by a result clause in the conditional, as in the example.

EXEMPLE   Si on mangeait beaucoup de frites, on ne maigrirait pas.

Exemple

manger... / maigrir

1

manger... / maigrir

2

manger... / éviter les matières grasses

3

boire... / rester en bonne santé

4

manger... / grossir

5

boire... / devenir plus fort

1. _____

   _____

2. _____

   _____

3. _____

   _____

4. _____

   _____

5. _____

   _____

G. Dans ces conditions. What would these people do in the following circumstances? Complete each sentence with the logical ending from the list, putting the verb in the conditional.

ne pas prendre beaucoup de dessert   boire de l'eau

mettre un chandail   manger quelque chose

ne pas se marier   faire la sieste *(to take a nap)*

    EXEMPLE   Si nous avions faim, **nous mangerions quelque chose.**

1. Si les enfants avaient sommeil, ils _____.
2. Si nous avions soif, nous _____.
3. Si j'avais froid, je _____.
4. Si Rose voulait maigrir, elle _____.
5. Si Rosalie et André avaient peur du mariage, ils _____.

*H. Si... Say what you would do under the following circumstances. Complete each sentence with the indicated verb in the conditional.

    EXEMPLE   Si je sortais ce soir, **j'irais au cinéma** (aller).

1. Si je sortais ce soir pour un souper spécial, _____

_____ (aller).

2. Si j'invitais mon professeur de français chez moi pour souper, _____

_____ (préparer).

3. Si j'avais plus de temps libre, _____

_____ (aimer).

4. Si je ne faisais pas mes devoirs en ce moment, _____

_____ (pouvoir).

---

*Journal. How would your life be if things were perfect? Write at least six sentences saying what changes there would be and what would stay the same as now **(comme maintenant).**

Si ma vie était parfaite... _____

_____

_____

_____

_____

_____

_____

_____

_____

_____

Partie auditive

 A. Que veulent-ils faire? Listen to what changes these people are making in their lifestyle and fill in the missing words. Then indicate what each wants to do: lose weight **(maigrir),** gain weight **(grossir),** become stronger **(devenir plus fort[e]),** or improve his or her health **(améliorer sa santé).** You may choose more than one response in some cases. Pause the recording between items to allow enough time to respond.

1. Henri essaie d'éviter _____, _____

   et _____.

   Il voudrait: maigrir ____ / grossir ____ / devenir plus fort ____ / améliorer sa santé ____.

2. Yannick fait _____ et prend

   _____.

   Il voudrait: maigrir ____ / grossir ____ / devenir plus fort ____ / améliorer sa santé ____.

3. Rosalie mange moins de _____ et plus de plats

   _____ et _____.

   Elle voudrait: maigrir ____ / grossir ____ / devenir plus forte ____ / améliorer sa santé ____.

4. Rose _____, _____

   et _____ tous les jours.

   Elle voudrait: maigrir ____ / grossir ____ / devenir plus forte ____ / améliorer sa santé ____.

5. André fait _____ tous les jours.

   Il voudrait: maigrir ____ / grossir ____ / devenir plus fort ____ / améliorer sa santé ____.

 B. Prononciation: La consonne *r* et le conditionnel. Pause the recording and review the *Prononciation* section on page 321 of the textbook. Look at these sentences and decide whether people who want to improve their health would do these things. If they would, leave the sentence as it is. If they would not, place **ne... pas** in the blanks. Then turn on the recording and check your answers by repeating the statements after the speaker. Pay particular attention to the pronunciation of the endings of the verbs in the conditional.

Moi, je (j') _____ éviterais _____ le tabac.

Toi, tu _____ prendrais _____ de(s) repas copieux tous les jours.

Nous _____ irions _____ plus souvent au club de gym.

Vous _____ feriez _____ plus souvent de l'exercice.

Mes amis _____ mangeraient _____ beaucoup de matières grasses.

C. Résolutions. André has decided to improve his health. Here is what he told Rosalie he would do. Listen to each phrase and fill in the missing verb in the conditional.

J'ai dit à Rosalie…

1. que je _____ plus de fruits et de légumes.

2. que je _____ des plats plus sains.

3. que mes repas _____ moins copieux.

4. que nous _____ plus souvent au club de gym.

5. qu'on _____ de l'exercice ensemble tous les jours.

D. Rosalie et Rose préparent le repas. Listen as Rosalie (**mamie**) and Rose discuss the dinner they are preparing. Then pause the recording and complete these sentences according to what they say.

1. Pour prendre beaucoup de vitamines, on peut manger _____.

2. Comme exercice, Rosalie fait des promenades et Rose _____

   _____.

3. Rosalie voudrait diminuer *(to cut back)* _____.

4. Rose mange trop de _____.

E. Conseils. You are giving advice to a friend. Complete each sentence you hear with the logical ending. Then, as you hear the answer, identify the correct ending.

EXEMPLE   VOUS VOYEZ :   tu dormirais mieux ____ / tu dormirais moins ____

VOUS ENTENDEZ :   Si tu buvais moins de café…

VOUS DITES :   **Si tu buvais moins de café, tu dormirais mieux.**

VOUS ENTENDEZ :   Si tu buvais moins de café, tu dormirais mieux.

VOUS INDIQUEZ :   tu dormirais mieux ✓ / tu dormirais moins ____

1. tu te sentirais plus fatigué ____   tu te sentirais moins fatigué ____

2. tu maigrirais ____   tu grossirais ____

3. tu serais en mauvaise forme ____   tu serais plus fort ____

4. tu éviterais l'alcool ____   tu éviterais le tabac ____

5. tu te sentirais moins nerveux ____   tu te sentirais plus nerveux ____

6. tu oublierais mes conseils ____   tu écouterais mes conseils ____

***F. Et vous ?** Answer the questions *with complete sentences.*

1. _____

2. _____

3. _____

4. _____

5. _____

6. _____

En vacances

Chapitre 9

Talking about vacation

By the time you finish this *Compétence,* you should be able to talk about future vacation plans.

Partie écrite

A. Où aiment-ils passer leurs vacances? Say where the indicated people like to spend their vacation and what they like to do there. Complete the sentences with the name of a place from the first box and the most logical pair of activities from the second box.

à la maison
sur une île tropicale
à la montagne
dans une grande ville
dans un autre pays

se reposer et travailler dans le jardin
courir le long des plages et nager
visiter des sites historiques et goûter la cuisine locale
faire du ski et admirer les paysages
aller au théâtre et profiter des activités culturelles

EXEMPLE   Mes parents aiment passer leurs vacances **à la maison.**
Ils aiment **se reposer et travailler dans le jardin.**

1. Maryse aime passer ses vacances _____.
   Elle aime _____.

2. Éric et Thomas aiment passer leurs vacances _____.
   Ils aiment _____.

3. Mon frère aime passer ses vacances _____.
   Il aime _____.

4. Mes cousins aiment passer leurs vacances _____.
   Ils aiment _____.

B. Conversation. Reread the conversation between Luc and Alain on page 338 of the textbook. Then, complete this conversation between two friends.

AHMAD : Je vais bientôt _____ **(1).**
(leave on vacation)

KARIMA : Et tu vas où ?

AHMAD : _____ **(2)** aller _____ **(3).**
(I'm planning on / I'm counting on)   *(to the mountains)*

KARIMA : _____ **(4)** !
(What luck)

AHMAD : Et toi, qu'est-ce que tu vas faire ?

KARIMA : Je vais passer 10 jours près de _____ **(5).** J'aime
(the sea)

_____ **(6)** le long des plages et _____ **(7)**
(to run)   *(taste)*

les spécialités de la région.

AHMAD : Super ! _____ **(8).**
(I hope you'll like it)

C. Voyage avec nous ! Some friends are going to the Antilles on vacation. They are trying to convince another friend to go with them and are telling him all the things he will see and do if he goes, as well as what their travel plans are. Complete what they say by putting the indicated verbs into the *future* tense.

Si tu viens en vacances avec nous, tu _____ **(1)** (voir) des choses

magnifiques. En Guadeloupe, on _____ **(2)** (rencontrer) beaucoup de

gens intéressants et on _____ **(3)** (goûter) la cuisine créole. Le paysage

_____ **(4)** (être) beau aussi. On _____ **(5)**

(aller) au parc national et on _____ **(6)** (faire) du bateau dans l'eau

claire de la mer des Antilles. On _____ **(7)** (s'amuser) bien et tu

_____ **(8)** (aimer) beaucoup la Guadeloupe. Après notre séjour

(stay) en Guadeloupe, nous _____ **(9)** (aller) en Martinique.

Nous _____ **(10)** (arriver) en Martinique le 15 août. Nous

_____ **(11)** (être) à l'hôtel Bakoua jusqu'au 20 août, le jour où nous

_____ **(12)** (partir). Les enfants et Martine _____ **(13)**

(rentrer) de Guadeloupe le 25 août, mais moi, je _____ **(14)** (faire) un voyage à

Saint-Martin et à la Désirade. J' _____ **(15)** (aller) d'abord à Saint-Martin ; ensuite

je _____ **(16)** (passer) deux jours à la Désirade.

D. Dans ce cas... Review the use of the present and future tenses with clauses with **si** and **quand** on page 340 of the textbook. Then complete the following sentences in which Luc talks about his plans with Micheline for tomorrow with the correct form of the verb in parentheses.

Si Micheline n'a pas trop de travail à faire demain, nous _____ (1) (passer) la soirée ensemble. Quand elle _____ (2) (finir) son travail, elle viendra tout de suite chez moi. Si j' _____ (3) (avoir) le temps demain, je préparerai un bon petit souper. Quand elle arrivera chez moi, je _____ (4) (servir) le souper. Après, s'il fait beau, nous _____ (5) (faire) une promenade. S'il _____ (6) (faire) mauvais, nous irons au cinéma. Quand elle _____ (7) (devoir) rentrer, je la raccompagnerai chez elle.

E. Pour mieux lire: *Recognizing compound tenses.* Reread the explanation on recognizing compound tenses on page 342 of the textbook. Then translate into English the italicized parts of these sentences based on Luc's vacation.

1. Le 11 août, j'*aurai presque fini* mes vacances, mais je *ne serai pas encore rentré* au Canada.

   On August 11, I _____ *my vacation, but*

   I _____ *to Canada.*

2. J'*aurai passé* trois semaines en Guadeloupe et j'*aurai vu* des choses intéressantes.

   I _____ *three weeks in Guadeloupe and I*

   _____ *some interesting things.*

3. Si je *n'avais pas rencontré* Micheline, mes vacances *auraient été* moins intéressantes.

   If I _____ *Micheline, my vacation*

   _____ *less interesting.*

4. Si je *n'avais pas fait* une bêtise au parc national, nous *n'aurions jamais commencé* à parler.

   If I _____ *a silly thing at the national*

   park, we _____ *to talk.*

F. Quelle aventure! Now reread Luc's message to Alain on page 343 of the textbook and answer these questions *in a few words in French.*

1. Qui est-ce que Luc a rencontré au parc national? Comment est-ce qu'il la trouve?

   _____

2. Pourquoi est-ce que Luc a pensé que le volcan allait exploser?

   _____

3. Qu'est-ce que Micheline a dit pour calmer les touristes?

   _____

4. Comment était la vue du sommet?

   _____

5. Pourquoi est-ce que Luc dit: «Tout est bien qui finit bien»?

   _____

*G. Des vacances virtuelles. Will computers and virtual reality give us new vacation options in the future (**à l'avenir**)? Complete the questions with the given verbs in the future tense. Then, answer the questions.

1. À l'avenir, est-ce qu'on _____ (pouvoir) faire des voyages virtuels sans

   quitter la maison? Est-ce que la réalité virtuelle _____ (être) aussi

   réelle *(real)* que la réalité un jour?

   _____

   _____

   _____

2. Est-ce qu'il y _____ (avoir) des choses qu'on ne pourra jamais faire en

   réalité virtuelle, par exemple goûter la cuisine, ou est-ce qu'on _____

   (pouvoir) tout faire en réalité virtuelle un jour?

   _____

   _____

3. Si un jour on peut voyager dans le temps, _____-vous (faire) des

   voyages dans le temps?

   _____

4. Si un jour il y a un parc jurassique, est-ce que vous le _____ (visiter)?

   _____

5. Est-ce qu'on _____ (visiter) d'autres planètes à l'avenir?

   _____-vous (faire) un voyage sur une autre planète un jour?

   _____

   _____

6. Est-ce qu'on _____ (avoir) plus de vacances à l'avenir parce que

   les nouvelles technologies _____ (faire) tout le travail ou est-ce qu'on

   _____ (devoir) travailler plus que maintenant?

   _____

   _____

Partie auditive

 A. Que faire? Listen to what several people like to do on vacation. Label each picture with the name of the person who likes the illustrated activity.

| Pierre | Alain | Antoinette | Anne | Daniel | Vincent |

a. _____

b. _____

c. _____

d. _____

e. _____

f. _____

Now replay the recording and listen again. This time, indicate where, according to the activities mentioned, the person named should spend his or her vacation.

1. ___ dans une grande ville / ___ à la mer

2. ___ dans un pays étranger / ___ à la montagne

3. ___ sur une île tropicale / ___ dans une grande ville

4. ___ à la montagne / ___ dans un pays exotique

5. ___ à la campagne / ___ dans une grande ville

6. ___ dans une grande ville / ___ à la mer

 B. Prononciation: Le futur. Practise saying verbs in the future tense by repeating these sentences after the speaker.

Je ferai un voyage en Guadeloupe cet été.

Tu viendras me chercher à l'aéroport.

Le voyage sera assez long.

Nous passerons beaucoup de temps sur la plage.

Ton amie Micheline et toi, vous visiterez la région avec moi.

Les gens seront très sympas.

C. Elle est dynamique! Micheline is very active and prefers physical activities when she travels. You will hear two activities named. Complete the sentences to say which one she will do, *using the future tense.* Pause the recording as needed. You will then hear the correct answer. Verify your response and repeat.

> **EXEMPLE**   VOUS ENTENDEZ: rester à l'hôtel / faire une randonnée
> VOUS ÉCRIVEZ: Elle **fera une randonnée.**
> VOUS ENTENDEZ: Elle fera une randonnée.
> VOUS RÉPÉTEZ: **Elle fera une randonnée.**

1. Elle _____.

2. Elle _____.

3. Elle _____.

4. Elle _____.

5. Elle _____.

6. Elle _____.

D. Les vacances de Luc. Listen as Luc talks to a friend about how his vacation will be. The first time, just listen to the conversation at regular speed. You will then hear it again with pauses for you to fill in the missing words.

_____ **(1)** pour la Guadeloupe le 20 juillet. Le voyage

_____ **(2)** plutôt long et _____ **(3)** trois semaines

là-bas. _____ **(4)** le 12 août. _____ **(5)** dans

un hôtel près de la plage. _____ **(6)** plein de choses: _____ **(7)**

à la plage, _____ **(8)** tous les sites et _____ **(9)**

la cuisine locale. Et toi? Où _____ **(10)** tes vacances?

_____ **(11)** un voyage?

*E. Et vous? A friend is asking you about your vacation travel plans this year. Answer your friend's questions *in the future tense,* explaining what you will do. If you do not have vacation plans yet, use your imagination.

1. _____

2. _____

3. _____

4. _____

5. _____

6. _____

7. _____

8. _____

COMPÉTENCE 2

Preparing for a trip

By the time you finish this **Compétence,** you should be able to describe preparations for a trip and say with whom you stay in communication.

Partie écrite

A. Préparatifs. A friend will soon leave on a trip. What will he do? Rewrite each pair of activities *in the future tense* and place them in the logical order in which he will do them.

> **EXEMPLE**   partir en voyage / demander à sa voisine de garder son chien
> **Il demandera à sa voisine de garder son chien. Il partira en voyage.**

1. dire à sa famille où il ira / décider où aller

   _____

2. choisir un vol *(flight)* / acheter son billet électronique

   _____

3. réserver une chambre / s'informer sur les hôtels

   _____

4. lire un guide touristique / faire un itinéraire *(to plan an itinerary)*

   _____

5. faire sa valise / partir pour l'aéroport

   _____

6. prendre un taxi pour aller à son hôtel / quitter l'aéroport

   _____

B. Conversation. Reread the conversation between Catherine and Alain on page 345 of the textbook. Then, complete this paragraph from an e-mail from Alain to Luc.

_____ **(1)** ton courriel et devine quoi *(guess what)*! On a décidé de venir
      (I received)

te rejoindre en Guadeloupe. Nous aussi, nous voudrions _____
                                            (to see the tropical scenery)

_____ **(2)** et _____ **(3)** du beau _____ **(4).**
     (to take advantage)   *(weather)*

Catherine adore les fruits de mer et l'idée de _____ **(5)** la cuisine antillaise
                                   (to taste)

_____ **(6).** Moi, je voudrais faire la connaissance de la
   (pleases him / is appealing to him [use **plaire**]*)*

Guadeloupéenne que _____ **(7)** là-bas.
              (you met)

C. *Dire, lire et écrire.* Some friends are talking about people they know that say, read, and write certain things. Complete their statements with the correct form of the verbs in parentheses and the translation of the other indicated words.

1. Dans ma famille, nous _____ (lire) beaucoup. Moi, je _____ (lire) souvent des _____ *(stories)* d'aventure et ma sœur _____ (lire) souvent des _____ *(novels)* d'amour et des _____ *(poems)*.

2. Mes parents _____ (lire) des articles dans le _____ *(newspaper)* et des _____ *(magazines)*.

3. Vous _____ (lire) beaucoup dans votre famille? Et toi? Qu'est-ce que tu _____ (lire) le plus souvent? Qu'est-ce que tu _____ (lire: passé composé) récemment?

4. En cours de français, nous _____ (écrire) des _____ *(compositions)* quelquefois et en fait *(in fact)*, nous en _____ (écrire: passé composé) une hier.

5. Moi, j'_____ (écrire) mieux en anglais qu'en français. Et toi? Est-ce que tu _____ (écrire) bien en français?

6. Les étudiants dans mon cours _____ (s'écrire) des messages sur Facebook quelquefois. Tes camarades de classe et toi, est-ce que vous _____ (s'écrire) des messages ou des commentaires sur Facebook quelquefois?

7. Quand j'arrive en cours de français, je _____ (dire) bonjour et quand le prof arrive en cours, il _____ (dire) bonjour aussi. Nous _____ (dire) tous bonjour au prof, bien sûr. Est-ce que tu _____ (dire) bonjour quand tu arrives en cours?

8. À la fin *(end)* du cours, les étudiants _____ (se dire) au revoir. Tes camarades de classe et toi, est-ce que vous _____ (se dire) au revoir à la fin du cours? Qu'est-ce que tu _____ (dire: passé composé) quand tu as quitté le cours aujourd'hui?

D. Le voyage de Luc. Restate what Luc does, using the verb in the initial sentence and a direct object pronoun **(le, la, l', les)** to replace the italicized noun. Then indicate whether he does the activity **a. avant le voyage, b. à son arrivée** *(arrival),* or **c. à son retour** *(return)* in the blank after your response.

   EXEMPLE Luc fait *sa valise.* Luc **la fait.** **a.**

1. Il réserve *sa chambre d'hôtel.* Il _____. _____

2. Il achète *son billet* sur Internet. Il _____ sur Internet. _____

3. Il montre *son passeport.* Il _____. _____

4. Il montre *ses photos* à sa famille. Il _____ à sa famille. _____

Now continue with the following sentences, using an indirect object pronoun (**lui, leur**) to replace the italicized noun.

>   **EXEMPLE**   Luc écrit une carte postale *à ses amis.* Luc **leur écrit** une carte postale.   **b.**

1. Il dit *à ses parents* où il va. Il _____ où il va.   _____

2. Il demande *à son voisin* de garder son chien. Il _____
   _____ de garder son chien.   _____

3. Il téléphone *à ses parents* de Guadeloupe. Il _____
   de Guadeloupe.   _____

4. Il téléphone *à sa sœur* pour dire qu'il est rentré. Il _____
   pour dire qu'il est rentré.   _____

E. Votre temps libre.
Say whether you often do or do not often do these things during your free time. Use a direct or an indirect object pronoun to replace each italicized noun.

>   **EXEMPLE**   inviter *vos amis* à la maison
>   **Je les invite souvent à la maison. / Je ne les invite pas souvent à la maison.**

1. regarder *la télé* _____

2. faire *vos devoirs* devant la télé _____

3. téléphoner *à votre meilleur(e) ami(e)* _____

4. rendre visite *à vos amis* _____

5. écouter *votre iPod* _____

Review the position of the object pronouns on page 348 in the textbook and say whether or not you are going to do the things listed above later today. Use the *future proche.*

>   **EXEMPLE**   inviter vos amis à la maison
>   **Je vais les inviter à la maison. / Je ne vais pas les inviter à la maison.**

1. _____
2. _____
3. _____
4. _____
5. _____

Now review the position of the object pronouns and the agreement of the past participle in the **passé composé** on page 348 in the textbook. Say whether or not you did the things listed above last night.

>   **EXEMPLE**   inviter *vos amis* à la maison
>   **Je les ai invités à la maison. / Je ne les ai pas invités à la maison.**

1. _____
2. _____
3. _____
4. _____
5. _____

*F. Et toi? Answer a friend's questions about your travel habits, replacing each italicized phrase with a direct or indirect object pronoun.

1. Est-ce que tu prépares *tes voyages* bien à l'avance? Fais-tu *ta valise* à l'avance ou au dernier moment? Dis-tu *à tes parents* où tu vas généralement quand tu pars en vacances? Demandes-tu *à ton voisin* de garder tes animaux?

   _____

   _____

   _____

   _____

2. Est-ce que tu achètes *ton billet* sur Internet ou dans une agence de voyages? Où est-ce que tu as acheté *ton billet* la dernière fois que tu as voyagé?

   _____

   _____

3. Est-ce que tu préfères réserver *ta chambre* en ligne ou par téléphone? La dernière fois que tu es descendu(e) à l'hôtel, comment as-tu trouvé *ta chambre*? Est-ce que tu avais réservé *cette chambre* à l'avance?

   _____

   _____

   _____

---

*Journal. Describe someone with whom you stay in touch. Using indirect object pronouns, tell how often you telephone or visit him/her, write him/her e-mails, and send him/her text messages. Also say what you talk to him/her about **(parler de)** and what you ask him/her to do **(demander de faire)**.

Je suis souvent en contact avec...

_____

_____

_____

_____

_____

_____

_____

_____

_____

_____

Partie auditive

A. Avant le départ ou à l'arrivée? A Canadian tourist is preparing for a trip to France. Decide whether each sentence you hear describes something she does **avant son départ** or **à son arrivée** at the airport in Paris. Indicate the correct choice.

1. ____ avant son départ   ____ à son arrivée
2. ____ avant son départ   ____ à son arrivée
3. ____ avant son départ   ____ à son arrivée
4. ____ avant son départ   ____ à son arrivée
5. ____ avant son départ   ____ à son arrivée

Now play this section again. Indicate which of the options would be the most logical thing for the tourist to do next. Repeat this section as needed, pausing the recording between items to allow enough time to respond.

1. Maintenant, elle devrait…   ____ **a.** montrer son passeport et passer la douane.

                                     ____ **b.** faire un itinéraire *(make an itinerary)*.

2. Maintenant, elle devrait…   ____ **a.** réserver son billet.

                                     ____ **b.** montrer son passeport et passer la douane.

3. Maintenant, elle devrait…   ____ **a.** faire ses valises.

                                     ____ **b.** montrer son passeport.

4. Maintenant, elle devrait…   ____ **a.** faire sa valise.

                                     ____ **b.** acheter des devises étrangères.

5. Maintenant, elle devrait…   ____ **a.** acheter un plan *(map)* de la ville.

                                     ____ **b.** acheter des devises étrangères.

B. Prononciation: Les verbes *dire, lire* et *écrire*. You will hear someone talk about the reading and writing habits of his family. Just listen the first time as the passage is read at normal speed. It will then be repeated slowly with pauses for you to fill in the missing words.

Dans ma famille, nous _____ **(1)** beaucoup. Quand j'étais petit, je ne

_____ **(2)** pas beaucoup, mais maintenant je _____ **(3)** assez

souvent. Hier soir, j'_____ **(4)** un magazine et j'en _____

(5) sans doute un autre ce soir. Mes parents _____ **(6)** souvent des romans. Ma sœur

préfère _____ **(7)** des poèmes. Tous ses amis _____ **(8)**

qu'elle _____ **(9)** bien. Moi, je ne _____ **(10)** rien parce

que je _____ **(11)** ses poèmes et je n'_____ **(12)**

que *(only)* des courriels.

C. Qu'est-ce que Luc fait? Luc is answering a friend's questions about how he generally prepares for a trip. Listen to the questions. After each one, pause the recording and complete Luc's answer with the verb and a direct object pronoun (**le, la, l', les**). Then, turn on the recording and listen and repeat as you hear the correct answer.

EXEMPLE	VOUS ENTENDEZ:	D'habitude, tu achètes *ton billet* bien à l'avance?
	VOUS ÉCRIVEZ:	Oui, je **l'achète** bien à l'avance.
	VOUS ENTENDEZ:	Oui, je l'achète bien à l'avance.
	VOUS RÉPÉTEZ:	**Oui, je l'achète bien à l'avance.**

1. Non, je _____ rarement sur Internet.

2. Oui, bien sûr, je _____ avant de partir en voyage.

3. Non, je ne _____ pas souvent à voyager avec moi.

4. Non, je ne _____ pas au dernier moment.

5. Oui, je _____ à mes parents.

Now Luc is answering questions about his communication with others during his trip. After each one, pause the recording and complete Luc's answer with the verb and an indirect object pronoun (**lui, leur**). Then, turn on the recording and listen and repeat as you hear the correct answer.

1. Oui, je _____ souvent des courriels.

2. Oui, je _____ tous les jours.

3. Oui, je _____ souvent qu'elle est belle.

4. Non, je _____ ne pas souvent de cartes postales.

5. Oui, je _____ de ma vie au Canada.

*D. Et vous? Answer the questions you hear about your vacations and preparations. Use *the appropriate direct or indirect object pronoun* in your responses. Pause the recording between items to allow enough time to respond.

1. _____

2. _____

3. _____

4. _____

5. _____

COMPÉTENCE 3

Buying your ticket

By the time you finish this *Compétence,* you should be able to make arrangements for a trip.

Partie écrite

A. Pour voyager. Complete each of these sentences with the logical expression from the box.

d'embarquement	d'arrivée	crédit
devises étrangères	bancaire	un passeport
un billet d'avion	le numéro de votre vol	
départ	les transports en commun	

1. Pour faire preuve de *(to prove)* votre identité et de votre nationalité, il vous faut

   _____.

2. Pour monter dans l'avion, on a besoin d' _____ et d'une carte

   d'embarquement *(boarding pass).*

3. À l'aéroport quand on va prendre l'avion, il faut aller à la porte _____.

   On descend de l'avion à la porte _____.

4. Pour savoir à quelle heure votre vol partira, il faut savoir _____

   _____ et vérifier l'heure de _____

5. On peut aller à la banque pour acheter des _____.

6. On peut payer ses achats *(purchases)* par carte de _____ ou par carte

   _____.

7. Pour visiter la région, on peut louer une voiture ou on peut utiliser _____

   _____.

*B. Achetez votre billet. Reread the conversation between Luc and the travel agent on page 350 of the textbook. Then, imagine that you are leaving on a trip. Complete this conversation to buy a round-trip plane ticket from Montreal to the city of your choice.

Vous: Bonjour, monsieur. Je voudrais acheter un billet pour aller de Montréal à

_____, s'il vous plaît.

L'agent de voyages: Très bien, monsieur/madame. Vous voulez un billet aller-retour ou un aller simple?

Vous: _____.

L'agent de voyages: À quelle date est-ce que vous voulez partir?

Vous: _____.

L'AGENT DE VOYAGES : Quand est-ce que vous voudriez rentrer ?

VOUS : _____.

L'AGENT DE VOYAGES : Vous voulez un billet de première classe, de classe Tango, Flex ou affaires ?

VOUS : _____.

L'AGENT DE VOYAGES : Très bien. Voilà des vols possibles. Ça vous convient ?

VOUS : Oui, c'est parfait. Combien coûte le billet ?

L'AGENT DE VOYAGES : C'est _____ dollars.

VOUS : Bon. Alors, faites ma réservation. Voici ma carte de crédit.

Now explain what you will do during this trip by creating sentences *in the future* with the following verbs.

EXEMPLE   aller à *[what city]* : **J'irai à…**

1. aller à *[what city]* : _____

2. voyager *[with whom]* : _____

3. partir *[when]* : _____

4. être en *[what class]* : _____

5. prendre *[what meals]* pendant le vol : _____

6. arriver à *[what time]* : _____

7. descendre/rester *[where]* : _____

8. rester *[how long]* : _____

9. rentrer *[when]* : _____

C. Luc est prêt. Luc is talking to Alain about his trip. Fill in the blanks with the correct form of the verb **savoir** *in the present tense.*

ALAIN : Tu _____ **(1)** quand tu vas partir ?

LUC : Oui, je _____ **(2)** la date et l'heure exacte de mon départ. J'ai téléphoné à ma

sœur. Elle _____ **(3)** quand elle doit m'amener *(to take me)* à l'aéroport.

ALAIN : Vous _____ **(4)** de quel aéroport tu pars ?

LUC : Bien sûr et nous _____ **(5)** aussi qu'il faut arriver à l'aéroport

bien à l'avance. Ne t'inquiète pas !

ALAIN : Oui, mais les compagnies aériennes _____ **(6)** bien que tous les

touristes ne vont pas arriver à l'avance !

Now fill in the blanks in these sentences with the correct form of the verb **connaître** *in the present tense.*

1. J'ai demandé à ma sœur de m'amener à l'aéroport parce qu'elle _____ bien la

route. Mes parents la _____ moins bien.

2. J'ai lu plusieurs guides et je _____ assez bien l'histoire et la culture de la

Guadeloupe. Et toi, tu _____ la Guadeloupe ?

3. Non, mais ma famille et moi, nous _____ d'autres îles des Caraïbes.

Ta famille et toi, quelles îles _____-vous ?

D. *Connaître* ou *savoir*? Luc's neighbour has just moved in, but he knows a lot about the neighbourhood already. Fill in the blanks with **il sait** or **il connaît**.

1. _____ bien le quartier et _____ les meilleures routes

   pour aller au centre-ville.

2. _____ où il y a un bon restaurant et _____

   ce qu'ils servent chaque jour, mais _____ aussi faire la cuisine.

3. _____ tous ses voisins. _____ que certains de ses voisins

   sont américains, mais ce n'est pas un problème parce qu' _____ le français.

4. _____ le numéro de téléphone de Luc et _____ à

   quelle heure Luc est chez lui d'habitude.

5. _____ bien les parcs du quartier et _____ si les chiens

   sont permis *(permitted)* dans ces parcs.

E. Quel verbe? Luc has problems the day of his departure. Complete the following passage with the correct forms of **savoir** or **connaître** *in the present tense.*

Luc a quelques problèmes le jour de son départ pour la Guadeloupe. D'abord, il ne

_____ **(1)** pas où il a laissé son billet et son passeport, mais son père

_____ **(2)** très bien son fils et les trouve tout de suite. Au dernier moment,

sa sœur ne peut pas l'amener *(take him)* à l'aéroport et il doit prendre un taxi. Le chauffeur de taxi ne

_____ **(3)** pas bien le quartier de Luc et il se perd et arrive en retard *(late)*.

Ils ne _____ **(4)** pas si Luc va arriver à l'aéroport à temps pour prendre

son avion. Arrivé à l'aéroport, Luc ne _____ **(5)** pas où aller parce qu'il

ne _____ **(6)** pas l'aérogare *(terminal)*. Un employé de l'aéroport, qui

_____ **(7)** très bien les touristes, _____ **(8)** ce qu'il faut

faire pour l'aider et Luc arrive à la porte d'embarquement juste à temps pour prendre son avion.

F. Entre amis. Using the pronoun **me,** answer the questions about your relationship with your best friend.

> **EXEMPLE** Il/Elle t'accompagne quelquefois en vacances?
> **Oui, il/elle m'accompagne quelquefois en vacances.**
> **Non, il/elle ne m'accompagne jamais en vacances.**

1. Il/Elle te rend souvent visite? _____

2. Il/Elle t'invite souvent à sortir?_____

3. Il/Elle va te rendre visite ce soir? _____

4. Il/Elle va t'aider à faire tes devoirs? _____

5. Il/Elle t'a téléphoné récemment? _____

6. Quand est-ce qu'il/elle t'a vu(e) récemment? _____

G. En cours. Using the pronoun **nous,** answer these questions about the interactions your French professor has with you and the other students.

> **EXEMPLE**   Votre professeur vous pose beaucoup de questions en cours?
> **Oui, il/elle nous pose beaucoup de questions.**
> **Non, il/elle ne nous pose pas beaucoup de questions.**

1. Est-ce qu'il/elle vous donne des devoirs tous les jours?

    _____

2. Il/Elle vous rend vos examens au début *(beginning)* ou à la fin *(end)* du cours?

    _____

3. Quand vous posez des questions à votre professeur(e) en anglais, est-ce qu'il/elle vous répond en anglais ou en français?

    _____

4. Il/Elle vous explique *(explains)* le cours en anglais ou en français la plupart du temps?

    _____

*H. Beaucoup de questions! The classmate who sits next to you is asking you these questions. Answer them using the indirect object pronouns **me, te, nous, vous, lui,** and **leur.**

1. Quand tes parents partent en vacances, est-ce qu'ils *te* disent où ils vont?

    _____

2. Et toi? Quand tu pars en vacances, est-ce que tu dis *à tes parents* où tu vas?

    _____

3. Est-ce que tu écris des cartes postales *à ton meilleur ami (ta meilleure amie)?*

    _____

4. Est-ce que ton meilleur ami (ta meilleure amie) écrit des cartes postales *à tes autres amis et à toi* quand il/elle voyage?

    _____

5. La prochaine fois que tu partiras en vacances, est-ce que tu *m'*écriras? Est-ce que tu *m'*achèteras un cadeau *(gift)?*

    _____

    _____

Nom _____ Date _____

Partie auditive

 A. Il faut... You will hear lists of what one needs to have and to know to travel abroad. Fill in the missing words. Pause the recording as needed.

1. Il faut avoir un billet, une carte _____, une carte

   _____, des _____

   et _____.

2. Il faut savoir le numéro du _____, l'heure

   _____, l'heure _____,

   la porte _____

   et la porte _____.

3. Il faut connaître _____ et

   _____ de la région,

   _____ et leur culture et

   _____ en commun.

 B. Luc organise son voyage. Listen as Luc makes some inquiries and arrangements for his trip. Pause the recording and indicate whether these statements are true or false by selecting **vrai** or **faux.**

Luc téléphone à l'agence de voyages.

1. Il y a encore de la place sur le vol du 21 juillet.   _____ VRAI _____ FAUX

2. Luc veut rester huit jours en Guadeloupe.   _____ VRAI _____ FAUX

3. Luc va voyager en classe affaires.   _____ VRAI _____ FAUX

4. Luc décide de faire ses réservations.   _____ VRAI _____ FAUX

Now play this section again. Then pause the recording and complete these statements.

1. Le vol pour Pointe-à-Pitre part le _____ à ___ h ___.

2. Luc va quitter Pointe-à-Pitre le _____.

   Il arrivera à Montréal à ___ h ___.

3. Le billet aller-retour coûte _____ $.

C. Prononciation : Les verbes *savoir* et *connaître*. Pause the recording and complete each sentence with the appropriate form of either **savoir** or **connaître**. Then turn on the recording and verify your answers by repeating the sentences after the speaker.

1. Je _____ une femme qui travaille en Guadeloupe, mais je ne

   _____ pas dans quelle ville elle est allée.

2. Est-ce que tu _____ ? Tu _____

   où elle travaille ?

3. Elle ne te _____ pas, mais elle _____ qui tu es.

4. Nous _____ ce qu'il faut faire, mais nous ne

   _____ pas la région.

5. _____ -vous la région ? _____ -vous

   où on peut acheter un guide ?

6. Les gens d'ici _____ toute la région. Ils _____

   où tout se trouve *(is located)*.

D. Entre amis. Luc is asking Micheline about her friend Suzanne. After each question, pause the recording and complete Micheline's response. Then turn on the recording and listen and repeat as you hear the correct answer.

EXEMPLE   VOUS ENTENDEZ :   Elle te téléphone tous les jours ?

               VOUS COMPLÉTEZ :   Non, elle **ne me téléphone pas** tous les jours.

               VOUS ENTENDEZ :   Non, elle ne me téléphone pas tous les jours.

               VOUS RÉPÉTEZ :   **Non, elle ne me téléphone pas tous les jours.**

1. Oui, elle _____ assez souvent.

2. Oui, elle _____ souvent des courriels.

3. Non, elle _____ souvent de lettres.

4. Non, elle _____ toujours.

5. Non, elle _____ de choses méchantes.

***E. Et ton meilleur ami ?** Another friend is asking about what your best male friend does for you. Answer the questions *with complete sentences in French*.

EXEMPLE   Ton meilleur ami te comprend toujours ?

               Oui, il me comprend toujours. / Non, il ne me comprend pas toujours.

1. _____

2. _____

3. _____

4. _____

5. _____

COMPÉTENCE 4

Deciding where to go on a trip

By the time you finish this **Compétence,** you should be able to talk about where you went on vacation in the past and where you plan to go in the future.

Partie écrite

*A. Quels pays aimeriez-vous visiter? Say which two countries, from the list of countries on page 356 of the textbook, you would most like to visit for each continent.

En Afrique, j'aimerais visiter _____ **(1)** et

_____ **(2).** En Asie, je voudrais visiter _____ **(3)**

et _____ **(4).** En Amérique du Nord ou en Amérique centrale, j'ai envie de

visiter _____ **(5)** et _____ **(6).** En Amérique

du Sud, j'aimerais le mieux visiter _____ **(7)** et

_____ **(8).** En Océanie, je préférerais visiter

_____ **(9)** et _____ **(10).** En Europe,

je voudrais visiter _____ **(11)** et _____ **(12).**

B. Quels pays? Reread the conversation between Micheline and Luc on page 357 of the textbook. Then, complete this conversation as indicated.

ANNICK: _____ **(1)** as-tu visités?
(What foreign countries)

LIN: J'ai visité _____ **(2)** et _____ **(3).**
(Peru) *(Mexico)*

Et toi? Tu aimes voyager _____ **(4)**?
(in a foreign country / abroad)

ANNICK: Oui, beaucoup. L'année prochaine, _____ **(5)**
(I would like to visit)

l'Afrique. Je voudrais voir _____ **(6)**
(Egypt)

et _____ **(7).**
(Senegal)

C. Pays et continents.
Review the use of articles with geographical places on page 358 of the textbook. Then, fill in the blank before the name of each place with the appropriate article (**le, la, l', les**).

> **EXEMPLE**   En Océanie:
>
> _____l'_____ Australie, ____la____ Nouvelle-Calédonie, ____la____ Polynésie française

1. En Afrique:

   _____ Maroc, _____ Algérie, _____ Sénégal, _____ Côte d'Ivoire

2. En Asie et au Moyen-Orient:

   _____ Chine, _____ Japon, _____ Vietnam

3. En Amérique du Nord et en Amérique centrale:

   _____ Antilles, _____ Canada, _____ États-Unis, _____ Mexique

4. En Amérique du Sud:

   _____ Argentine, _____ Pérou, _____ Colombie, _____ Chili, _____ Brésil, _____ Guyane

5. En Europe:

   _____ Allemagne, _____ Belgique, _____ Espagne, _____ France,

   _____ Royaume-Uni, _____ Suisse

Now list the names of the preceding countries or regions where French is spoken or where there is an important francophone cultural influence. Refer to the map in the front of your textbook if necessary.

<u>la Nouvelle-Calédonie, la Polynésie française,</u> _____

_____

_____

D. Voyages et préférences.
Fill in the blank before each place with the appropriate article (**le, la, l', les**). *If no article is needed, leave it blank.*

1. J'aimerais visiter _____ France, surtout _____ Paris, _____ Lyon et _____ Côte d'Azur.

2. J'ai visité _____ Italie. J'ai beaucoup aimé _____ Rome.

3. En Asie, j'ai visité _____ Japon. J'aimerais voir _____ Chine aussi.

4. En Amérique, j'ai visité _____ États-Unis, _____ Canada et _____ Mexique. J'ai adoré _____ Montréal et _____ Californie.

E. Où?
Review the chart on page 358 of the textbook on how to say *to* or *in* with geographical places. Say in which country from the choices given the following cities are located.

> **EXEMPLE**   (Italie / France): Lyon est **en France.**

1. (Mexique / Argentine): Buenos Aires est _____.

2. (Chine / Vietnam): Bejing est _____.

3. (Côte d'Ivoire / Maroc): Casablanca est _____.

4. (Royaume-Uni / Allemagne): Berlin est _____.

5. (Australie / Nouvelle-Calédonie): Sydney est _____.

6. (Canada / États-Unis): Toronto est _____.

7. (Algérie / Sénégal): Dakar est _____.

F. Les voyages de Christian. Complete the paragraph with the appropriate preposition for each geographical place mentioned. The first one has been done as an example.

Christian habite **aux** États-Unis mais il a voyagé partout! L'année dernière, il est allé _____ (1) Mexique,

_____ (2) Antilles et _____ (3) France! Il a habité _____ (4) Canada où il est allé à l'Université de

Montréal. Ensuite, il a voyagé partout _____ (5) Europe et il a passé quelques semaines _____ (6) Paris où

il a visité beaucoup de monuments historiques et de musées. Ensuite, il est allé _____ (7) Royaume-Uni,

_____ (8) Allemagne et _____ (9) Espagne. Mais finalement, il n'avait plus d'argent et il a dû revenir

_____ (10) États-Unis.

G. Pays francophones. Look back at the places listed in *C. Pays et continents* on the preceding page and complete these statements to say which countries on each continent are considered part of the francophone world.

> **EXEMPLE**   En Océanie, on parle français **en Nouvelle-Calédonie** et **en Polynésie française.**

1. En Afrique du Nord, on parle arabe et français _____

   et _____.

2. En Afrique de l'Ouest *(West),* on parle français _____

   et _____.

3. En Asie, il y a une influence française _____.

4. En Amérique du Nord et en Amérique centrale, on parle français

   _____, et en Louisiane!

5. En Amérique du Sud, on parle français _____.

6. En Europe, on parle français, _____

   et _____.

*H. Où vont-ils aller? A friend is talking about where various people are going on vacation. Complete these sentences saying where they are going to go and what they will do there.

> **EXEMPLE**   Mes parents vont aller **en Espagne. Ils visiteront des sites historiques.**

Espagne

1. Mon meilleur ami va aller _____

   _____

France

2. Mes cousins vont aller _____

   _____

Égypte

Nom _____ Date _____

3. Mes amis et moi, nous allons aller _____

_____

Canada

4. Ma voisine va aller _____

_____

Antilles

*I. Préférences. Complete the following questions with the correct prepositions. Then answer each question.

1. Est-ce que vous habitez _____ États-Unis, _____ Canada ou dans un autre pays ?

_____

2. Aimeriez-vous mieux passer vos vacances _____ Californie ou _____ Colorado ?

_____

3. Préféreriez-vous faire un voyage _____ Montréal, _____ Paris ou _____ Abidjan ?

_____

4. Est-ce que vous aimeriez mieux passer vos vacances _____ Asie ou _____ Afrique ?

_____

5. Êtes-vous allé(e) _____ Europe ? Si oui, quels pays avez-vous visités ?

_____

_____

*Journal. Describe an interesting vacation you took, saying where you went, with whom, when, what you did there, whether you liked it (**Ça m'a plu. / Ça ne m'a pas plu.**) and why. Then name two places outside of your own country that you would like to visit and explain why.

_____

_____

_____

_____

_____

_____

_____

_____

_____

Partie auditive

 A. Où sont-ils ? List the name of each place you hear under the name of its continent.

1. **L'AFRIQUE**

_____

_____

2. **L'ASIE ET
    LE MOYEN-ORIENT**

_____

_____

3. **L'AMÉRIQUE DU NORD
    OU L'AMÉRIQUE CENTRALE**

_____

_____

4. **L'AMÉRIQUE DU SUD**

_____

_____

5. **L'OCÉANIE**

_____

_____

6. **L'EUROPE**

_____

_____

 B. Un tour du monde. You will hear a tourist describing his trip around the world. Number the places 1 to 8 on the map in the order that he goes to each one. The first one has been done as an example.

EXEMPLE VOUS ENTENDEZ : Je suis parti de Paris le 25 mai. D'abord, j'ai pris le train pour la Belgique où j'ai passé deux jours à Bruxelles...

VOUS MARQUEZ :

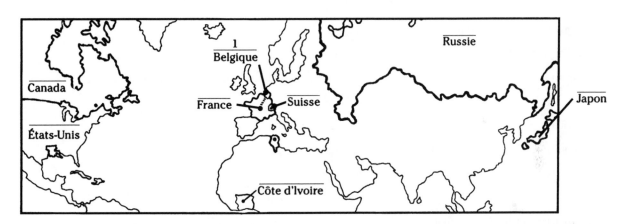

Now pause the recording and complete these sentences with the name of the appropriate country preceded by the correct preposition.

EXEMPLE   Le 25 mai, il a pris le train de Paris à Bruxelles, *en Belgique*

1. Le 28 mai, il a pris l'avion de Bruxelles à Montréal, _____.

2. Après, il a visité la Louisiane, _____.

3. Ensuite, il est allé à Tokyo, _____.

4. Après un séjour *(stay)* en Russie, il a pris le train pour Genève, _____.

5. Avant son retour à Paris, il a visité Abidjan, _____.

🔘 **C. Visitons le monde francophone !** A friend suggests various places to visit. Suggest that you go to the *francophone* place by completing the statements that follow with the correct preposition and the logical place. After a pause, you will hear the correct answer.

EXEMPLE	VOUS ENTENDEZ :	On visite l'Égypte ou le Maroc ?
	VOUS COMPLÉTEZ :	Allons **au Maroc** !
	VOUS ENTENDEZ :	Allons au Maroc !
	VOUS RÉPÉTEZ :	**Allons au Maroc** !

1. Allons _____!   4. Allons _____!

2. Allons _____!   5. Allons _____!

3. Allons _____!

🔘 **D. Qu'est-ce qu'ils deviendront ?** What will become of the various characters you have met in the different chapters of *Horizons*? Listen to what will happen to them and fill in the missing words.

1. **Chapitres 1 et 2 :** Emma _____ à Montréal, au Québec, où elle

   _____ professeure d'anglais à l'Université de Montréal.

   Félix et elle _____.

2. **Chapitres 3 et 4 :** Philippe _____ ses études à

   l'Université d'Ottawa, _____ Ontario. Ensuite, il _____ à

   Paris où il _____ pour une grande société internationale.

3. **Chapitres 5 et 6 :** Alice Tremblay et sa famille _____ à

   Baie-Comeau, _____ Québec, et elle _____ beaucoup de

   succès dans le commerce international.

4. **Chapitres 7 et 8 :** Rosalie Blais et André Dupont _____

   le reste de leur vie _____ Suisse. Rosalie _____

   souvent _____ Canada pour voir sa famille

   _____ Vancouver, _____ Colombie-Britannique.

5. **Chapitres 9 et 10 :** Micheline _____ voir Luc _____ Canada.

   Ils _____ beaucoup de temps ensemble et ils

   _____ bien.

À l'hôtel

Chapitre 10

COMPÉTENCE 1

Deciding where to stay

By the time you finish this **Compétence,** you should be able to describe a stay at a hotel and make suggestions about travel.

Partie écrite

A. Logements de vacances. Create sentences explaining where these people are staying and how they are going to pay their bill.

> **EXEMPLE** Robert **descend dans une auberge de jeunesse. Il va régler la note comptant.**

1. M. et Mme Lefric _____
_____
_____
_____

2. Mes amis et moi _____
_____
_____
_____

B. À l'hôtel. Reread the conversation between Alain and the hotel receptionist on pages 370–371 of the textbook. Then, complete this conversation, in which another tourist is asking for a room.

LA TOURISTE : Bonjour, monsieur. Avez-vous _____ **(1)** avec un grand lit pour ce soir ?
(a room)

L'HÔTELIER : Oui, nous avons _____ **(2)** avec
(a room)

_____ **(3)** avec _____ **(4)** à 120 euros la nuit.
(bathroom) *(shower and bathtub)*

LA TOURISTE : Est-ce que _____ **(5)** ?
(breakfast is included)

L'HÔTELIER : Non, il faut payer _____ **(6)** de 7 euros.
(extra charge)

La touriste : Bon, c'est très bien. Je prends cette chambre.

L'hôtelier : Ah, attendez. Nous avons aussi une chambre avec _____ (7)

                                                      (shower)

         à 105 euros si vous préférez. C'est _____ (8).

                                               (courtyard side)

La touriste : Oui, je préfère ça.

L'hôtelier : Très bien. Comment voulez-vous _____ (9),

                                             (to pay the bill)

      _____ (10), _____ (11)?

               (in cash)   *(by credit card)*

La touriste : _____ (12).

                     (In cash)

L'hôtelier : Alors, vous avez la chambre numéro 12, _____ (13).

                                        (at the end of the hallway)

         Voici _____ (14) pour ouvrir la porte de votre chambre.

                           (the key card)

La touriste : Merci, monsieur.

L'hôtelier : Je vous en prie. _____ (15)!

                           (Enjoy your stay!)

C. Règlements.
If you were staying at a hotel in a francophone country, would they tell you that one must or must not do the following things? Complete each sentence with **il faut** or **il ne faut pas**.

    EXEMPLE   Pour assurer que votre chambre soit *(is)* prête à votre arrivée, **il ne faut pas** arriver avant 14 h.

1. _____ quitter la chambre à midi le jour de votre départ pour éviter des frais supplémentaires *(extra charges)*.

2. _____ payer un supplément de 18 euros par jour pour les animaux.

3. En cas d'incendie *(In case of fire)*, _____ prendre l'ascenseur.

4. _____ faire trop de bruit dans les couloirs.

5. _____ régler la note à votre départ.

6. _____ hésiter à contacter la réception si vous avez besoin de quelque chose.

D. Conseils. Based on what your friend says, give her suggestions by completing the statements with one of the choices given.

choisir une chambre côté jardin / faire une réservation / changer d'hôtel / téléphoner à l'ambassade *(embassy)* / prendre l'ascenseur / régler la note par carte de crédit / demander une chambre à deux lits

> **EXEMPLE** — **Je préfère une chambre calme.**
> — Alors, il vaut mieux **choisir une chambre côté jardin.**

1. — Le restaurant où on va dîner est très fréquenté *(busy).*

   — Alors, il vaut mieux _____.

2. — J'ai perdu mon passeport!

   — Alors, il faut _____.

3. — Je ne dors pas bien quand je dois partager mon lit.

   — Alors, il vaut mieux _____.

4. — Je n'aime pas du tout cet hôtel.

   — Alors, il faut _____.

5. — Je n'ai pas assez d'argent pour payer l'hôtel.

   — Alors, il faut _____.

6. — Ma chambre est au cinquième étage et j'ai beaucoup de bagages.

   — Alors, il vaut mieux _____.

E. En voyage. Luc has made two lists of things to do or not to do before and during a trip and has ordered each list according to how important it is to do the things mentioned. The first item in each list is the most important to do and the last one is the least important or should be avoided. Fill in the blank in each sentence with the appropriate expression from the box that precedes it.

Avant de partir…

il vaut mieux	il faut absolument	il ne faut pas	il n'est pas important de (d')

1. _____ réserver une chambre.

2. _____ acheter son billet bien à l'avance pour payer moins cher.

3. _____ préparer un itinéraire pour tout le voyage parce que les projets changent toujours.

4. _____ oublier de demander à quelqu'un de garder son animal.

Pendant le voyage…

il est important de (d')	il n'est pas bon de (d')	il faut	il ne faut jamais

1. _____ faire attention à ses bagages et à son argent.

2. _____ utiliser sa carte de crédit.

3. _____ voyager avec beaucoup d'argent en espèces.

4. _____ laisser ses bagages sans surveillance à l'aéroport.

Nom _____   Date _____

*F. De nouveaux étudiants. A group of new students has arrived at your school. Complete these statements with suggestions as to what they need to do to be successful.

1. Il faut _____.

2. Il ne faut pas _____.

3. Il vaut mieux _____.

4. C'est bien de (d') _____.

5. Il est essentiel de (d') _____.

*G. Et vous? Describe your last stay (or an imaginary stay) at a hotel by answering the following questions *with complete sentences.*

1. À quel hôtel êtes-vous descendu(e)? Aviez-vous une réservation quand vous êtes arrivé(e)?

_____

_____

2. Comment était votre chambre? Est-ce que c'était une chambre avec ou sans climatisation? Est-ce qu'il y avait un grand lit ou deux lits?

_____

_____

_____

3. Est-ce qu'il y avait un mini-bar dans la chambre? Une télévision à écran plat? Est-ce qu'il y avait le wi-fi gratuit?

_____

_____

_____

4. À quel étage était votre chambre? Est-ce qu'il y avait un ascenseur à l'hôtel? Que pouviez-vous voir de la fenêtre de votre chambre? Est-ce qu'il y avait un balcon?

_____

_____

_____

5. Est-ce qu'il y avait un restaurant à l'hôtel? Est-ce que vous avez pris vos repas dans votre chambre?

_____

_____

6. Quel était le prix de votre chambre? Comment avez-vous réglé la note?

_____

_____

Nom _____ Date _____

Partie auditive

A. Quel genre d'hôtel ? You will hear short
descriptions of several hotels. Indicate the category of each
hotel by selecting **un hôtel peu cher** or **un hôtel de luxe**.

1. UN HÔTEL PEU CHER _____ UN HÔTEL DE LUXE _____

2. UN HÔTEL PEU CHER _____ UN HÔTEL DE LUXE _____

3. UN HÔTEL PEU CHER _____ UN HÔTEL DE LUXE _____

un hôtel peu cher   **un hôtel de luxe**

Repeat this section and listen to the description of each hotel again. Fill in the blanks with the information about each hotel.

L'hôtel Carayou : Il y a _____ **(1)** chambres à l'hôtel. _____ **(2)**

chambres sont avec salle de bains, toilettes séparées, téléphone, télévision, accès Internet wi-fi, mini-bar, radio

et balcon donnant sur les jardins. L'hôtel se trouve *(is located)* _____ **(3)**. Une

chambre coûte _____ **(4)** euros la nuit.

L'hôtel Amantine : Il y a _____ **(1)** chambres à l'hôtel. _____ **(2)**

chambres sont avec salle de bains. L'hôtel se trouve _____ **(3)**. Une

chambre coûte _____ **(4)** euros la nuit.

L'hôtel Diamant : Il y a _____ **(1)** chambres à l'hôtel. _____ **(2)**

chambres sont avec salle de bains, balcon, cuisine équipée et téléphone. L'hôtel se trouve, à

_____ **(3)** minutes du centre-ville. Une chambre coûte _____ **(4)**

euros la nuit.

B. Pour mieux comprendre : *Anticipating a response.* You will hear various tourists talking about
hotels. Identify the sentence that would logically follow next. Then, check your work as you hear the statement
again followed by the correct answer.

EXEMPLE   VOUS ENTENDEZ :   L'ascenseur à côté de notre chambre fait trop de bruit. Je n'ai pas dormi du tout.
                VOUS INDIQUEZ :   ___✓___ Il faut demander une autre chambre.
                                   _____ Il faut revenir à cet hôtel la prochaine fois.
                VOUS ENTENDEZ :   L'ascenseur à côté de notre chambre fait trop de bruit. Je n'ai pas dormi du
                                   tout. Il faut demander une autre chambre.

1. _____ Il faut demander une autre chambre.

   _____ Il faut revenir à cet hôtel la prochaine fois.

2. _____ Il faut chercher un autre hôtel.

   _____ Il faut réserver une deuxième nuit.

3. _____ Il faut payer par carte de crédit.

   _____ Il vaut mieux payer comptant.

4. _____ Il est important de réserver bien à l'avance.

_____ Il n'est pas nécessaire de faire une réservation.

5. _____ Il vaut mieux demander une chambre côté rue.

_____ Il vaut mieux demander une chambre côté jardin.

C. La chambre. Listen as a tourist talks about her hotel room. Then pause the recording and indicate whether these statements are true or false by selecting **vrai** or **faux.**

1. La chambre est grande.   VRAI _____   FAUX _____

2. La touriste ne va pas passer beaucoup de temps dans la chambre.   VRAI _____   FAUX _____

3. Il y a une salle de bains, mais il n'y a pas de douche.   VRAI _____   FAUX _____

4. Il y a une belle vue sur la ville.   VRAI _____   FAUX _____

D. À l'hôtel. Listen to a conversation between two tourists about their hotel room and fill in the missing words. Pause the recording as needed in order to have enough time to respond.

ANNE-MARIE :   Tu sais, je suis vraiment déçue *(disappointed)* ! Regarde cette chambre ! Nous payons

_____ **(1)** la nuit et _____ **(2)**

est toute petite.

SOPHIE :   La prochaine fois, _____ **(3)** nous informer mieux que ça avant de

choisir un hôtel.

ANNE-MARIE :   Tu as raison. Cette chambre n'est pas agréable du tout et en plus elle est côté rue et

_____ **(4).**

SOPHIE :   Oui, _____ **(5)** demander une autre chambre pour

ce soir — quelque chose _____ **(6).** Pour pouvoir bien

profiter de notre séjour, _____ **(7)** bien

dormir la nuit.

ANNE-MARIE :   As-tu essayé _____ **(8)** ? Ils ne sont vraiment pas très

confortables !

SOPHIE :   Écoute, demain _____ **(9).**

ANNE-MARIE :   Bonne idée. Alors, vaut-il mieux _____ **(10)** ce soir ?

SOPHIE :   Non, pas ce soir. J'ai _____ **(11)** et je peux la

_____ **(12)** demain matin.

ANNE-MARIE :   Bon, d'accord. Et demain on cherche un autre hôtel !

COMPÉTENCE 2

Going to the doctor

By the time you finish this *Compétence,* you should be able to describe how you feel when you are ill and give recommendations about what to do.

Partie écrite

A. Le corps. Label the following body parts *in French.* Use the definite article with each body part **(le, la, l', les).**

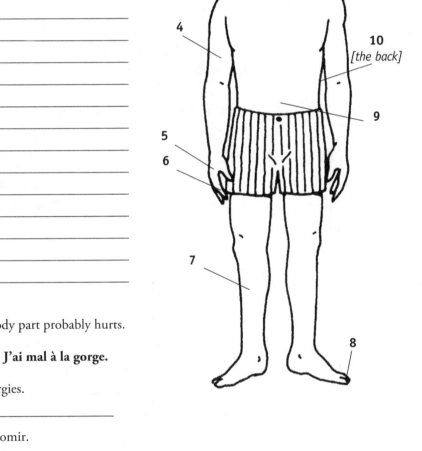

1. _____
2. _____
3. _____
4. _____
5. _____
6. _____
7. _____
8. _____
9. _____
10. _____
11. _____
12. _____
13. _____
14. _____

B. Où ont-ils mal ? Say what body part probably hurts.

EXEMPLE Je tousse beaucoup. **J'ai mal à la gorge.**

1. J'éternue beaucoup. J'ai des allergies.

   _____

2. J'ai trop mangé et j'ai envie de vomir.

   _____

3. J'ai fait un marathon ce matin.

   _____

4. J'ai bu trop de bière hier soir. Ce matin, _____.

5. Je dois aller chez le dentiste parce que _____.

6. Je vais chez l'oculiste *(eye doctor)* parce que _____.

C. Conversation. Reread the conversation between Alain and the doctor on page 380 of the textbook. Then, complete this conversation between another patient and the doctor with the indicated words.

LE MÉDECIN : Bonjour, madame. _____ **(1)** ?
(What's wrong)

MME GARNIER : _____ **(2).** _____ **(3)**
(I feel bad)   *(I have the shivers)*

et _____ **(4)** tout le temps.
(my head hurts)

LE MÉDECIN : Vous avez une forte fièvre *(fever)* aussi. Je pense que c'est _____ **(5).**
(the flu)

MME GARNIER : Qu'est-ce que je dois faire ?

LE MÉDECIN : Voici _____ **(6).** Il faut que vous preniez ces
(a prescription)

médicaments _____ **(7)** et _____ **(8)**
(three times per day)   *(it's essential)*

que vous vous reposiez.

D. Il faut se soigner ! Suggest something to help the following people feel better by completing each recommendation with the logical phrase from the list. Put the verb in the subjunctive.

manger des plats plus légers le soir   porter des gants *(gloves)* la prochaine fois

boire moins d'alcool   arrêter de fumer

prendre de l'aspirine   utiliser de la crème solaire la prochaine fois

acheter de nouvelles chaussures

    EXEMPLE   — J'ai toujours mal aux yeux.
                     — Il faut que vous **changiez de lunettes.**

1.   — J'ai souvent mal aux pieds à la fin de la journée.

     — Il faut que vous _____.

2.   — Mon mari a toujours mal à la gorge et il tousse beaucoup.

     — Il faut qu'il _____.

3.   — Mon fils est sorti avec ses amis hier soir et il a mal à la tête ce matin.

     — Il faut qu'il _____

     et qu'il _____.

4.   — Je ne digère pas bien et j'ai souvent mal au ventre quand je me couche.

     — Il faut que vous _____.

5.   — Ma fille a passé la journée à la plage. Maintenant, elle a eu un coup de soleil *(sunburn)*.

     — Il faut qu'elle _____.

6.   — J'ai travaillé dans le jardin ce matin et maintenant, j'ai mal aux mains à cause des rosiers *(rose bushes)*.

     — Il faut que vous _____.

Nom _____ Date _____

E. Chez le médecin. Imagine the doctor's reactions to these remarks by his patients. Complete the statements with the logical phrase in parentheses. Put the verb in the subjunctive.

EXEMPLE   Nous sommes souvent très fatigués. (rentrer tard, se coucher plus tôt)
Il faut que vous **vous couchiez plus tôt.**
Il ne faut pas que vous **rentriez tard.**

1. Mes enfants sont souvent très fatigués. (sortir tous les soirs, prendre des vitamines)

   Il faut qu'ils _____.

   Il ne faut pas qu'ils _____.

2. Ma femme est très stressée. (se reposer, réfléchir trop à ses problèmes)

   Il faut qu'elle _____.

   Il ne faut pas qu'elle _____.

3. Mon fils a grossi récemment. (choisir des plats légers, manger beaucoup)

   Il faut qu'il _____.

   Il ne faut pas qu'il _____.

4. Je suis enceinte. (boire de l'alcool, dormir assez)

   Il faut que vous _____.

   Il ne faut pas que vous _____.

5. Mon mari a besoin d'améliorer sa santé. (boire trop d'alcool, maigrir un peu)

   Il faut qu'il _____.

   Il ne faut pas qu'il _____.

F. Une bonne santé. Give a friend who wants to improve his health advice by completing the following statements with the logical ending from each pair. Remember to use the subjunctive.

EXEMPLE   (être toujours nerveux / boire moins de café)
Il vaut mieux que tu **boives moins de café.**
Il n'est pas bon que tu **sois toujours nerveux.**

1. (faire attention à ce que tu manges / manger trop de sucre)

   Il faut que tu _____.

   Il ne faut pas que tu _____.

2. (savoir combien de calories il y a dans chaque plat, prendre des plats avec trop de calories)

   Il est important que tu _____.

   Il n'est pas bon que tu _____.

3. (maigrir trop vite / perdre quelques kilos)

   C'est bien que tu _____.

   Il est mauvais que tu _____.

4. (faire de l'exercice / aller tous les jours au gym)

Il faut que tu _____.

Il n'est pas nécessaire que tu _____.

5. (pouvoir te reposer de temps en temps, être trop stressé)

Il faut que tu _____.

Il ne faut pas que tu _____.

G. Dans l'avion.

You are training to be a flight attendant and you are going over the regulations. Complete each sentence logically with **il faut** or **il ne faut pas** in the first blank and the subjunctive of the verb in parentheses in the second one.

> **EXEMPLE** **Il faut** que le dossier du siège *(seatback)* de chaque passager **soit** (être) en position verticale au décollage et à l'atterrissage *(on take-off and landing)*.

1. _____ que chaque passager _____

(avoir) une carte d'embarquement *(boarding pass)* pour monter dans l'avion.

2. _____ que les passagers _____

(utiliser) leur cellulaire ou d'autres appareils électroniques au décollage ou à l'atterrissage.

3. _____ que les passagers _____

(savoir) utiliser les masques à oxygène en cas de dépressurisation de la cabine.

4. _____ que tous les bagages à main *(carry-on luggage)*

_____ (être) dans les compartiments à bagages ou sous le siège *(seat)*

situé devant les passagers.

5. _____ que les passagers _____

(fumer) dans les toilettes.

---

*Journal. Remember the last time you were sick and imagine that you have come down with the same illness again. Write a conversation between you and the doctor in which you describe your symptoms and the doctor tells you what you need to do. Be sure to use the subjunctive as needed.

_____

_____

_____

_____

_____

_____

_____

_____

_____

Partie auditive

A. Le corps. Repeat each part of the body you hear and put the corresponding number in the appropriate blank.

LE CORPS

EXEMPLE   VOUS ENTENDEZ: les dents
VOUS RÉPÉTEZ: **les dents**
VOUS NOTEZ:

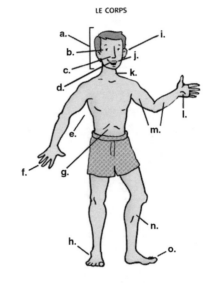

a. _____   i. _____

b. _____   j. _____

c. _____   k. _____

d. _Exemple_____   l. _____

e. _____   m. _____

f. _____   n. _____

g. _____   o. _____

h. _____

B. J'ai mal partout! Where do the following people hurt? Repeat each sentence you hear and put the corresponding number with the appropriate illustration.

EXEMPLE   VOUS ENTENDEZ: Il a mal à la main.
VOUS RÉPÉTEZ: **Il a mal à la main.**
VOUS NOTEZ:

a. _____

b. _____

c. _Exemple_____

d. _____

e. _____

f. _____

g. _____

h. _____

C. Pour avoir une bonne santé. A doctor is explaining to a patient how to feel better and have more energy. Repeat each sentence and indicate whether the doctor is expressing what should be done (**oui**) or what shouldn't be done (**non**) by putting the number of each statement and **oui** or **non** in the blank for the corresponding illustration.

EXEMPLE   VOUS ENTENDEZ: Il vaut mieux que vous évitiez les matières grasses.

           VOUS RÉPÉTEZ: **Il vaut mieux que vous évitiez les matières grasses.**

           VOUS NOTEZ:

a. _____   b. _____   c. _____

d. **Exemple: oui**   e. _____   f. _____

D. Que faut-il faire? Which of the solutions from each pair below would a doctor logically recommend to his patients so that they will feel better? Use **il faut que vous...**, as in the example. You will then hear the correct response. Check your answer and indicate the correct option.

EXEMPLE   VOUS LISEZ: aller chez le dentiste ____ / boire moins de café ____

           VOUS ENTENDEZ: J'ai souvent mal à la tête et je dors mal.

           VOUS DITES: **Il faut que vous buviez moins de café.**

           VOUS ENTENDEZ: Il faut que vous buviez moins de café.

           VOUS INDIQUEZ: aller chez le dentiste ____ / boire moins de café ✓

1. acheter d'autres chaussures ____ / boire moins ____

2. écrire moins ____ / changer de lunettes ____

3. dormir plus ____ / manger moins rapidement ____

4. cesser de fumer ____ / boire moins d'eau ____

5. nager plus souvent ____ / boire moins de café ____

6. travailler moins ____ / aller chez le dentiste ____

*E. Et vous? Answer the following questions *with complete sentences*.

1. _____

2. _____

3. _____

4. _____

COMPÉTENCE 3

Running errands on a trip

By the time you finish this **Compétence,** you should be able to talk about running errands on a trip and say what you want yourself and others to do.

Partie écrite

A. Pourquoi? Luc is saying where he and Micheline went and why. Complete his statements.

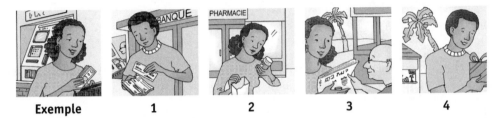

| Exemple | 1 | 2 | 3 | 4 |

acheter de l'aspirine

acheter des devises étrangères

retirer de l'argent

acheter un journal et une carte téléphonique

acheter un cadeau

EXEMPLE   Micheline est allée **au guichet automatique** pour **retirer de l'argent.**

1. Je suis allé _____ pour _____.

2. Micheline est allée _____ pour _____.

3. Micheline est allée _____ pour _____

   _____.

4. Je suis allé _____ pour _____

   _____.

B. Conversation. Reread the conversation between Catherine and Alain on page 386 of the textbook. Then, complete this conversation where two friends are making plans for a visit.

AURÉLIE: _____ **(1)** tu viennes me voir. Quand vas-tu arriver?
(I'm happy that, I'm glad that)

FLORENCE: Je pars lundi matin.

AURÉLIE: À quelle heure est-ce que je devrais _____ **(2)** à l'aéroport?
(to go pick you up)

FLORENCE: Non, ne viens pas _____ **(3).** Je peux prendre
(to pick me up)

_____ **(4).** Je ne veux pas que tu perdes ton temps à
(the shuttle)

l'aéroport si l'avion arrive _____ **(5).**
(late)

Nom _____ Date _____

AurÉlie: Mais non, _____ (6)! L'avion arrive à quelle heure ?
                              (I insist)

Florence: À 18 h 15.

AurÉlie: _____ (7), nous pouvons aller souper
                  (If you don't have other plans)

en ville. _____ (8) un bon petit restaurant pas loin de l'aéroport.
                  (I know)

Florence: Bonne idée! J'aurai faim _____ (9).
                              (after my flight)

AurÉlie: _____ (10). À lundi, alors!
                  (Perfect)

Florence: Oui, au revoir, à lundi!

C. Réactions.

How would you respond if a travel companion with whom you were planning to spend the day told you the following things? Begin each response with the logical expression in parentheses and do not forget to use the subjunctive.

> **EXEMPLE**   Je n'aime pas du tout ma chambre. (C'est dommage que… / Je suis content[e] que…)
> **C'est dommage que tu n'aimes pas du tout ta chambre.**

1. Le restaurant à l'hôtel est excellent. (Je suis content[e] que… / C'est dommage que…)

    _____

2. Il y a trop de bruit la nuit. (Je suis heureux [heureuse] que… / Je regrette que…)

    _____

3. Je ne peux pas bien dormir. (Je suis désolé[e] que… / Je suis content[e] que…)

    _____

4. Je suis fatigué(e). (C'est dommage que… / Je suis content[e] que…)

    _____

5. Je n'ai pas envie de sortir. (Je suis heureux [heureuse] que… / Je regrette que…)

    _____

6. Je veux passer toute la journée à l'hôtel. (Je suis surpris[e] que… / Je suis content[e] que…)

    _____

7. Je commence à me sentir mieux. (Je suis désolé[e] que… / Je suis heureux [heureuse] que…)

    _____

8. Je t'invite au restaurant ce soir. (Je regrette que… / Je suis content[e] que…)

    _____

D. Quel temps fait-il? The weather can often change vacation plans. Give your feelings about the weather, using the French equivalent of each expression from page 388 of the textbook.

EXEMPLE   **Je suis surpris(e) qu'il fasse mauvais.**

Exemple   **1.** *It's too bad that ...*   **2.** *I'm sorry that ...*   **3.** *I'm happy that ...*   **4.** *I regret that ...*
I'm surprised that ...

1. _____

2. _____

3. _____

4. _____

*E. L'idéal. What traits do you require in your ideal partner? Complete each sentence with the phrase from the list that best expresses your feelings and the subjunctive of the verb in parentheses.

Je veux que…   **Je préfère que…**   **Il n'est pas important que…**   **Je ne veux pas que…**

EXEMPLE   **Il n'est pas important qu'**il/elle **soit** (être) riche.

1. _____ il/elle _____ (vouloir) avoir
   des enfants.

2. _____ il/elle _____ (avoir) déjà
   beaucoup d'enfants.

3. _____ il/elle _____ (pouvoir) sortir
   avec moi tous les soirs.

4. _____ il/elle _____ (gagner)
   beaucoup d'argent.

5. _____ il/elle _____ (savoir) parler
   une autre langue.

6. _____ il/elle _____ (être) plus ou
   moins du même âge que moi.

7. _____ il/elle _____ (finir) ses
   études universitaires.

8. _____ il/elle _____ (faire) des
   études supérieures *(postgraduate)*.

9. _____ il/elle _____ (avoir) un bon
   sens de l'humour.

10. _____ il/elle _____ (s'intéresser) aux
    mêmes choses que moi.

F. Un voyage. One friend is making plans with another to go on a trip. Complete the following sentences with the verbs in parentheses, using either the infinitive or the subjunctive.

    EXEMPLE   Je voudrais **aller** (aller) en Guadeloupe et je voudrais que tu y **ailles** (aller) avec moi.

1. Je veux que tu _____ (choisir) l'hôtel, mais je ne veux pas _____ (payer) trop cher.

2. Je voudrais _____ (être) dans un hôtel près de la plage et je préfère que l'hôtel

    _____ (ne pas être) trop grand.

3. J'aimerais _____ (partir) le matin, mais je ne veux pas que notre vol

    _____ (partir) trop tôt.

4. En avion, je préfère _____ (dormir) et je ne veux pas que les autres passagers à côté

    de moi _____ (faire) beaucoup de bruit.

5. Je veux que tu me _____ (dire) ce que tu veux _____ (faire) en

    Guadeloupe parce que je veux _____ (préparer) un itinéraire détaillé avant de partir.

6. Je veux que ce voyage _____ (être) agréable et je ne veux pas

    _____ (avoir) de problèmes.

7. Je veux que tu _____ (prendre) beaucoup de photos avec ton nouvel appareil photo

    (camera) parce que j'aimerais _____ (faire) un album de photos.

8. Je suis content que tu _____ (faire) ce voyage avec moi parce que je ne veux pas le

    _____ (faire) tout seul.

*G. Et vous ? Answer the following questions about traveling *with complete sentences.*

1. Où voudriez-vous passer vos prochaines vacances ? Aimez-vous avoir un itinéraire détaillé quand vous voyagez ou préférez-vous faire des projets au jour le jour *(day by day)* ?

    _____

    _____

    _____

2. Préférez-vous être dans un hôtel peu cher mais loin du centre-ville ou préférez-vous que l'hôtel soit près de tout, même si *(even if)* vous devez payer plus cher ?

    _____

    _____

3. Préférez-vous avoir une chambre non-fumeur *(non-smoking)* ou préférez-vous pouvoir fumer ?

    _____

4. Aimez-vous mieux que le déjeuner soit compris dans le prix de votre chambre ou préférez-vous ne pas prendre le déjeuner à l'hôtel ? Si vous visitez un autre pays, aimez-vous goûter des plats exotiques ou préférez-vous que la cuisine ne soit pas trop différente de chez vous ?

    _____

    _____

    _____

Partie auditive

 A. Des courses. You will hear what errands Luc and Micheline ran today. Repeat what you hear, then put the number of the sentence with the corresponding illustration.

EXEMPLE   VOUS ENTENDEZ: Luc est allé à la boutique de cadeaux.
           VOUS RÉPÉTEZ: **Luc est allé à la boutique de cadeaux.**
           VOUS NOTEZ:

a. _____

b. _____

c. _____

d. _____

e. _____

f. **EXEMPLE**

 B. Des touristes en vacances. You will hear several tourists say what they need to do today. Based on what they say, tell them where they need to go, using **il faut**. After a pause for you to respond, you will hear the correct response. Fill in the missing words in the sentences as you listen.

EXEMPLE   VOUS ENTENDEZ: Je veux acheter un journal.
           VOUS RÉPONDEZ: **Pour acheter un journal, il faut que vous alliez chez le marchand de journaux.**
           VOUS ENTENDEZ: Pour acheter un journal, il faut que vous alliez chez le marchand de journaux.
           VOUS ÉCRIVEZ: Pour **acheter un journal,** il faut que vous alliez chez le marchand de journaux.

1. Pour _____, il faut que vous alliez au bureau

   de poste.

2. Pour _____, il faut que vous alliez au bureau

   de poste.

3. Pour _____, il faut que vous alliez à la boutique

   de cadeaux.

4. Pour _____, il faut que vous alliez au guichet

   automatique ou à la banque.

5. Pour _____, il faut que vous alliez à la

   banque.

C. Qui va le faire? Luc's parents are leaving on vacation and his mother is talking to her husband, Lucien, about who is going to do what. Based on the lists that are shown, say whether she asks him to do each thing you hear named or whether she prefers to do it herself. Note that she forgets to mention two of the listed items.

EXEMPLES VOUS ENTENDEZ: acheter un journal
VOUS RÉPONDEZ: **Je veux que tu achètes un journal.**
VOUS ENTENDEZ: Je veux que tu achètes un journal.
VOUS ENTENDEZ: acheter un guide
VOUS RÉPONDEZ: **Je préfère acheter un guide moi-même (*myself*).**
VOUS ENTENDEZ: Je préfère acheter un guide moi-même.

Now complete the following two sentences for the two items that Luc's mother forgot to mention.

Je veux que tu _____.

Je préfère _____ moi-même.

> **Moi**
> acheter un guide
> lire le guide
> préparer l'itinéraire
> réserver une chambre
> faire les valises
>
> **Lucien**
> acheter un journal
> préparer la voiture pour le voyage
> dire aux voisins la date de notre départ
> acheter une carte téléphonique
> aller chercker tes médicaments à la pharmacie

D. L'arrivée. Pause the recording and review the conversation on page 386 of the textbook. A friend of Catherine's, Monique, is coming to visit her. Turn on the recording and listen to their conversation. You will hear their conversation twice. The first time, just listen at normal speed. Then listen as it is repeated in short phrases at a slower speed, with pauses for you to fill in the missing words. Play this section again as needed.

CATHERINE: Comme je suis contente _____

_____ **(1)** chez moi. Tu arrives quand?

MONIQUE: Jeudi matin _____ **(2)**.

CATHERINE: Tu veux _____ **(3)** à l'aéroport?

MONIQUE: C'est gentil, mais je ne veux pas _____ **(4)** à

l'aéroport si jamais *(in case)* _____ **(5)**.

Il y a _____ **(6)**, non?

CATHERINE: Non, non, j' _____ **(7)**. Mais je préfère _____ **(8)**

juste devant la sortie principale. Comme ça, je n'aurai pas besoin de trouver un stationnement.

Disons vers _____ **(9)**?

MONIQUE: C'est parfait. À jeudi, alors!

CATHERINE: Oui, à très bientôt!

COMPÉTENCE 4

Giving directions

By the time you finish this *Compétence,* you should be able to give and follow directions in French.

Partie écrite

A. En ville. Complete the following sentences with a logical preposition according to the illustration. You are standing in the street, facing the **Hôtel Molière.**

à côté / à gauche / à droite / en face / entre / au bout / au coin

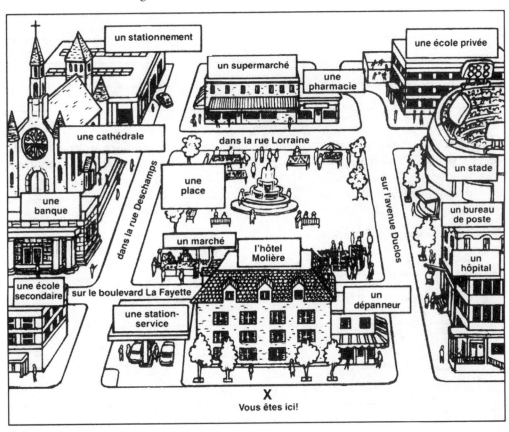

1. La station-service est _____ de l'hôtel Molière et le dépanneur

   (convenience store) est _____ de l'hôtel.

2. Il y a un bureau de poste _____ de l'hôpital.

3. Le stade est _____ le bureau de poste et l'école privée.

4. Il y a un stationnement _____ de la rue Lorraine et de la rue Deschamps.

5. _____ du stationnement, de l'autre côté de la rue Deschamps, il y

   a un supermarché.

6. _____ de l'avenue Duclos, il y a une école privée.

*B. Pour aller à... You are standing in the street, facing the **Hôtel Molière** in the illustration in *A. En ville.* Give directions to the following places.

> **EXEMPLE** le stationnement:
> **Montez la rue Deschamps et continuez tout droit**
> **jusqu'au bout de la rue. Le stationnement est à gauche au**
> **coin de la rue Lorraine et de la rue Deschamps.**

1. le supermarché: _____

_____

_____

2. le stade: _____

_____

_____

3. la pharmacie: _____

_____

_____

C. Conversation. Reread the conversation between Micheline and the employee at the tourist office on page 395 of the textbook. Then, complete this conversation where another tourist is asking for directions.

L'EMPLOYÉ :   Bonjour, mademoiselle, _____ **(1)**?
                                                    (may I help you)

LA TOURISTE :   Oui, s'il vous plaît, monsieur, _____ **(2)**
                                                    (could you explain to me)

                comment aller à la gare routière *(bus station)*?

L'EMPLOYÉ :   Bien sûr, mademoiselle, c'est très simple. C'est tout près.

                _____ **(3)**
                                        (Go up)

                la rue Provence _____ **(4)**
                                        (until, up to)

                la rue Duplessis et _____ **(5)**.
                                        (turn left)

LA TOURISTE :   _____ **(6)** la rue Provence et
                        (I go up)

                _____ **(7)**?
                                        (I turn left)

L'EMPLOYÉ :   Oui, c'est ça. _____ **(8)** et la gare routière sera
                                        (Continue straight)

                _____ **(9)** la rue Dubouchage.
                                (on your right, just after)

LA TOURISTE :   _____ **(10)**, monsieur.
                                        (Thank you)

L'EMPLOYÉ :   Je vous en prie, mademoiselle.

D. Un safari. A group of tourists is receiving instructions before leaving on a safari in Senegal. Give logical commands telling them to do or not to do the following things using a direct object pronoun (**le, la, l', les**), an indirect object pronoun (**lui, leur**), **y**, or **en** for the italicized words.

  EXEMPLES oublier *votre passeport* : **Ne l'oubliez pas.**
  garder *(to keep)* *votre passeport* avec vous : **Gardez-le avec vous.**

1. boire *de l'eau du robinet (tap water)* : _____

2. acheter *de l'eau* en bouteille : _____

3. écouter le *guide* pendant le safari : _____

4. perdre *le guide* de vue : _____

5. aller *dans la jungle* tout seul : _____

6. toucher *les animaux* : _____

7. donner à manger *aux animaux* : _____

8. donner un pourboire *(tip)* *au guide* : _____

9. oublier *le pourboire* : _____

E. Et toi ? Tell a friend who is leaving on vacation to do or not to do the following things by changing the statements in the subjunctive to commands.

  EXEMPLES Il ne faut pas que tu t'ennuies !
  Ne t'ennuie pas !

  Je veux que tu m'écrives.
  Écris-moi !

1. Je veux que tu t'amuses !

   _____

2. Je veux que tu me montres tes photos !

   _____

3. Il ne faut pas que tu me demandes de l'argent pour le voyage !

   _____

4. Il ne faut pas que tu te perdes !

   _____

5. Je veux que tu m'invites la prochaine fois !

   _____

6. Je voudrais que tu me téléphones quand tu arriveras !

   _____

7. J'aimerais que tu m'achètes un souvenir !

   _____

8. Je ne veux pas que tu m'oublies !

   _____

Nom _____ Date _____

F. Faisons-le ensemble! You tell your brother/sister to do the following things, but he/she does not feel like doing them, so you suggest doing them together. In the last two sentences for each one, replace the italicized words with a direct object pronoun **(le, la, l', les)**, an indirect object pronoun **(lui, leur)**, or with **y** or **en.** Follow the example.

> **EXEMPLE** faire *les valises*
> — **Fais les valises!**
> — **Je n'ai pas envie de les faire.**
> — **Alors, faisons-les ensemble!**

1. choisir *l'hôtel*

   — _____

   — _____

   — _____

2. aller *à la banque*

   — _____

   — _____

   — _____

3. acheter *des devises étrangères*

   — _____

   — _____

   — _____

4. téléphoner *à l'agent de voyages*

   — _____

   — _____

   — _____

*Journal. You are inviting some classmates to your place after class. Write precise directions telling how to get there from the university.

_____

_____

_____

_____

_____

_____

_____

_____

Partie auditive

A. Des indications. Imagine that you are at the hotel on the **boulevard Angoulvant.** (Look for the X on the following map.) Listen to the directions and determine where you end up. In the list below, put the number of the directions given next to the place you end up. Directions will be given to only two destinations.

EXEMPLE   VOUS ENTENDEZ : Sortez de l'hôtel et tournez à droite. Descendez le boulevard Angoulvant jusqu'à l'avenue Terrasson de Fougères. Tournez à gauche et continuez tout droit. Traversez le boulevard Clozel et ça va être sur votre gauche.

   VOUS NOTEZ :   **Exemple** *by* **bureau de poste**

Assemblée nationale ____   Bureau de poste ~~Exemple~~

Cathédrale St-Paul ____   Palais de Justice ____

Place Climbié ____   Restaurant Climbié ____

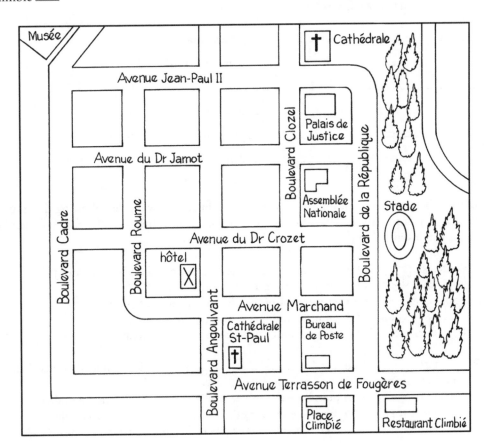

Now play this section again and fill in the missing words in each set of directions. Pause the recording as needed.

1. Sortez de l'hôtel et _____ sur le boulevard Angoulvant.

Au premier coin, _____

sur l'avenue du Dr Crozet. Ensuite, _____

sur le boulevard Clozel et ce sera _____.

2. Sortez de l'hôtel et _____ sur le boulevard Angoulvant.

_____ l'avenue Jean-Paul II.

Là, _____. _____

le boulevard Clozel et ce sera _____.

B. En voyage. You are traveling with a friend who always puts everything off as long as possible. What does your friend say to do in each case? Answer with a **nous**-form command and a direct object pronoun. You will then hear the correct response. As you listen, complete the sentences with the missing words.

EXEMPLE   VOUS ENTENDEZ: On réserve la chambre d'hôtel avant de partir ou on la cherche à notre arrivée ?

VOUS DITES: **Cherchons-la à notre arrivée!**

VOUS ENTENDEZ: Cherchons-la à notre arrivée!

VOUS COMPLÉTEZ: **Cherchons-la** à notre arrivée!

1. _____ au restaurant!

2. _____ demain matin!

3. _____ plus tard!

4. _____ plus tard!

5. _____ plus tard dans une banque!

6. _____ demain matin!

C. À la réception. The clerk at your hotel's front desk is asking if you want the following things done for you. Answer affirmatively or negatively with a **vous**-form command, as in the example. You will then hear the correct response. As you listen, fill in the missing words in each sentence.

EXEMPLE 1 VOUS LISEZ: Oui, _____ ma chambre, s'il vous plaît.

VOUS ENTENDEZ: On vous montre votre chambre ?

VOUS DITES: **Oui, montrez-moi ma chambre, s'il vous plaît.**

VOUS ENTENDEZ: Oui, montrez-moi ma chambre, s'il vous plaît.

VOUS ÉCRIVEZ: Oui, **montrez-moi** ma chambre, s'il vous plaît.

EXEMPLE 2 VOUS LISEZ: Non merci, _____ le déjeuner dans ma chambre.

VOUS ENTENDEZ: On vous sert le déjeuner dans votre chambre ?

VOUS DITES: **Non merci, ne me servez pas le déjeuner dans ma chambre.**

VOUS ENTENDEZ: Non merci, ne me servez pas le déjeuner dans ma chambre.

VOUS ÉCRIVEZ: Non merci, **ne me servez pas** le déjeuner dans ma chambre.

1. Oui, _____ une autre carte clé, s'il vous plaît.

2. Non merci, _____ demain matin.

3. Oui, _____ avec les bagages, s'il vous plaît.

4. Non merci, _____ le souper dans ma chambre.

5. Oui, _____ le nom d'un bon restaurant, s'il vous plaît.

6. Oui, _____ comment aller à ce restaurant, s'il vous plaît.

7. Non merci, _____ demain matin.